Family Histories of World War II

Family Histories of World War II

Survivors and Descendants

**EDITED BY
RÓISÍN HEALY AND
GEARÓID BARRY**

Leabharlanna Chathair Bhaile Átha Cliath
Dublin City Libraries

BLOOMSBURY ACADEMIC
LONDON • NEW YORK • OXFORD • NEW DELHI • SYDNEY

BLOOMSBURY ACADEMIC
Bloomsbury Publishing Plc
50 Bedford Square, London, WC1B 3DP, UK
1385 Broadway, New York, NY 10018, USA
29 Earlsfort Terrace, Dublin 2, Ireland

BLOOMSBURY, BLOOMSBURY ACADEMIC and the Diana logo are trademarks of
Bloomsbury Publishing Plc

First published in Great Britain 2021

Cover images: Middle left © Catnap72 / Getty Images
Top left/right, bottom left/right © Rouzes / Getty Images
Cover Design by Toby Way

A catalogue record for this book is available from the British Library.

A catalog record for this book is available from the Library of Congress.

ISBN: HB: 978-1-3502-0194-1
PB: 978-1-3502-0195-8
ePDF: 978-1-3502-0196-5
eBook: 978-1-3502-0197-2

Typeset by Newgen KnowledgeWorks Pvt. Ltd., Chennai, India
Printed and bound in Great Britain

To find out more about our authors and books visit www.bloomsbury.com
and sign up for our newsletters.

Contents

Illustrations

Figures

Table

Acknowledgements

This book would not have been possible without the generous response of colleagues at National University of Ireland (NUI) Galway, to our call to write about their families' experiences of World War II. It is a source of great regret that we could not accommodate all those who responded and we thank both those whose stories do not appear here as well as those whose stories do. The authors whose work appears in this volume received generous assistance from other members of their families and we extend thanks to them too.

We would also like to express our gratitude to Bloomsbury and its anonymous reviewers for their help in bringing these stories to a wider audience. We note with appreciation all those, whether living or deceased, who took the photographs that appear in this book. We thank Cillian Joy and Peter Corrigan in the James Hardiman Library of NUI Galway, for their technical assistance in preparing these photographs for publication.

Contributors

Marina Ansaldo works in NUI Galway, as researcher development manager. She was born and grew up in Genoa, Italy, and first arrived in NUI Galway, as an Erasmus student, but fell in love with the west of Ireland and never left. She finished her BA studies and subsequently completed a PhD in Medieval and Early Modern English and Italian Literature. She then spent a few years working as a researcher and teaching at university, both in Galway and Dublin, and now works to support other researchers with their career development.

Gearóid Barry is a lecturer in modern French and European history at NUI Galway. He has published a monograph on modern French history, *The Disarmament of Hatred: Marc Sangnier, French Catholicism and the Legacy of the First World War, 1914–1945* (2012) and thematic articles for the 1914–1918-online International Encyclopedia of the First World War. He has also co-edited two volumes of essays, *Small Nations, and Colonial Peripheries in World War I* (2016) and *1916 in Global Context* (2018).

Ciara Boylan is a researcher at the UNESCO Child and Family Research Centre, NUI Galway. A native of Galway city, she studied history and philosophy at NUIG before completing a masters in Imperial and Commonwealth History and a DPhil (PhD) in nineteenth-century Irish history at the University of Oxford. She worked in a number of libraries in Dublin and as a postdoctoral research fellow at Trinity College, Dublin, before returning to Galway and to NUIG. She is co-editor of *Family Histories of the Irish Revolution* (2017).

Enrico Dal Lago is a professor of American history at the NUI Galway, and a member of the Royal Irish Academy. He has published extensively in the fields of slavery, comparative history and the nineteenth-century United States and Italy. He was born in 1966 in Ivrea, Italy, where he lived for the first twenty-five years of his life. His parents experienced World War II when they were children in two different Italian regions, both subject to Nazi occupation and both centres of Resistance activities during 1943–5: Piedmont in the northwest and Veneto in the northeast.

Constantinos G. Efthymiou is a researcher in the School of Chemistry, NUI Galway. He was born and grew up in Platystomo, Greece. He received his BSc in chemistry from University of Patras (Greece), where he also obtained his PhD (inorganic chemistry). He was a postdoctoral fellow at the University of Florida (Gainesville, USA) (2008–11) and at the University of Cyprus (2011–15). In 2016, he moved to Galway. His research interests are focused on the synthesis of novel multifunctional hybrid materials with interesting technological, medicinal and environmental properties.

Sara Farrona was born and grew up in Mérida, a small and very old city in the region of Extremadura in western Spain. In 1994 she moved to Badajoz, a city very close to Mérida on the border with Portugal, to study biology. After finishing her studies there, she did a PhD in biology in Seville and subsequently lived in Germany for almost ten years. Together with her Spanish husband, she moved to Galway in 2015. She works as a lecturer at the College of Science and Engineering at NUI Galway, and leads her own laboratory in plant developmental epigenetics.

Gill Fennell holds a diploma from Edinburgh College of Domestic Science. She moved with her husband, Robert, and family from Dublin to West Cork in the 1980s. After her mother Pat died, her father, Cecil, a World War II veteran, came to live with them. The papers pertaining to his and Pat's wartime experiences were discovered upon Cecil's death, and Gill has worked tirelessly to transcribe them.

Sheena Fennell is a senior technician in oceanography at the School of Natural Sciences, NUI Galway. She holds a BSc from the University of Southampton and an MSc from NUI Galway. When her grandfather Cecil moved to West Cork they spent many hours together. Sheena especially remembers happy times spent together fishing and building beehives for their garden.

Róisín Healy is a senior lecturer in modern German and European history at NUI Galway. She is the author of two monographs, *The Jesuit Specter in Imperial Germany* (2003) and *Poland in the Irish Nationalist Imagination, 1772–1922* (2017) and the editor or co-editor of four volumes of essays. She has contributed a chapter on her grandfather's role in the Easter 1916 Rising to the volume, *Family Histories of the Irish Revolution* (2018).

Colleen Maloney Williamson is a retired Pittsburgh Public School elementary teacher and math teacher trainer, who has always lived in Pittsburgh, Pennsylvania.

Maureen Maloney is a lecturer in human resource management in the J. E. Cairnes School of Business and Economics at NUI Galway. She lived in Pittsburgh, Pennsylvania, before moving to Ireland in 1988.

Sylvie Mossay is a modern foreign language teacher with twenty years of experience in second- and third-level education. Originally from Belgium, she studied languages with a specific emphasis on Germanic literature at the Université de Liège, where she received a BA and MA, before gaining a Higher Diploma in Education and a further MA at NUI Galway, Ireland. She has been teaching French there since 2004. She has a particular research interest in comics and explores the representation of World War II in East German comics in a current Global Language Studies module.

Cormac Ó Loideáin is a native of An Cheathrú Rua, Co. na Gaillimhe, where he lives with his wife and three children. He is a graduate of NUI Galway, where he received his masters in education in 2008. He is a teacher, tutor and translator who contributes to various Irish language courses offered by Acadamh na hOllscolaíochta Gaeilge at NUIG and at St. Joseph's Patrician College in Galway city. He has long had an interest in family history, an interest which has informed his contribution to this volume.

Hermann Rasche was born in 1942 and brought up in a small provincial town in northwest Germany. He studied German literature, English philology and literature, and philosophy at Freiburg University and did further study at University College Dublin in the mid-1960s. Appointed to NUI Galway (then University College Galway) in the early 1970s, he taught German literature of the eighteenth to twentieth centuries, German language and cultural studies, and linguistics at NUI Galway, until his retirement as senior lecturer in 2007. He has numerous publications in the fields of German-Irish cultural relations, exile studies and travel writing.

Irina (Ira) Ruppo teaches English and manages the Academic Writing Centre at NUI Galway. A graduate of the Hebrew University of Jerusalem, Trinity College, Dublin and NUI Galway, she is the author of *Ibsen and the Irish Revival* (2010) and several other publications on Irish theatre, cross-national reception of literary works and modernism. She was born in Russia in 1978, moved to Israel when she was 12 and moved to Ireland in her early twenties.

Hans-Walter Schmidt-Hannisa is professor of German at NUI Galway. He grew up in Kulmbach, Upper Franconia, and is a graduate of the University of Freiburg i.Br. (MA 1984, PhD 1989) and the University of Bayreuth (Habilitation, 2000). Before his appointment in Galway in 2005, he taught at universities in Bayreuth, Taegu (South Korea), Shanghai, Würzburg and at University College, Cork. His research interests include the cultural and literary history of the dream, German Enlightenment and Romanticism, and media theory. He has published German translations of major contemporary French philosophers. Since 2011 he is honorary consul representing Germany in the west of Ireland.

Patricia Scully is a lecturer in physics at NUIG. She moved to Ireland in 2018 after having held academic positions at several UK universities. She was born to Irish parents, John Scully from Kerry and Myra Cuffe from Sligo, who met at NHS hospitals in the UK. John grew up in the UK, and Myra came to the UK to train as a nurse. Patricia grew up in a small market town, Leek in the Staffordshire Moorlands, and studied physics at the University of Manchester, UK, followed by a PhD in engineering at the University of Liverpool, UK.

1

From generation to generation: World War II narratives in transition

Róisín Healy and Gearóid Barry

Life during World War II was, for many millions of people across the globe, the equivalent of experiencing hell on earth. While, as historian Ian Kershaw points out, the continent of Europe went 'to hell and back' between 1914 and 1949, it was in the years between 1939 and 1945 that Europeans really plumbed the 'bottomless pit of inhumanity'.[1] Extreme hatreds based on ethnonationalism or class, incipient in the continent since World War I, had by 1939 coagulated into the warped utopianisms of Nazism and Stalinism, along with a host of local variants. Social engineering in the name of racial purity or wartime security ordained the direst cruelty towards perceived internal enemies. Even representatives of the Axis powers themselves were occasionally shocked by the depravity of their allies, as in the case of the treatment of the Orthodox Serbs by the Croat Fascist Ustaše regime.[2] That is not to say, as Norman Davies reminds us, that World War II was a straightforward morality tale: the Allied victory was itself 'no simple victory'. The Allies had also played a part in further obliterating the civilian-combatant distinction in wartime, as the civilian dead of the 'strategic bombing' of German cities, such as the thirty thousand who died in Hamburg in 1943, could have attested.[3] World War II as a whole ended only with Japan's defeat in August 1945, when the world entered a frightening new atomic age with the American bombings of Hiroshima and Nagasaki. The first-hand account of

Irishman Aidan MacCarthy, then a British prisoner of war (POW) in Japanese captivity, of the destruction of Nagasaki on 9 August 1945 and the suffering of its people which, as a medical doctor, he tried to salve, captures well the manner in which World War II could literally defy human understanding. MacCarthy recorded in his memoir his initial conviction that he was witnessing the Apocalypse at first hand.[4]

Within Europe alone fighting killed about forty million people, both soldiers and civilians, and the war left in its wake about another thirty million uprooted people, including camp survivors.[5] War-related deaths of civilians and combatants had been unequally distributed. For instance, out of the estimated fourteen million military deaths on the Allied side in World War II, 70 per cent had been sustained by the Soviet Union whereas Britain and France lost fewer soldiers than they had in World War I.[6] Suffering did not end with the defeat of the Axis powers. Mark Mazower speaks of a 'brutal peace' emerging from the war marked by internal civil wars, hunger and a looming Cold War divide in Europe.[7] Ethnic cleansing, of which the Holocaust was the most flagrant example, began during the war and continued for several years afterwards, violently reordering central and eastern Europe into more homogenous territories. Indeed, World War II was decisive in a number of key respects in remaking Europe and the world geopolitically. In contrast to 1918, in 1945 the Allies were in a position to inflict an absolute defeat on Germany and overthrow its domestic regime. Both the western Allies – Britain, the United States and France – and the Soviet Union imposed, in the parts of Germany they controlled, political regimes in their own image and likeness. Another major consequence of World War II was the expansion of Soviet power into eastern Europe, a dominance that lasted until 1989.

Biography and memoir

The enormous impact of the war in political, social, economic and cultural terms has encouraged a view of the war as a quintessentially collective experience. In Britain, the popular notion of the 'spirit of the blitz' testifies to the value placed on solidarity in the face of Nazi aggression, especially the bombings of British cities.[8] The Holocaust was conceived as an attack on all Jews and remembered as a collective experience. The Final Solution threw Jewish citizens of different nationalities, different language communities and different levels of commitment to Judaism together in camps, killing fields and gas chambers. The horror of these years and the mass emigration of survivors from Europe helped to forge a transnational Jewish identity in places like Israel and North America. Moreover, the aftermath of the war in eastern

Europe – the exchange of Nazi rule for Soviet rule – encouraged a popular regional narrative that considered World War II as the start of a fifty-year period of collective oppression.[9]

Yet no two individuals had the same war experience. Even within national, racial or regional communities, experiences differed according to a host of factors such as gender, age, profession, location and, not least, chance. There is a long tradition of documenting the individual experiences of World War II produced by these multiple variations. Some of those who lived through the war took on the role of active witnesses, deliberately recording their own experiences for posterity. Anne Frank is the best-known example, although there were many others whose works were published long after the war, if at all.[10] Peacetime provided a more conducive context in which to recount the often-traumatic experiences of the war. Soon after it ended, a host of memoirs appeared, largely focusing on combat activities and acts of resistance. Many were written by politicians and senior military officers, keen to celebrate their own prowess and, in the case of the losers, dissociate themselves from the Nazi cause.[11] The demand for examples of great heroism allowed some lesser-ranking soldiers and civilians active in the resistance to publish their accounts too.[12] The horror of the Nazis' campaign of mass murder also gave rise to individual memoirs. Holocaust survivors Viktor Frankl and Primo Levi felt particular urgency in committing their experiences to paper immediately after the war.[13] Biography also became an important means of communicating individual experiences of the war. For many years, only the key political and military figures were deemed worthy of attention.[14] Numerous biographies of Churchill and Hitler were published in different languages within just a few years of the war's end.[15]

These individual histories of the war proved popular with readers. It is not hard to understand why. Historian Lois W. Banner has pointed out that biography encourages 'transference', a process by which readers identify with past lives to ask questions of their own.[16] Readers responded particularly well to *Band of Brothers*, the collective biography of Easy Company, a US Army crack rifle unit that fought its way through France, the Netherlands and Germany in the last year of the war. The familial note struck by this title emphasized that individual and collective experiences of the war were intertwined.[17] Autobiographical writings enjoy even more immediate resonance. It is no coincidence that the Holocaust is taught in schools largely through first-person accounts such as those by Primo Levi, Elie Wiesel and Anne Frank.[18]

The decades since 1990 have seen a significant increase in accounts of individual experiences of the war, especially those of Jews. By 2020, the seventy-fifth anniversary of the end of the war, the genre of World War II biography and memoir accounted for over nine thousand entries on Amazon. Much of this boom is to do with the interest sparked in the Holocaust by popular films like *Schindler's List*, which was released in 1993.[19] The fall of the Berlin Wall and the end of Soviet dominance in eastern Europe also play a role. The ending of the official taboo on comparisons between Nazi and Stalinist terror allowed eastern Europeans to speak more openly about their wartime experiences. The mere passage of time has helped too. The impulse to record experiences in anticipation of death in old age has prompted an increasing number of survivors to pen their accounts.[20] Some survivors whose wartime experiences were politically awkward, even if they themselves perpetrated no crimes, felt the need to explain their actions and bear witness to their wartime suffering. Although sent to Germany against their will, the half a million French labour deportees were an embarrassing reminder of the collaborationist Vichy regime and only began writing their experiences decades after the initial rush of resisters' narratives.[21] The emotional distance from painful experiences has also enabled other new publications. The family of Renia Spiegel, a Jewish woman murdered in Poland in 1942, found her diary too difficult to process for many years after the war and arranged for its publication only in 2019.[22] It is hard to tell when the seam of personal accounts will be exhausted, given that diaries continue to be discovered, often upon the death of those with direct experience of wartime.[23]

Changes within the historical profession have also been influential in popularizing individual accounts. A greater appreciation of the significance of the experiences of ordinary people, and women in particular, has broadened the range of stories told.[24] Indeed, along with the opening of classified files on the Allied side, these developments mean that there are now enough memoirs and biographies about female spies in World War II to constitute a subgenre of their own.[25] The so-called 'biographical turn' in history at the turn of the twenty-first century has, moreover, allowed historians to explore individual experiences of World War II without needing to make excessive claims for the relevance of or typicality of these stories.[26] Historian Sheila Fitzpatrick recently published an account of a Latvian man's experiences in Nazi-occupied Europe, including episodes where he witnessed the persecution of the Jews. She describes his life as singular rather than representative.[27]

Family history

Fitzpatrick's subject was her own late husband, Mischka Danos. Her book is one of an increasing number written by relatives of those who lived through the war, although they are more commonly penned by children or grandchildren than by spouses. These fall into the category of family history, a genre which describes the experiences of an ancestor or ancestors and their impact on subsequent generations of the family. The impulse to write a family history of World War II reflects in part the fact that family history has become 'the fastest growing hobby in both Britain and America, as well as mainland Europe, Canada and Australia'.[28] The overriding motive appears to be a desire for a sense of belonging, often spurred by the experience of dislocation. Recent developments including increased geographical mobility, precarious labour practices and new patterns of socialization shaped by social media have created a more general sense of disorientation that family history may be thought to heal. The process of writing family history has an integrative function in that it involves conversations between and within different generations, an exchange that may be especially important for globally dispersed families.[29]

Given the popularity of family history, we were not surprised by the enthusiastic response when, in anticipation of the seventy-fifth anniversary of the end of the war, we issued a call in 2019 for essays on family memories of World War II to colleagues at our university, National University of Ireland, Galway. An earlier volume of family memories of colleagues demonstrated the interest in family history and the value of a university as a sample base.[30] It transpired that some colleagues were already engaged in the process of researching ancestors' roles in World War II. For others, the call provided a welcome opportunity to embark upon such an exploration. The very phenomenon of globally dispersed families is reflected in the highly international staff at our university. Our contributors include two Germans, two Italians, a Greek and others with a mixture of Russian, Israeli, Ukrainian, Belgian, Spanish, Portuguese, French and Irish backgrounds. Although Ireland was neutral in World War II, many Irishmen and women partook directly in the British or American war efforts and some of their stories are represented here.

World War II had a major impact on families as well as individuals. While early adult deaths, as a result of events like childbirth, work accidents or infection, were a constant source of family disruption in peacetime, the war brought unprecedented levels of death and separation for families. The Nazis' genocidal policy towards Jews meant that, in some cases, all members of a family were killed, making it impossible for their stories to be told from the perspective of direct descendants. For many of those who did survive and their descendants, often scattered across the globe, telling the story of wartime survival became a means of coming to terms with the 'presence of an absence', as Alan and Naomi Berger describe it.[31] Inherited trauma has been shown to have a major influence on subsequent generations.[32] The children of Holocaust survivors emerged as an identifiable group in the United States in the 1970s, organizing themselves into the International Network of Children of Jewish Holocaust Survivors in 1981, and were responsible for a sizeable portion of Holocaust memoirs.[33] Several decades later, the grandchildren of survivors have begun to play their part in recounting individual Holocaust experiences.[34]

Of course, non-Jews also experienced the loss of individual family members. The memoir by German writer Uwe Timm, *In My Brother's Shadow*, is a poignant evocation of the absence of his brother, a Waffen-SS soldier killed in the war. Yet, coming from a German perspective, it also addresses the possibility that his brother was in fact a perpetrator of war crimes.[35] Not surprisingly, accounts by Germans acknowledging this complicated legacy appeared only from the 1990s, decades after the victims of Nazism had begun describing their own experiences.[36] By now, in the early decades of the twenty-first century memoirs by the third generation have been published, most notably, *Heimat* by Nora Krug. This best-selling account, written in the form of a family album, describes how her maternal grandfather profited from the Nazis' dispossession of Jews.[37] Even in the absence of collective burdens like those borne by Germans, World War II provides rich material for family histories, not least the dynamics of family relationships.[38] American author Louise DeSalvo explored her father's experience aboard an aircraft carrier in the Pacific in order to better comprehend his failings as a father. Her discovery of his wartime trauma helped her understand him more fully.[39]

Family histories rely heavily on memories transmitted from one generation to the next. The processes both of remembering and of transmitting memories are complex. Not all experiences are remembered and only some of those remembered are communicated to others. Indeed memories are typically fragmentary, a collection of anecdotes rather than a coherent narrative. Moments of emotional intensity tend to crowd out the mundane. In his contribution to this volume, Hans-Walter Schmidt-Hannisa describes his mother's frequent recounting of the humiliation of having to beg for food after being expelled with other ethnic Germans from Czechoslovakia at the end of the war.[40] By contrast, fellow German Hermann Rasche's mother had joyful memories of the aftermath, exemplified by the pride she felt when Field Marshal Montgomery stopped his motorcade to have her and her son photographed.[41]

The context in which memories are recalled plays an important role. Events that took place between those recalled and the present can frame the memory of the original experience in significant ways. Holocaust scholar Stephan Lehnstaedt has shown, for instance, how the extreme experience of the death camps suppressed less harsh aspects of ghetto life beforehand in accounts by survivors. He notes that they forgot they had received payment for some labour services performed in the ghetto.[42] The adoption of popular narrative tropes also leads to the smoothing out of memories, whereby experiences that do not fit the interpretive framework are omitted or elided. Once framed as a story of triumph over adversity, for instance, wartime memories leave little room for moments of personal weakness or shame.

That survivors tell their stories at all is not a given. Some of the war witnesses described here spoke little of their experiences, others more than their relatives wanted to hear. Scholarship suggests that public events had an impact on the trajectory of recounting memories within some families. Cinema releases and television programmes could provide powerful impetuses to asking questions about wartime experiences. The iconoclastic four-hour documentary, *The Sorrow and the Pity*, encouraged a more honest assessment of the degree of collaboration and anti-Semitism in wartime France.[43] In Germany, the student revolution of 1968 prompted a nationwide reckoning with the past, which in some cases translated into difficult questions for fathers and grandfathers.[44] The essays in this case show that, in many cases, the impetus was more personal. Rasche notes that his uncle began to open up about his years in combat and captivity in Russia only after his retirement and the death of his wife. Schmidt-Hannisa's decision to opt for community service instead of military service as a youth provoked his grandfather into revealing the extent of his commitment to the Nazis' anti-Semitic agenda. Occasionally, the starting point for stories was accidental. In their essay, the Maloney sisters describe how the arrival of an Italian woman who had helped to hide their American father during the war first sparked family conversations about his experiences.[45] Cormac Ó Loideáin's relative, a Royal Navy volunteer married to his grand-aunt, began to talk when someone thought to ask about his early life.[46]

The fact that survivors communicate their wartime memories to relatives rather than outsiders shapes what is told and not told. For Enrico Dal Lago's father, it was a natural extension of his role as a parent to speak with his children about the war, suffusing their early years with stories of the Italian Resistance.[47] There may be a special effort to avoid certain topics in order to protect relatives from memories with painful implications or simply because these are culturally taboo – our stories tell little about the experience of sexuality during wartime, for instance.[48] There may also be an effort to teach lessons through past experience. A recent study of historical memory in Czech families showed that the stories transmitted, many of them about World War II, usually articulated positive values like moral righteousness, bravery or ingenuity, as embodied by the survivor. The repetition of these stories suggested that these values were to be embraced by all subsequent family generations too.[49] As Marina Ansaldo explains in her contribution to this volume, her Italian grandfather expanded the notes he took in wartime captivity into a tale of fortitude as a means of helping his daughter to overcome an episode of depression.[50] Lessons from the past may also be communicated in more subtle ways, in parenting practices like the tendency towards protectiveness frequently found among Holocaust survivors or a preoccupation with ensuring sufficient supplies of food. In speaking of begging for food, Schmidt-Hannisa's mother was also teaching her children gratitude for plenty.

Those hearing stories of the past also bring their own feelings and values to the process. In the case of World War II, many of those who heard these stories depended for their very existence on their ancestors' survival in wartime. Family histories are shaped by 'affect and loyalty'; that is, a strong tendency on the part of descendants to identify and empathize with their subjects.[51] In a series of interviews with three generations of German families in the 1990s, Harald Welzer identified a phenomenon of 'cumulative heroization' of wartime perpetrators. Blinded by bonds of affection and loyalty, grandchildren ignored evidence of their grandparents' complicity in Nazi crimes and depicted them as apolitical or even critical of Nazism.[52] Welzer later identified a similar phenomenon in countries occupied by the Nazis. Young people in Norway, Denmark and the Netherlands emphasized their grandparents' resistance to Nazism. While this was more plausible than in the German case, interviewees explained away evidence to the contrary, for instance, by dismissing an admission of collaboration as the product of senility.[53]

The force of emotion evident in these studies of the intergenerational transmission of historical memory threatens to undermine the credibility of family history. Indeed the historical profession was long sceptical of family history, seeing it also as narrow in focus and decontextualized. An appreciation of the role of emotions in the past and indeed in history-writing generally has lessened this scepticism in recent years. Historian Ivan Jablonka emphasizes that all history, not just family history, is subjective.[54] Alongside Sheila Fitzpatrick, he is one of an increasing number of professional historians who have themselves written family histories.[55] The greater readiness of historians to experiment with different scales of historical experience has also boosted the status of family history. Historians have come to appreciate it as a means of exploring the complex interaction of history and memory in ways that often diverge from official national narratives and popular memory.[56] Part of the fascination of Welzer's work is that he shows how these different levels clash in the German case, where the official narrative acknowledged the crimes of the Nazi era, and coalesce in the case of occupied countries, where official narratives emphasized national resistance. Family histories, while generally written in just one voice as opposed to the multiple voices of Welzer's studies, provide useful points of comparison with collective memories. The three stories of Irish war veterans in this volume provide an additional example of the relationship between official and private narratives. The private memories of Irish service in the British Army, while articulated in family and veteran circles, were not valourized as part of the Republic of Ireland's national story.

Another argument in defence of family history is its increasing professionalism. The digitization of archival sources and the generally higher levels of education of post-war generations have allowed non-historians to piece together the experiences of their relatives and craft them into coherent narratives with some level of critical reflection. The contributors to this volume, mainly academics in various disciplines, are particularly proficient in this respect. They use many of the sources employed by professional biographers. A handful of contributors are able to draw on sources dating back to the war itself. These include official documents not only like the labour registration card issued to Sylvie Mossay's grandfather in Ukraine in 1943, but also personal ones like the notes taken by Ansaldo's grandfather on cigarette paper in a POW camp during his captivity from 1943 to 1945.[57] Nearly all contributors were able to source old family photographs, some of which were taken in the 1930s and 1940s. All of the photos and facsimiles of surviving wartime documents that accompany the chapters in this volume are from the private collections of our contributors unless otherwise stated. Letters between soldiers and their families back home yield rich information for a number of authors too, such as Schmidt-Hannisa, Sheena and Gill Fennell, and Ciara Boylan.[58] Several authors exploit accounts written by their ancestors after the war. For instance, Irina Ruppo makes extensive use of her grandmother's memoir about the Siege of Leningrad and Dal Lago of his aunt's published account of her brothers' resistance activities in northern Italy.[59] Other contributors base their accounts primarily on stories transmitted orally. Rasche, although born during the war, learned mostly about the events of the time from stories related by his mother's family. Ó Loideáin's account relies heavily on an interview his father recorded with his great-uncle-in-law. Some contributors engaged in additional research into official sources to fill in gaps in the stories passed down to them. One of the unexpected benefits of this project was that Mossay's mother saw her birth certificate for the first time.

Our contributors have sought to corroborate the stories they inherited and the editors have ensured that all stories are plausible; that is, they were within the bounds of the possible in World War II. That is not to say, however, that the authors or the editors can stand over every detail. Survivor memories can be unreliable, as Ruppo demonstrates when comparing accounts from within her own family of their evacuation from Leningrad.[60] For our purposes, this is not as important as it might seem. Family history is about the transmission of values and emotions as much as facts about the past. Our authors describe not just the lives of their ancestors, but the impact that these lives had on them. In nearly all cases, the authors knew those who had lived through the war, although few of them are alive today. They use the process of rediscovery to reflect on these relationships. Many frame their stories as lessons for subsequent generations, suggesting a continuum of values identified with the family. Only in Schmidt-Hannisa's case is this a negative one. His rejection of his grandfather's anti-Semitism is designed to create a new family narrative based on the acceptance of others.

The course of World War II

The main events of the war are undisputed and provide the indispensable historical context for the family stories at the heart of this volume. Between 1939 and 1945, the war was fought out in multiple theatres, often in several campaigns simultaneously.[61] For Europe, the war may be broadly divided into two periods. The first, from 1939 to 1942, was dominated by the expansion of Nazi Germany's control over large swathes of the European continent. A second phase, from mid-1942 to 1945, was marked simultaneously by the Reich's implementation of the Holocaust and by the decline of German power and the final collapse of the Reich in May 1945. Outside Europe, a different periodization applies. As far back as 1937, Imperial Japan was loosely allied with Nazi Germany and Fascist Italy by means of an Anti-Comintern Pact; a cycle of Japanese expansion began, in fact, with aggression against China in the 1930s. Japan's war against the United States and against European nations' empires in Asia lasted from December 1941 to August 1945 following a similar pattern to Germany's rise and fall. Within this broad sweep there was a succession of military campaigns, occupations and key moments. The thirteen chapters in this volume touch upon most major theatres of war – western Europe, Scandinavia, the eastern front, Italy, the Balkans, North Africa and the eastern Mediterranean. Given its important place in the historiography of World War II and its uniqueness, it is perhaps surprising that the Holocaust barely features in this volume. This absence not only owes something to the low levels of post-war Jewish immigration into Ireland but, more substantially, it also reflects the war's scale of devastation across Europe. As noted earlier, up to seventy million Europeans were either killed or displaced as a consequence of the conflict.

As is well known, the German attack on Poland in September 1939 marked the beginning of the war in Europe. This was followed later that same month by the attack of the Soviet Union on eastern Poland in accordance with secret terms of the Nazi-Soviet Non-Aggression Pact of August 1939. Mossay's family's first experience of the war was of Soviet occupation. Poland's considerable resistance in these weeks was no match for the Wehrmacht and the Red Army. Although pledged to support Poland, Britain and France could do little to aid the Poles who were now the subject of a brutal race war at German hands. The Soviets meanwhile altered their western borders not only by taking over eastern Poland but also, shortly thereafter, by invading Finland and later, in 1940, forcibly incorporating the three Baltic states into the Union of Soviet Socialist Republics (USSR).

Meanwhile British and French policymakers, becalmed in what became known as the Phoney War of 1939–40, settled on a long-war strategy whereby they would build up their strength and move against Germany around 1941. The disastrous Anglo-French failure to keep the Norwegian port of Narvik out of German hands in the spring of 1940 opened a season of humiliation for the western Allies. The two German contributors to this volume, Schmidt-Hannisa and Rasche, describe their relatives' tours of duty in Narvik. Applying the blitzkrieg formula of combined aerial, tank and infantry assault used previously in Poland, Hitler launched an attack in the west on 10 May 1940. Having already taken over Denmark, the Wehrmacht rolled into the Low Countries and, spectacularly defying expectations, defeated France in just six weeks with minimal German losses. The Fall of France had a range of consequences, not least the division of France into an occupied zone and a 'free' zone which became known as Vichy France. Contributor Sara Farrona describes the implications for her grand-uncle living there as a Spanish communist refugee.[62] The attack on France had also occasioned Mussolini's entry into the war on Germany's side. Italian troops proceeded to expand eastward into the Balkans. Meanwhile, the place of 1940 in the British national epic hardly needs emphasis. The undoubted achievement of the Royal Air Force (RAF) in preventing German control of British skies, followed by the failure of the blitz to crack British morale, allowed Britain to bounce back from the ropes. London became host to a range of exiled governments such as those of the Netherlands and Poland and liberation movements such as Charles De Gaulle's Free French.

Following on from Hitler's fateful choice to attack the Soviet Union in June 1941, the Wehrmacht cut through swathes of Soviet territory facilitating the murderous racial war of SS Einsatzgruppen. The thousand-day Siege of Leningrad, so powerfully recounted from family memories in the essay by Ruppo in this volume, was one of many cruel episodes in the enormous German-Soviet War. From the very beginning of World War II in 1939, the travails of the populations living in the territories between Nazi Germany and the Soviet Union had been great. Between 1939 and 1945 some ten million civilians were killed in Poland, Ukraine, Belarus, the Baltic countries and the western parts of the Soviet Union.[63] Undergoing occupations by Hitler and Stalin, in some cases both in succession, this region has been dubbed 'bloodlands' by historian Timothy Snyder. It was the site of the Nazis' six death camps and of ruthless imperial exploitation, of which slave labour was one aspect, described here in wrenching detail by Mossay.[64]

Churchill's unlikely offer of alliance to the Soviet Union in the face of the German attack linked two European opponents of Germany. Six months later, in December 1941, American entry into the war brought a military and economic sleeping giant on to their side. Intelligence breakthroughs helped tip the Battle of the Atlantic in Britain's favour, facilitating the transport of troops, food and matériel to Britain. All the same, by the midpoint in the war in 1942, fortunes in several theatres were delicately balanced. The German surrender in the icy hell of Stalingrad in January 1943 belied Germany's invincibility. In North Africa, British and German forces fought for control of Italy's colonial possession in Libya and to safeguard the British-controlled Suez Canal. The struggle turned in the Allies' favour at the two battles of El Alamein in 1942. Boylan recounts how her grandfather, an Irish dentist in the British Army, tended to the dental needs of Axis soldiers interned after the battles in a POW camp in Fayid, Egypt. Along with American military advances from the west, these battles secured North Africa for the Allies.

This in turn facilitated the Anglo-American invasion of Italy, beginning with landings in Sicily in July 1943, attacking what Churchill called the 'soft underbelly' of the Axis. Gill Fennell and her daughter Sheena recount here how Gill's father, an RAF pilot from Ireland, participated in the bombardment of Italy's tiny offshore redoubt of Pantelleria in preparation for the landings in Sicily. The Allies' long, slow progress up the Italian peninsula had a number of fateful implications for Italians. In July 1943, the Italian king and elements in the governing elites deposed Mussolini as head of government and in October clumsily attempted to switch sides to the Allies. Nazi Germany had already found Fascist Italy a burdensome ally and decided to occupy the country itself. Italians themselves separated into anti-Fascists and supporters of a continuity of the Fascist Italian Social Republic led by Mussolini, recently sprung from captivity by German commandos. The brutality of the German occupation of Italy is reflected here in the contribution of Dal Lago about his father's family's role in the resistance, Ansaldo's tribute to her grandfather, an Italian Army officer-turned-military internee in German custody and in the Maloney sisters' account of their father, a downed American airman sheltered at great risk by Italian villagers in 1945.

June 1944 is indelibly associated in Western minds with D-Day, the American-led multinational Normandy landings, the biggest amphibious assault in history. That same month the Red Army launched Operation Bagration, an enormous counter-attack against Germany to retake Soviet territory from Germany. The Red Army proceeded to conquer eastern and central Europe, culminating in the entry into Berlin in April 1945. At their Casablanca conference in January 1943, Stalin, Roosevelt and Churchill had fatefully decided to insist upon the unconditional surrender of Nazi Germany. This resolve in turn fed the fanatical resistance of some Nazis to the bitter end. The failed attempt on Hitler's life on 20 July 1944 reinforced a sense of personal loyalty to the Führer amongst the broader pro-Nazi population. Allied strategic bombing of Germany intensified in the last years of the war, pulverizing German targets – military and civilian. The war's end in Europe, on 8 May 1945, brought relief for many, if not respite from shortage or from concern for the future. The war against Germany's ally, Japan, came to an end on 15 August, shortly after the bombings of Hiroshima and Nagasaki.

Wartime experiences

The chapters in our volume provide perspectives on the war from the ground up. As such, they provide telling details that convey the lived experience of the war. Fighting was a common, but not universal, wartime experience for adult men across the world at war. There were, of course, variations in the nature and intensity of combat over time. Extensive training was required to make soldiers battle-ready. Pilots like Gill Fennell's father underwent intense and exhilarating technical training to fly Spitfires. Ó Loideáin's grand-uncle-in-law learned to use cutting-edge technology to guide bombs. Combat itself tested the endurance of soldiers. The progress of Allied troops up through Italy, efforts to break German defences in the Normandy *bocage* in the summer of 1944 and the takeover of Berlin in 1945 required dogged fighting for every patch of ground. Fighting could also include moments of great drama. Gill Fennell's father was shot down while strafing a troop train in German-occupied Yugoslavia. The Maloney sisters' father, a US Army Air Forces pilot, parachuted out of his plane just before it crashed into a mountain. Military service, however, could also encompass moments of respite or even leisure. Quieter postings allowed German officers to act for a time like tourists as much as occupiers.[65] Schmidt-Hannisa's father recalled the pleasure of taking saunas and making ice-cream during his tour of duty in Finland. The same held for Allied officers. Boylan's grandfather wrote home about playing golf in Alexandria, duck-shooting on the Nile and swimming in the Suez Canal.

Interpersonal violence occurred on most fighting fronts at some stage. Ansaldo provides a dramatic account of how her grandfather and twenty-five other Italian soldiers exchanged an hour-long hail of bullets with German troops before surrendering. Indeed German soldiers, in conversations among themselves, admitted to conducting a merciless war, especially on the eastern front.[66] Personalized violence featured strongly in the asymmetric war fought between resistance fighters across Europe and the superior force of Axis armies. Its localized and very personal nature is seen vividly in Constantinos G. Efthymiou's depiction of German-occupied central Greece and in Dal Lago's chapter on occupied north-eastern Italy.[67] To take the second example, Dal Lago's father's young cousins were shot dead near their home by German soldiers hunting for partisans. The author's father, a boy of ten, had himself to dodge German machine-gun fire on the family farm to pass messages or avoid disclosing to raiding soldiers the hiding place of a partisan arms cache.

The actions of partisans reflected the dissatisfaction of many Europeans with German occupation and the decision of elements of these European populations to resist occupation.[68] The recourse to acts of sabotage and explosions by armed resisters against the Germans is seen in Farrona's account of her uncle's role in the French Resistance and in Efthymiou's account of attacks on strategic railway lines and troop trains in central Greece. Deemed illegitimate forms of warfare by the occupiers, such acts contributed to a cycle of repression in occupied Europe. In the Italian case, Dal Lago's father described how the countryside of the Veneto was, in contemporary parlance, 'raked' for resisters. Efthymiou provides a vivid example of how partisan activity could provoke German atrocities. The execution of a dozen captured German soldiers on a mountaintop near his village prompted all able-bodied villagers to flee their homes. Although only six years of age, Efthymiou's mother has vivid memories of flight. Their fears were well founded. Four elderly villagers, including a bed-ridden local priest, were put to death in the subsequent German raid.

Understandably, being captured was one of the greatest fears of members of conventional armies or resistance units. Several of the protagonists who feature in our volume managed to avoid capture by going into hiding. The terror of being discovered made for powerful memories. The Maloneys' father found refuge from the Germans in the last months of the war in the Italian Alps, cared for by the local community. His deliverance from danger became an important foundation story for his children and remains a source of immense pride for the village to this day. Dal Lago's uncle Danilo's daring escape also became the stuff of family legend. He escaped from the regular Italian Army as it fell into the clutches of the Wehrmacht in September 1943 and returned home dazed. Nonetheless he quickly took up arms as a Resistance partisan.

Some others were not so lucky. Several of the survivors mentioned in our stories faced periods of captivity. POW camps varied greatly. While Boylan's grandfather remembered humane, if crowded, conditions in the British camp in Egypt in which he served, Ansaldo's grandfather recalled horrific conditions in a German camp. Not surprisingly, for the latter, the experience of captivity dominated his memories of the war. The experiences of Rasche's two uncles demonstrate that the camps established by the Allies to punish Germans after the war also differed considerably. One uncle returned from British captivity relatively unscathed, while the other returned from Soviet captivity so physically weakened that his parents barely recognized him. The former was accordingly less critical of the Nazis' war campaign in discussions after the war.

The shadow of death hung over all those who lived through World War II either on fighting fronts or home fronts. Ansaldo's grandfather and about three hundred other Italian Military Internees in Germany in April 1945 experienced the narrowest of escapes from death. The commander of their camp refused to carry out the order from Berlin to kill the prisoners, whether out of an impulse rooted in humanity or self-protection in light of Germany's imminent defeat. Only afterwards, when he discovered the extent of German killings of Italian internees, did her grandfather appreciate how fortunate he and his comrades had been. Gill Fennell's father had the burden of witnessing some of his fellow Allied POWs being killed as they were marching through Germany in the final months of the war by friendly fire from Allied planes. The Fennells report that this was the wartime incident that had the most profound effect on him. For those on the home front, the prospect of their loved ones' deaths in battle was a constant worry. His own future wife, a volunteer ambulance driver in Scotland, became alarmed when she heard that he had been shot down in Yugoslavia in April 1943 and was missing. She wrote to his mother to say: 'Please God missing is so much better than missing believed killed.' News later came that he had survived. By contrast, Rasche's mother had to deal with word of her husband's death. Like millions of others, she and her son had to live with the consequences for decades to come.[69] Even in the absence of death, war could cause serious and sustained loss. Mossay's grandmother had to cope with the very painful experience of separation from her daughter for over thirty years because of political conditions in Ukraine after the war. Some of our contributors also had to confront the war's legacy of death on a mass scale. Boylan's grandfather, recalled to Germany after the war's end to help in the gruesome task of ascertaining the number of victims in Bergen-Belsen on the basis of dental remains, could barely speak of the experience afterwards. One of the most arresting details in our collection is the instruction by British navy commanders to their men in early 1946, recounted by Ó Loideáin's grand-uncle-in-law, not to swim in Tripoli harbour because it was filled with half a million corpses.

For those who remained at home, aerial bombardment was one of the most scarring aspects of World War II both in terms of physical destruction and lost lives. Bombing certainly occurred as part of conventional military operations but more often it became an end in its own right, as seen in the German attempt to break British resistance during the blitz of 1940–1. This having failed, Britain and the United States subsequently used the growing Allied air superiority to conduct the 'area bombing' of Germany. This meant attacking German workers as well as crippling German industry: British planes dropped more bombs there in the month of March 1945 than in the first three years of the war combined.[70] While the military effectiveness of the Allied and German bombing campaigns was questionable, they left an indelible mark on those who lived through them, as the family memories in this volume show.[71] In the Scottish port of Aberdeen, Gill Fennell's mother and her ambulance colleagues tended to the injured from an air raid and saw a grown man weep at the loss of his home. She wrote: 'I finally got back at 4 a.m. having seen dreadful things.' In early January 1945, Ó Loideáin's grand-uncle-in-law heard first-hand from family friends in Manchester of their home's narrow escape from having being hit by a German V1 flying bomb the previous Christmas

Eve. In these same weeks, he saw the British Lancaster bombers lined up at Skegness on the east coast of England ready to take part in the attack on Dresden, with notorious consequences for German civilians.

Death in World War II could also come slowly, as a result of malnutrition and resultant disease. Food was a constant preoccupation for both soldiers and civilians during the war and features strongly in the memories of war survivors. The military campaigns of World War II disrupted traditional food supply chains, as agricultural sites were destroyed and millions of people displaced. Food had never been distributed evenly, not even within the allegedly egalitarian Soviet Union, but the disparities between the amount and quality of food available to different kinds of people grew to colossal proportions during the war.[72] Distance from the front was a distinct advantage. Gill Fennell's mother admitted that she was putting on weight in Britain and Rasche records that his family in northern Germany had plenty to eat. Ruppo's grandmother, by contrast, nearly died of starvation while Leningrad was under siege by German troops. The priorities of those in charge were also an important determinant of access to food, and thus ultimately survival. Wherever it ruled, Germany exercised a strategy of brutal exploitation based on political calculation and racial hierarchies. Ansaldo's grandfather was constantly on the hunt for food during his time as a military internee in a German camp. One of his greatest achievements was to source ingredients for what might pass as a Christmas cake. Slave labourers working for German families fared little better. Mossay's grandmother resorted to eating the scraps for dogs because she received so little food from her employer. Indeed Schmidt-Hannisa notes that his own grandfather objected to the Belarusian slave labourer working for his family being given the same amount of food as family members. Fortunately, the author's great-grandmother overruled her son. The tables turned after the war, of course, as the Allies privileged the victims of Nazism by giving them higher rations than the Germans.[73] Yet food could also serve as a valuable tool for the Allies in seeking to win over Germans during the post-war occupation. Both our German authors provide stories of receiving sweets from Allied soldiers. Indeed, the benevolence of the British post-war occupation regime made a sufficient impression on Rasche to encourage him to study English later in life.

The chapters in this volume show a great breadth of attitudes towards the enemy. The experience of the war led Patricia Scully's grandfather to refuse to read books or watch television programmes about Germany and Japan. Other chapters in this volume suggest that the war generated less hatred for the enemy than might be expected of such a bloody conflict. Even though animosities ran high during the war, our contributors note moments of magnanimity towards the enemy. Gill Fennell's mother had resolved to give inferior treatment to German POWs, should they ever come under her supervision but, when faced with them in the flesh, human sympathy led her to give them the best of care. Efthymiou's mother recalls with compassion the loneliness of a Wehrmacht officer, who, missing his own children while on duty in Greece, was moved to tears by her and her young friends. Decades later when the son of another Wehrmacht officer visited the village, the local community helped him in his quest to reconstruct the final moments of his father who had been executed by partisans nearby. Schmidt-Hannisa's father, also a member of the Wehrmacht, felt no bitterness towards France or the French farmers for whom he worked as a German POW in the immediate aftermath of the war. Indeed he brought his own family to the farm for a visit around 1970. The exchange of personal visits, both at an individual and town level, helped to underpin the larger, political process of Franco-German reconciliation in the context of European integration.

In retrieving this collection of family memories, we as editors have been pushing an open door. It is by now well recognized that the impact of World War II was not limited only to those who lived through it, but also extended to subsequent generations. For that reason, we have subtitled our volume *Survivors and Descendants*. Our authors, the descendants, variously, of refugees, soldiers, slave labourers, POWs, military internees and civilians, bear witness to the enormous impact of the events from 1939 to 1945 on their families. The very fact that descendants chose to write about their ancestors over seventy-five years after the war demonstrates the enduring legacy of wartime events. The current strength of engagement with the war by families across the globe shows no sign of abating.

Notes

1 Ian Kershaw, *To Hell and Back: Europe, 1914–1949* (London: Penguin, 2016), 356.

2 Mark Mazower, *Hitler's Empire: Nazi Rule in Occupied Europe* (London: Penguin, 2009), 347.

3 Norman Davies, *Europe at War, 1939–1945: No Simple Victory* (London: Pan, 2007).

4 Aidan MacCarthy, *A Doctor's War* (Cork: Collins Press, 2006), 130.

5 Konrad H. Jarausch, *Out of Ashes: A New History of Europe in the Twentieth Century* (Princeton: Princeton University Press, 2015), 395.

6 Kershaw, *To Hell and Back*, 346.

7 Mark Mazower, *Dark Continent: Europe's Twentieth Century* (London: Penguin, 1999).

8 Angus Calder, *The Myth of the Blitz* (London: Pimlico, 1997).

9 Anna Wolff-Powęska and Piotr Forecki, eds, *World War II and Two Occupations: Dilemmas of Polish Memory* (Frankfurt: Peter Lang, 2016).

10 Moshe Flinker, *Young Moshe's Diary: The Spiritual Torment of a Jewish Boy in Nazi Europe* (Jerusalem: Yad Vashem, 1971), originally published in Hebrew in 1958; Micheline Bood, *Les Années Doubles: journal d'une lycéenne sous l'occupation* (Paris: Robert Laffont, 1974).

11 Francis de Guingand, *Operation Victory* (London: Hodder & Stoughton, 1947) and Heinz Guderian, *Panzer Leader* (New York: Ballantine Books, 1952), originally published in German in 1950.

12 For military adventures, see Fitzroy Maclean, *Eastern Approaches* (New York: Time, 1949). For a resistance memoir, see Agnès Humbert, *Résistance: Memoirs of Occupied France* (London: Bloomsbury, 2009), originally published in French in 1946.

13 Viktor Frankl, *Man's Search for Meaning: An Introduction to Logotherapy* (New York: Houghton Mifflin, 2000), originally published in German in 1946 and in English translation later in 1946; Primo Levi, *If This Is a Man* (London: Little Brown, 2013), originally published in Italian in 1947 and in English translation in 1958.

14 See, for example, Alden Hatch, *George Patton, General in Spurs* (New York: Messner, 1950).

15 For a comprehensive list, see WorldCat.org. Examples from the last year of the war include Jean Allary, *Winston Churchill* (Paris: Hachette, 1945), in French, and Bo Enander, *Adolf Hitler* (Stockholm: Bonnier, 1945), in Swedish.

16 Lois W. Banner, 'Biography as History', *American Historical Review* 114, no. 3 (2009): 585.

17 Stephen E. Ambrose, *Band of Brothers: E Company, 506th Regiment, 101st Airborne from Normandy to Hitler's Eagle's Nest* (London: Simon and Schuster, 1992).

18 Elie Wiesel, *Night* (London: Penguin, 2008), originally published in French in 1958 and in English translation in 1960. Anne Frank, *The Diary of a Young Girl* (New York: Bantam Books, 1993), originally published in Dutch in 1947 and in English translation in 1952. For Levi, see above.

19 On the trajectory of popular interest in the Holocaust, see Peter Novick, *The Holocaust in American Life* (New York: Houghton Mifflin, 1999).

20 See the best-selling memoir, Edith Eger, *The Choice: Embrace the Possible* (New York: Scribner, 2017).

21 Elie Poulard, *A French Slave in Nazi Germany: A Testimony*, trans. and ed. Jean V. Poulard (Notre Dame, IN: University of Notre Dame Press, 2016), originally published in French in 2005. On the trajectory of deportee accounts, see Richard Vinen, *The Unfree French: The Tragedy of the Occupation, 1940–44* (London: Allen Lane, 2006), 363.

22 Renia Spiegel, *Renia's Diary: A Girl's Life in the Shadow of the Holocaust* (London: Ebury Press, 2019). For German veterans' memories, see Christian Hardinghaus, *Die verdammte Generation: Gespräche mit den letzten Soldaten des Zweiten Weltkriegs* (Berlin: Europa Verlag, 2020). Between 2003 and 2006 the BBC ran a project collecting memories of the war among

those then aged 60 or more. This project harnessed over 47,000 stories. See www.bbc.co.uk/history/ww2peopleswar/ (accessed 2 July 2020).

23 Hugh Trevor Roper, *Wartime Journals*, ed. Richard Davenport-Hines (London: I. B. Tauris, 2011).

24 As early as 1985, Nobel Prize winner Svetlana Alexievich published accounts of the wartime experiences of Russian women and children, *War's Unwomanly Face* (Moscow: Progress Publishers, 1988) and *Last Witnesses: An Oral History of the Children of World War II* (London: Penguin, 2019).

25 One example is Sonia Purnell, *A Woman of No Importance: The Untold Story of the American Spy Who Helped Win World War II* (London: Virago, 2019).

26 See 'History and Biography' special issue of *American Historical Review* 114, no. 3 (2009): 579–86; and Stephen M. Norris, 'A Biographical Turn?' *Kritika: Explorations in Russian and Eurasian History* 17, no. 1 (2016):163–79.

27 Sheila Fitzpatrick, *Mischka's War: A Story of Survival from War-Torn Europe to New York* (London: I. B. Tauris, 2017).

28 Fenella Cannell, 'English Ancestors: The Moral Possibilities of Popular Genealogy', *Journal of the Royal Anthropological Institute* 17, no. 3 (2011): 462, quoted in Emma Shaw, ' "Who We Are, and Why We Do It": A Demographic Overview and the Cited Motivations of Australia's Family Historians', *Journal of Family History* 45, no. 1 (2020): 109.

29 Cardell Jacobson, 'Social Dislocations and the Search for Genealogical Roots', *Human Relations* 39, no. 4 (1986): 347–56.

30 Ciara Boylan, Sarah-Anne Buckley and Pat Dolan, eds, *Family Histories of the Irish Revolution* (Dublin: Four Courts Press, 2018), to which Róisín Healy contributed a chapter on her grandfather. Boylan has written a chapter for this volume.

31 Alan L. Berger and Naomi Berger, 'Introduction', in *Second Generation Voices: Reflections by Children of Holocaust Survivors and Perpetrators*, ed. Alan L. Berger and Naomi Berger (Syracuse: Syracuse University Press, 2001), 1–12, at 1.

32 Berger and Berger, *Second Generation Voices*; Esther Jilovsky, Jordana Silverstein and David Slucki, eds, *In the Shadows of Memory: The Holocaust and the Third Generation* (Elstree, UK: Valentine Mitchell, 2015). On trauma, see Francesca Cappelletto, 'Long-Term Memory of Extreme Events: From Autobiography to History', *Journal of the Royal Anthropological Institute* 9, no. 2 (2003): 241–60.

33 Serialized between 1980 and 1991, Art Spiegelmann's graphic novel, *Maus: A Survivor's Tale* (New York: Pantheon Books, 1991), has proved very popular. See also Paula Fass, *Inheriting the Holocaust: A Second Generation Memoir* (New Brunswick, NJ: Rutgers University Press, 2008).

34 Ivan Jablonka, *A History of the Grandparents I Never Had* (Stanford: Stanford University Press, 2016) and Noah Lederman, *A World Erased: A Grandson's Search for His Family's Holocaust Secrets* (Lanham, MD: Rowman & Littlefield, 2017).

35 Uwe Timm, *In My Brother's Shadow* (London: Bloomsbury, 2006), originally published in German in 2003.

36 Berger and Berger, *Second Generation Voices*, 8. Harald Welzer, 'Schön unscharf: Über die Konjunktur der Familien – und Generationenromane', *Mittelweg 36*, no. 1 (2004): 53–64.

37 Nora Krug, *Heimat: A Family Album* (London: Particular Books, 2018).

38 On family disintegration as a spur to family history, see Katrina Hackstaff, 'Family Genealogy: A Sociological Imagination Reveals Intersectional Relations', *Sociology Compass* 4, no. 8 (2010): 660.

39 Louise DeSalvo, *Chasing Ghosts: A Memoir of a Father, Gone to War* (New York: Fordham University Press, 2016).

40 See Chapter 2, in this volume.

41 See Chapter 10, in this volume.

42 Stephan Lehnstaedt, 'Coercion and Incentive: Jewish Ghetto Labor in East Upper Silesia', *Holocaust and Genocide Studies* 24, no. 3 (2010): 420.

43 For the impact of the 1969 documentary and French memory of the occupation generally, see Julian Jackson, *The Dark Years: France, 1940–1944* (Oxford: Oxford University Press, 2001), 613–32 and Henry Rousso, *The Vichy Syndrome: History and Memory in France since 1944* (Cambridge, MA: Harvard University Press, 1991). For the impact of the television series, *Holocaust*, broadcast in Germany in 1979, see Wulf Kansteiner, *In Pursuit of German Memory: History, Television, and Politics after Auschwitz* (Athens, OH: Ohio University Press, 2006), 116–22.

44 A. Dirk Moses, *German Intellectuals and the Nazi Past* (Cambridge: Cambridge University Press, 2007), 186–218.

45 See Chapter 6, in this volume.

46 See Chapter 8, in this volume.

47 See Chapter 11, in this volume.

48 Friederieke Eigler, 'Writing in the New Germany: Cultural Memory and Family Narratives', *German Politics and Society* 23, no. 3 (2005): 23.

49 Radmila Švaříčková Slabáková, 'Moral Heroes or Suffering Persons? Ancestors in Family Intergenerational Stories and the Intersection of Family and National Memories', *Journal of Family History* 44, no. 4 (2019): 439–40.

50 See Chapter 5, in this volume.

51 Eigler, 'Writing in the New Germany', 22.

52 Harald Welzer, 'Re-Narrations: How Pasts Change in Conversational Remembering', *Memory Studies* 3, no. 1 (2010): 5–17; Harald Welzer, Sabine Moller and Karoline Tschuggnall, '*Opa war kein Nazi*': *Nationalsozialismus und Holocaust im Familiengedächtnis* (Frankfurt: Fischer Taschenbuch, 2002).

53 Harald Welzer, 'Family Memories of World War II and the Holocaust in Europe, or Is There a European Memory?' in *Cultural Memories: The Geographical Point of View*, ed. Peter Meusburger, Michael Heffernan and Edgar Wunder (Dordrecht: Springer, 2011), 171–88, at 183.

54 Ivan Jablonka, *History Is a Contemporary Literature: Manifesto for the Social Sciences* (Ithaca, NY: Cornell University Press, 2018).

55 Jablonka, *Grandparents I Never Had*; Mark Mazower, *What You Did Not Tell: A Father's Past and a Journey Home* (New York: Other Press, 2017); Stéphane Audoin-Rouzeau, *Quelle histoire: Un récit de filiation (1914–2014)* (Paris: Seuil, 2013).

56 Eigler, 'Writing in the New Germany'. On different levels of historical memory, see Jan Assmann and Aleida Assmann, 'Das Gestern im Heute: Medien des sozialen Gedächtnisses', in *Die Wirklichkeit der Medien*, ed. Siegfried J. Schmidt, Siegfried Weischenberg and Klaus Merten (Opladen: VS Verlag für Sozialwissenschaften, 1994), 114–40.

57 For Mossay, see Chapter 14, in this volume.

58 See Chapters 2, 3 and 7, in this volume.

59 For Ruppo, see Chapter 13; for Dal Lago, see Chapter 11, in this volume.

60 On the reliability of survivor memory, see Christopher Browning, *Collected Memories: Holocaust History and Postwar Testimony* (Madison, WI: University of Wisconsin Press, 2003).

61 For single-volume accounts of the global war, see Antony Beevor, *The Second World War* (London: Weidenfeld & Nicolson, 2012); Max Hastings, *Inferno: The World at War, 1939–1945* (London: Random House, 2012); Philip Bell, *Twelve Turning Points of the Second World War* (New Haven, CT: Yale University Press, 2011). On the war in Europe, see R. J. Overy, *The Bombing War: Europe 1939–1945* (London: Allen Lane, 2013). On the Pacific and East Asia, see John Costello, *The Pacific War, 1941–45* (New York, NY: William Morrow, 1982).

62 See Chapter 9, in this volume.

63 Kershaw, *To Hell and Back*, 346–7.

64 Timothy Snyder, *Bloodlands: Europe between Hitler and Stalin* (New York: Basic Books, 2012).

65 Anthony McElligott, '"German Servicemen See Europe": Cultural Mobilization of Troops on the Aegean "Quiet Front"', in *A World at War, 1911–1949: Explorations in the Cultural History of War*, ed. Caitriona Pennell and Filipe Ribeiro De Meneses (Leiden: Brill, 2019), 61–80.

66 Sönke Neitzel and Harald Welzer, *Soldaten – on Fighting, Killing and Dying: The Secret Second World War Transcripts of German POWs* (London: Simon and Schuster, 2012).

67 For Greece, see Chapter 12, in this volume.

68 Vesna Drapac and Gareth Pritchard, *Resistance and Collaboration in Hitler's Europe* (London: Palgrave Macmillan, 2017).

69 Richard Bessel, 'The Shadow of Death in Germany at the End of the Second World War', in *Between Mass Death and Individual Loss*, ed. Alon Confino, Paul Betts and Dirk Schumann (New York, NY: Berghahn, 2008), 51–68.

70 Kershaw, *To Hell and Back*, 355.

71 Overy, *The Bombing War*.

72 Tatjana Tönsmeyer, 'Supply Situations: National Socialist Policies of Exploitation and Economies of Shortage in Occupied Societies during World War II', in *Coping with Hunger and Shortage under German Occupation in World War II*, ed. Tatjana Tönsmeyer, Peter Haslinger and Agnes Laba (London: Palgrave Macmillan, 2018), 3–23.

73 Atina Grossmann, 'Grams, Calories, and Food: Languages of Victimization, Entitlement, and Human Rights in Occupied Germany, 1945–1949', *Central European History* 44, no. 1 (2011): 118–48.

PART ONE

Lives in uniform: Enduring combat and captivity

2

Nothing spectacular to remember? Dealing with wartime memories in a German family

Hans-Walter Schmidt-Hannisa

Seventy-five years after the end of World War II, in Germany, as elsewhere, the number of people who witnessed the atrocities of the war is dwindling. In the country of the perpetrators the development of a commemorative culture was a long and meandering process. Both German post-war states had their difficulties with what was called *Vergangenheitsbewältigung*, that is, coming to terms with the (Nazi) past. A watershed in this process was the famous speech by the-then West German president Richard von Weizsäcker in 1985, marking the fortieth anniversary of the end of the war, in which he emphasized the necessity for the Germans as a people to acknowledge their responsibility for the death and the suffering of millions. Since then, many debates have taken place, shedding more and more light on the twelve dark years of Nazi rule. Monuments such as the Holocaust Memorial in Berlin have been erected, historians have published tens of thousands of studies, and a legion of novelists, artists and filmmakers have helped to make the Nazi years a major theme within popular culture. In comparison with the population of other countries involved in genocides and stark war crimes, Germans now tend to view themselves as *Erinnerungsweltmeister* (world champions in commemoration).[1] However, it would be a mistake to assume that the undeniable strength of remembrance culture has made all Germans immune to voices trying to trivialize the significance of the Nazi era. Only in 2018 Alexander Gauland, leader of the German right-wing party, *Alternative für Deutschland* (AfD), declared that 'Hitler and the Nazis are just a speck of bird-shit in more than 1,000 years of successful German history'.[2] In light of such public remarks, it becomes clear that *Vergangenheitsbewältigung* will remain a cultural obligation for the Germans in the twenty-first century.

This cultural obligation is not just one for politicians, journalists and historians. *Vergangenheitsbewältigung* must be a twofold process; it has not only a public but also a personal dimension, and it can only be effective and thorough if relevant memories are passed on and shared between individuals. *Vergangenheitsbewältigung* therefore is, among other things, a family task. However, it is only in recent years that family memory, and in particular the ways in which German families engage with wartime memories, has become a topic of systematic sociological and psychological research.[3] Relevant studies have highlighted that there is often a divergence between the public discourse on Nazi and wartime topics that dominates the media and school curricula, on the one hand, and the narratives circulating within families, on the other. The latter are sometimes diametrically opposed, in an almost schizophrenic manner, to received historical knowledge. According to a recent survey conducted on behalf of the respected weekly newspaper, *Die Zeit*, only 3 per cent of Germans admitted that their ancestors had supported the Nazi regime, whereas 30 per cent believed they came from families who had opposed it. Another interesting figure underlines how ambivalent contemporary Germans are when it comes to the Nazi past: 77 per cent feel a duty to act against the forgetting of the Holocaust and the Nazi dictatorship, but at the same time 53 per cent say the ongoing engagement with the Nazi heritage should come to an end.[4]

In many families, talking about the wartime activities and experiences of family members was and sometimes still is an unspoken taboo. The generation that witnessed the war does not talk, the children and grandchildren do not ask questions and there is a consensus that family members of the wartime generation were 'exceptions', in the sense that they never did anything wrong. However, those who were traumatized during the war – be it, for example, as a soldier, as a victim of rape or as a witness of any kind of atrocities – often deal with their own trauma in a way that can cause traumatic stress responses in other family members, sometimes with consequences that strongly affect the functioning of the family. The trauma becomes transgenerational.[5]

This essay will try to make a small contribution to understanding how wartime memories were passed on and handled within German families. The following is an autobiographical account describing remembered events and how they were addressed and retold in my own family. In order to introduce myself, it may be sufficient to say that I was born in 1958 in Kulmbach, a small town in Upper Franconia, Bavaria, not far from the Czech border. I grew up there in a middle-class family, together with five siblings. The following will address the wartime activities and experiences of both my parents, Margareta and Georg Schmidt, and of my maternal grandfather, Hans Zenker. I grew up under the impression that my family was more on the side of the victims of war than the perpetrators. Apart from the fact that, in the aftermath of the war, my mother's family became refugees, there was, it seemed, nothing spectacular to remember. As in many German families, dealing with wartime memories in my own family was clearly gendered. Whereas my mother talked repeatedly about what had traumatized her, my father and grandfather did not speak very much about their involvement in the machinery of war. Many of the details I know about their activities between 1939 and 1945 I learned from my mother.

My mother

My mother was born in 1934 in the tiny village of Bärringen (now Pernink), high up in the Erzgebirge (Ore Mountains) in the Sudetenland region of Czechoslovakia. Only a few years later the family moved to another small village, Pirkenhammer (now Březová), near Karlsbad (now Karlovy Vary). In the summer of 1945 they had to leave their home when the government decreed the expulsion of all Germans from the re-established Czechoslovakian state. As refugees, they finally settled in Kulmbach. My mother, Margareta Zenker (later her married name was Schmidt), was 11 years old when they arrived.

It seems that she was lucky enough to avoid being excessively exposed to the physical dangers of the war. However, there was one event which left her with an enduring fear of death. It happened in the spring of 1945. My mother was on her way back home from school together with some other children when she suddenly spotted a low-flying airplane of the US Army Air Forces approaching quickly. As soon as the plane reached the group, it started to attack them and the bullets of a machine gun hit the ground. The children tried to seek shelter and jumped into a ditch until the plane disappeared. Nobody was injured, but this life-threatening event had such an impact on my mother that even today, in her mid-eighties and displaying all of the symptoms of progressing dementia, she regularly speaks about it, and all her children's requests, sentences such as 'please, mum, we have all heard this story a million times already', cannot stop her.

Karlsbad was initially occupied by American troops but was handed over to the Soviet Army on 11 May 1945. Hitler's portrait that had hung in the family's living room had been buried in the garden before their arrival. Several rooms of the family home, which was already accommodating some German refugees from eastern parts of the Reich, were confiscated by Russian officers. My mother and her brother were treated well and sometimes got sweets from them. Soldiers of lower rank, however, were less kind to the German population, and my mother remembers that a young girl living next door was raped. Soon the family was forced to abandon their house and hastily leave the Sudetenland as Czechoslovakia was re-established as a sovereign state. With a bare minimum of clothing and only the most essential personal belongings, they walked about 130 kilometres to Kulmbach in Upper Franconia, where my grandfather had spent most of his time during the war and where he had found a new wife after his first spouse had died in 1938. And there in Kulmbach, where the family settled, the most difficult time began, according to my mother. In the aftermath of the war she experienced the shortage of food: the family had to struggle daily for food. My mother's role in this critical situation was to beg for food in the villages around Kulmbach. Together with a friend she walked miles and miles every day, knocking at the doors of the farmhouses, hoping to get a slice of bread, a potato, an egg or a glass of milk – things she then had to share with the rest of the family.

During my childhood in particular, my siblings and I had to listen to these stories about her begging expeditions again and again, and their endless repetition had a deep impact on us. At some stage I understood that the experience of ongoing hunger and the humiliating necessity of asking strangers for food had traumatized my mother more than anything else. She was haunted by these memories, and their recurrence was beyond her control. However, these stories were also instrumentalized by her for pedagogical purposes. Whenever we were picky with food or left something on the plate, we were reminded that the abundance of food should not be taken for granted, that food should not be wasted, that we should be modest and grateful for what we had. On the surface she was just conveying to us a value system typical for refugees and for all those who have experienced the shortage of food, but in fact she was also passing on her personal trauma. This became manifest for example in her anxiety at the thought of running out of something or her obsession with keeping food in the fridge even when it was clear that it would never be eaten.

My father

My father's wartime memories are a much more complicated matter. Whereas my mother sometimes spoke too much, conversations with my father rarely transcended the level of small talk. I cannot remember him speaking about his wartime experience in any detail. What I know about it comes from other sources. My mother shared with her children what she knew, but whenever she was asked for details she could only confirm that my father had never spoken much about the time of the war. It was clear that her own interest in this matter was limited. After my father's death in 1994, we found revealing material such as photo albums (he was a keen photographer), letters to his parents and even diaries. Over the years, my younger brother, Thomas, increasingly adopted the role of custodian of the family archive and with him I could discuss details of our history.

My father, Georg Schmidt, born in 1922 in Speyer, grew up in Kulmbach where his parents owned a health food shop. Like many boys of his age group, he became a passionate member of the paramilitary *Hitlerjugend* (Hitler Youth). We found a photo album documenting a trip to the newly annexed Sudetenland organized by the local *Hitlerjugend* in August 1939, just days before the outbreak of the war. During the 1930s he began to collect illustrated propaganda books introducing the various departments of the Wehrmacht, their strengths and achievements. Later, works about victorious campaigns and military activities in particular geographical regions or about important battles were added to the collection.

Conscripted in 1941, my father was assigned to Mountain Troop Battalion 206, 7th Division (*Gebirgsjäger*), and his military ambitions, if he had any, did not take him any further than the rank of a lance corporal (*Obergefreiter*). His battalion was initially sent to Russia. According to his military identity card (*Wehrpass*), his first mission was to defend supply chains to the Demyansk Pocket near Novgorod, where about 100,000 German troops had been encircled by the Red Army. In the summer of 1942 he was transferred to Lapland (via Tallinn), where he served in a communications unit. His main task was to lay and maintain cables and secure connectivity between the widely scattered military units (see Figure 2.1). Finland had been attacked by the Soviet Union in 1939 and had lost a lot of its territory before a ceasefire was agreed in 1940. After the German attack on the Soviets in 1941 the Wehrmacht supported Finland's efforts to regain their lost territory.

On the rare occasions he spoke about his time in Finland, he would talk about the snow, the skiing, the saunas, the good comrades and how they produced a kind of ice cream by mixing snow, cream and jam. In September 1944 the alliance between Finland and Germany against the Soviet Union ended when Finland negotiated a ceasefire with the Soviets. As a consequence, the Lapland War broke out, in which the Germans and the Finns were no longer brothers in arms but enemies. In October my father was involved in the Battle of Tornio, which was the first major military engagement between the two armies. I remember that, as a boy, I was particularly curious to learn whether he had to shoot at people, but whenever I broached this subject he strenuously

FIGURE 2.1 *Georg Schmidt in Wehrmacht uniform, 1943*

denied it. In the course of the German withdrawal from Lapland, my father's battalion was transferred to Norway in January 1945, with the mission to defend northern Norway.[6] Soon after Germany's capitulation in May, they were shipped to Bremerhaven by British forces as prisoners of war (POWs). After an odyssey around Germany, they ended up in a prison camp in France.

As France was suffering from a labour shortage, it had a strong interest in forced labour. My father was taken to a farm near Besançon, where he had to work hard but was treated well. He sometimes praised the good food and the wine he was given. It was not until 1948 that he could finally return home. However, the story of the French connection does not end there. During my childhood our family rarely went abroad for holidays, but on a summer's day around 1970 the whole family was squeezed into our Opel and we drove 650 kilometres to visit the place where my father had to do forced labour for almost three years. And to the best of my knowledge this visit was made without any feelings of bitterness or resentment.

Among the letters we discovered after my father's death was one to his parents, sent on 22 July 1943 from Lapland, which is one of the rare documents giving some insight into my father's political views. He wrote:

Most people are too pessimistic now. Since we had to take some setbacks recently, everybody believes that, now, it is all over. They tend to forget our enormous achievements and conquests during the first three years of the war, which have to be defended now. We also have to prepare the next assaults. You cannot always be the winner. The Germans got used to being constantly successful and after a victory too easily achieved they might have quickly forgotten that our enemies are seeking to destroy us and that only our Führer's genius can save us. Only the complete extinction of our enemies (in particular Bolshevism) can guarantee a lasting peace.

This whole paragraph sounds like an excerpt from a propaganda pamphlet and it is difficult to assess whether it reflects my father's 'true' opinion. He knew that his letters were not read by his parents alone. However, although he was never a member of the Nazi party, it is not unlikely that he believed in the Führer at this stage. After the war his political orientation was always very conservative, and he did not try to keep his sympathy for far-right parties such as the National Democratic Party of Germany (NPD) and *Die Republikaner* (The Republicans) a secret. However, his nationalism was paired with a strict refusal of war. When, like my male contemporaries, I was called up for military service, I decided to take the route of a conscientious objector. This meant at the time that I had to undergo an interview by a special committee and had to provide evidence that my decision to refuse military service was indeed driven by my conscience. In this situation my father supported me by writing a declaration that as a veteran of the war he had educated me in the spirit of pacifism – and this was one of the moments when I felt truly close to him.

Such moments were, however, very rare. My father was a complicated character who struggled to relate to other people. He was not successful as a businessman, and he had difficulties in expressing his emotions (apart from anger!) and creating bonds with his children. Ultimately, his marriage broke up as well. It was much later, many years after he had passed away, that I began to wonder whether and to what extent my father had been a victim of the war. It was clear that, as a soldier and a prisoner of war, he had lost his freedom for seven years, that he had lost the best part of his youth and that all of this must have had a significant impact on the rest of his life. However, his wartime diaries and some letters sent to his parents suggested that he was in fact relatively lucky and not exposed to a great deal of violent military activity. What he wrote at that time is surprisingly banal, focusing mostly on food, activities with comrades, the books he read, the entertainment programme and the boring daily routine of military administration. The photos he took provide an almost idyllic picture of the war. In a letter from Lapland, dated 9 June 1943, he provides an account of a typical day:

5.30 am is waking-up time and at 7 we have to start work. My first task is to look after the outgoing mail and hand it over to a driver taking it to the post office. Then I have to take care of the documents arriving from the regiment. Besides this, regulations and official instructions have to be updated, rosters, applications and reports have to be drafted. At 9 am I fetch incoming news from the regiment and take care of them. Lists of code names have to be prepared, as well as material for radio communication and sketch-maps. At noon we have lunch; work starts again at 2 pm. Sometimes we are interrupted when the telephone rings. In the afternoon, the same tasks have to be performed again. In the evening I have to go to the officer who is responsible for signing the documents, and then I bring them back to the regiment. At 7 pm it is time for the muster, which is followed by dinner. As I am Duty Clerk at the moment I have to stay in the office. The *Unteroffizier vom Dienst* (Duty NCO) sleeps in the office as well. It is particularly annoying that occasionally there are incidents during the night.

When my siblings and I discussed my father's enigmatic character in later years, we had increasing doubts as to whether he really was spared any confrontation with the atrocities of the war. It seemed unlikely that my father's problems – his limited social skills, his inability to communicate emotions and to develop emotional bonds with his children – did not have at least some of their roots in traumatizing wartime experiences or in a deformation of personality caused by the long-term exposure to a non-civilian, extremely hierarchical environment. As my father had already passed away, all such questions will remain unanswered.

My maternal grandfather

Born in 1905, my grandfather, Hans Zenker was, it seems, an inveterate Nazi (Figure 2.2). Very little is known about his formative years and even less about his activities during the war. He never spoke about this time, and the source of all I know about it is my mother. I am not sure whether he was a member of the Nazi Party (NSDAP), but it seems quite likely. Two stories indicate that he had connections with the Nazis from early on. According to my mother, he left his home in Bärringen some days before the annexation of the Sudetenland (sanctioned by the Munich Agreement of September 1938), crossed the border into Germany and joined the Wehrmacht marching into the village. The other revealing story is about the house in Pirkenhammer which he acquired soon after this event: its previous owners were Jews – and Jewish property

FIGURE 2.2 *Margareta and Hans Zenker with their father, also Hans Zenker, c.1940*

was often given to party members at a greatly reduced price when the owner was forced to sell it at short notice.

At the beginning of the war Hans Zenker was a clerk for a recruitment board in Karlsbad; later he had a position at the Plassenburg, a castle in Kulmbach which served as a training centre for the NSDAP and was used for planning meetings by the *Organisation Todt*, a civil and military organization responsible for big building projects. Towards the end of the war he was sent to Nuremberg as part of the *Volkssturm*, a national militia set up in the last months of the war, and he had to man an anti-aircraft gun there. My mother repeatedly recounted how, one day while he was firing at attacking planes, his 16-year-old *Flakhelfer* was hit and died on the spot. It seems that the death of the boy, a member of an anti-aircraft auxiliary force consisting of child soldiers conscripted from 1943 onwards, had deeply moved him. However, it is probably no coincidence that it was precisely this story about an 'innocent' German victim and my grandfather's emotional reaction to it that found its way into family memory.

Two episodes shed some light on my grandfather's mindset. The starting point of the first one was that many years before, around 1918, his brother, Franz, had married Rosa, a Jewish woman. In the eyes of the Nazis such a liaison was *Rassenschande* or racial desecration, an unpermitted sexual relationship between an Aryan and a non-Aryan. What made things complicated was that Franz was a Nazi himself, someone, moreover with prospects within the party. When it was pointed out to him that he could only climb up the hierarchy if he was prepared to end this mésalliance, he stayed loyal to Rosa and refused to get a divorce. His brother, Hans, was one of those people who considered the relationship inappropriate and scandalous, and he too urged Franz to break with his wife. However, Franz sacrificed his career within the party in order to protect Rosa, who indeed was spared deportation.

The other episode centres on an argument my grandfather had with his own mother. During the war the family was allocated a forced labourer, a woman from Belarus. When my grandfather saw that his mother was serving her the same food as the members of the family, he was upset and insisted that she should get food of a lower quality. My great-grandmother however countered that the woman was doing very hard work and deserved to be treated well and to receive the same meals as the family members.

In 1976, at the age of 18, I ended all contact with my grandfather. This happened after a fierce argument which we had at a family party, in the presence of my parents and some of my uncles and aunts. When he heard that I had refused to join the army and intended to do community service instead, he called me 'a traitor to the fatherland'. I explained that the major reason for my decision was that so many crimes had been committed by the Wehrmacht in the name of patriotism. To this, my grandfather's response was: 'Hitler's only failure was that he did not extinguish all Jews.' I was completely speechless, and it was obvious from this moment on that any further discussion with a person displaying such fanatic views would have been pointless. At that time, my grandfather, born in 1905, was the head of a family with six children and a dozen or so grandchildren, a respectable member of the community and a shopkeeper with a reputation for being kind and trustworthy. None of my relatives seemed to have a problem with this justification or even glorification of genocide; none of them was willing to intervene and support me.

Retrospectively, I fail to understand why the significance and relevance of this incident began to dawn on me only decades later. Until I was about 40 years old I did not seriously question the narratives about my grandfather, which I had mostly heard from my mother. I was somehow content with what I had picked up from her, that he was an 'exception', that he did not have blood on his hands. And I assumed that due to his low rank he was not a decision maker or a *Schreibtischtäter* (desk murderer). I believed my mother that she did not know more than she had told me. So this is also the story of my own naiveté. For many years I did not make any further attempt to find out what he had really done during the war.

However, at some point I came to understand that, apart from this one appalling statement, another scandal had to be tackled in the family; the scandal that there was no reaction to my grandfather's fascist, racist and inhuman 'confession'. When I finally tried to initiate a conversation about the incident, and also about my grandfather's wartime activities, the responses were frustrating. My mother, representing the major source of 'family memory', had always had difficulties in facing the fact that her father had expressed an unacceptable view. My older sister argued that new information would not make any difference and pleaded for 'the whole story' not to be dug up again. What was the fear, I was wondering, that lay behind her reaction? At the same time, however, I was asking myself what exactly the point was of dredging everything up again or perhaps investigating it seriously for the first time. What is the value of unearthing a family history that cannot be changed and is likely to cause feelings of pain and shame?

There is certainly a difference between the abstract knowledge that 'the Germans' had started a war in which between fifty and seventy million people died, and the specific knowledge of 'my own family's' personal involvement in what went on during these dark years. The understanding of history is, at the end of the day, always a matter of perspective. And the perspective of the individual is strongly determined by the family in which he or she has their roots. And this is why I will pass on this essay to the next generation in my own family, to Aina, Freddy, Maria, Max and Lukas, who I constantly had in my mind while writing this text.[7]

Notes

1 See, for example: https://www.deutschlandfunkkultur.de/ vergangenheitsbewaeltigung-wir-sind-erinnerungsweltmeister.1008. de.html?dram:article_id=318468 (accessed 1 February 2020).

2 See https://www.afdbundestag.de/wortlaut-der-umstrittenen-passage-der- rede-von-alexander-gauland/ (accessed 15 February 2020).

3 See for example Harald Welzer, Sabine Moller and Karoline Tschuggnall, '*Opa war kein Nazi*': *Nationalsozialismus und Holocaust im Familiengedächtnis* (Frankfurt am Main: Fischer Taschenbuch, 2002). The focus of this project was not to clarify historical facts but to analyse patterns of recollection within families. See also Iris Wachsmuth, *NS-Vergangenheit in Ost und West: Tradierung und Sozialisation* (Berlin: Metropol, 2008).

4   See Christian Staas, 'Das Ende der Selbstgewissheit', *Die Zeit*, 29 April 2020, 17. In the survey, around one thousand Germans were asked about their attitude towards the Nazi regime.

5   The concept of the transgenerational transmission of trauma has sparked research both in psychology and in the area of cultural and historical studies. For the German situation, see, for example, Marianne Rauwald, ed., *Vererbte Wunden: Transgenerationale Weitergabe traumatischer Erfahrungen* (Weinheim, Basel: Beltz, 2013).

6   The activities of my father's battalion in Russia, Finland and Norway are listed in Roland Kaltenegger, *Die deutsche Gebirgstruppe 1935–1945* (Munich: Universitas, 1989), 74–7.

7   I wish to thank Sheila Dickson, Jeannine Jud and my brother, Thomas Schmidt, who helped me complete this essay.

3

The returning POW and a wartime volunteer: A love story

Sheena Fennell and Gill Fennell

In one way, the World War II stories of Irishman Cecil McCall and Irishwoman Patricia Fox – our ancestors – can be summarized in a few short sentences. Both left Ireland during the war. Cecil left to join Britain's Royal Air Force (RAF) and Patricia (known to her family as Pat) became an ambulance driver in Scotland with the American Ambulance Great Britain (AAGB). Both were therefore wartime volunteers, not conscripts. They both experienced large changes in their lives during the war years. In spite of these changes the affection they had felt for one another from before joining up endured. In 1945, Cecil and Pat got married (see Figure 3.1). Owing to that happy fact, we, Gill and Sheena Fennell, their daughter and granddaughter respectively, are here today and able to recount their wartime experiences in Britain and across Europe. Though their tale has a happy ending they both endured much in between with a variety of experiences, good and bad, along the way, experiences which require much more than a few sentences to recount! Piecing together family memories with the rich written evidence the couple left us, this chapter tells the story of one couple's war – a story which has similarities with those of so many other couples who would wed in the aftermath of the war.

FIGURE 3.1 *Cecil McCall and Patricia Fox, wedding day, Guildford, England, September 1945*

A private cupboard and a stash of 'war letters'

As descendants we are fortunate to have quite a good store of personal documentation and correspondence about Cecil's and Pat's wartime experiences. As is often the case, much of the material was found after the deaths of those concerned. As daughter, I, Gill, have been the primary custodian of my father's and mother's papers. As Gill's daughter, I, Sheena, can attest that we are only able to write this story in such detail thanks to my mother's years-long work of painstakingly transcribing and compiling this material into a series of spiral-bound volumes.[1] For us both, this chapter, therefore, has been a labour of love and very much a joint endeavour. However, for the ease of the reader, the main voice in what follows will be mine, Sheena's, as granddaughter of Cecil and Pat, not least as I weave in childhood memories of Cecil in particular into the story.

Grandmother Pat died when I (Sheena) was about a year old. At that point, my grandfather Cecil retired and came to live with us, the Fennell family, at our home on the scenic Mizen peninsula in West Cork. I remember Cecil fondly as a quiet man who loved fishing and woodwork. I have very happy memories of spending time fishing in our boat the *Sheelan*, where he would always hug me tight and keep me protected from the wind. I was extremely close to him and he taught me practical skills such as naming every tree in the garden, painting boats and mending nets. He also would buy me ice cream! My grandfather would never drink his tea from a mug but only from a cup and saucer and we all wondered why. Later, when we looked at his war records, it became clear that using mugs reminded him too much of that time. After Cecil passed away, his log book of flying, his diary and a book entitled 'A Wartime Log for British Prisoners' were found in his private cupboard. These stored his memories of that time, some happy, some full of adventure and some incredibly sad. Pat's story was recorded independently in the letters she sent home to her parents in County Cork during the war. They had been stored in two boxes and were known in the family as the 'War letters' but were never touched. It was only long after they had both died that my mother Gill started reading them, finding in them a young woman's life told in great detail – detailing a variety of people and activities she had never mentioned to my mother.

I have only one recollection of my grandfather actually talking about the war. I was about 7 years of age and we were sitting on the bench outside the hall door. We must have been talking about scars, as children do, and I must have asked him whether he had any. He pulled up the leg of his trousers to show me two scars across his knees and said that was where the cockpit of the Spitfire he was flying had gone into his knees when he crashed in World War II. I remember thinking that this was amazing but being a child I had no idea about the significance of it. If I had the opportunity again, I would ask this and many more questions though of course a lot of people chose not to speak about the trauma of the war. My grandfather was never comfortable talking about it and so he did not do so. My father often tried to prise him open on the subject but it was a closed chapter. In many ways, I can understand why he did not want to talk about it: it is impossible for us to imagine the horror and pain of what he and others experienced.

Cecil, Pat and their youthful ambitions

Cecil and Pat grew up in Cork, on Ireland's south coast, at a time of great change in Ireland. Cecil McCall was born in July 1919 in the town of Youghal, the eldest child of James and Emily McCall. He had three sisters. Cecil lost his father at the age of 13. Close male relatives of his had served in the British Army. Pat meanwhile was born in Monkstown, then a village near Cork city, in March 1920, the only child of James Booth Fox and Gertrude Mahony who both came from respected Cork business families, noted quilt manufacturers on her father's side and publishers on her mother's. Cecil and Pat were small children when, in 1922, the Irish Free State was established as an independent state with some residual political links to Britain. Growing up, Cecil and Pat, whose families belonged to the Church of Ireland tradition, attended Protestant schools – Bishop Foy's in Waterford for boys, Rochelle School in Cork for girls – for their secondary education. They and their families, part of a religious minority in the new state, were staunchly Irish and extremely patriotic. Pat, meanwhile, having finished secondary school, studied in Cork and gained a Performers' Diploma in Elocution awarded through Trinity College of Music London and also took paramedical courses through the Red Cross. Loving the stage, she joined the Good Companions Theatre Group in Cork. As a young woman she also volunteered as a Poppy Day collector as part of the British Legion's annual fundraising drive for former soldiers. Over twenty-five years Pat collected in Cork for the care of soldiers from both world wars. We still have her brooch that was presented to her for her quarter century of service to this charity.

Meeting and parting: Wartime choices

When war broke out in 1939, Cecil was 20 years old and taking an accountancy course. His mother and sisters had by then moved to Monkstown which was where Cecil and Pat met. They found they had much in common. Both had a wide group of friends and a good social life through tennis clubs, sailing and dances. They fell in love and got engaged and hoped to marry in 1941 or 1942 but the continuation of the war made them alter their plans. Cecil's and Pat's Irish patriotism coexisted with a strong sense of justice. Looking at the war in Europe in 1940 they considered it a contest of right versus wrong. Cecil himself crossed the border to go to Belfast, in Northern Ireland, still part of the UK, where, like many other southern Irishmen, he joined the RAF on 12 October 1940.[2] Cecil's sister Gabriel similarly left two years later in 1942 to join Britain's Women's Auxiliary Air Force (WAAFS). That same year Pat also crossed the Irish Sea to take up her wartime volunteer role. The war would separate the couple for some five years.

Cecil's RAF training was long and intense. At Padgate base in England, he and his fellow recruits were equipped and vaccinated before going to RAF Babacombe in Devon for basic training and flight training at nearby Paignton. His diary details weeks of intense study and training on topics such as navigation, signalling and aircraft recognition. At the end of the course there was a party where there were 'copious quantities of beer drunk'. During the graduation parade each name was called out and the bearer told to collect a tropical kit and one pair of boots. Within months he was aboard the troopship HMT *Dempo* along with 2,000 others bound for Cape Town in an uncomfortable month-long sea voyage from Liverpool, sleeping in hammocks and packed like sardines with all port holes locked. Travelling on by train to Rhodesia (present-day Zimbabwe) he underwent further gruelling training at a number of RAF bases. In the town of Bulawayo the men socialized and were well received by the locals. At RAF Belvedere, at Salisbury (now Harare), in July 1941, he got airborne for the first time in a Tiger Moth plane, a huge moment for him considering he had been training for it for nine months. The next six weeks saw him gain a great amount of experience and, impressively, he 'soloed' in a little over ten hours (out of the twenty-five hours training normally provided for this). He also did eight hours on the Link Trainer simulator which he referred to as 'this infernal contraption'. Of this challenge he wrote that

no matter how cool calm and collected you entered its cockpit when your time was up you emerged bathed in perspiration, shaky and disillusioned, [a] pupil pilot weakly avowing that nobody could fly that machine which persistently went first spinning one way and then the other, or else standing on its nose and then its tail or the whole lot combined. It is also the only machine in which you may land safely under the ground.

Rhodesia was not all hardship though. After his first solo flight – to Gatooma (now Kadoma) – six good ladies of the town had a tent erected and presented each arriving pilot with a cup of coffee, two jam tarts and fifty cigarettes as tokens of esteem. Here and at RAF Cranbourne, also in Rhodesia, both food and invitations to farms and homes were plentiful. In December 1941, Cecil gained his 'wings' and was promoted to full sergeant. The mess bar opened that night and he along with the others had the biggest party of their lives:

There will never be another day like it, all we strove for, swotted for, drilled for, and sweated it is there for all to see, just above the left breast pocket of our 'Per Adua ad Astra' (by labour to the stars). If any new pilot goes home sober that night, there are others who don't remember getting home at all. We are Lords of the Air and with envy do junior courses look on.

The next stop for Cecil and his fellow pilots was Suez, arriving in Egypt on 27 December 1941. Pitching a tent in the desert 90 miles from Cairo, the new pilots became, as he put it, 'homemakers':

Here we are. Four Pilots, Two English, One Irish, One Australian, twelve blankets, one tent and now one lamp. No one knows anything so we hitch-hiked to Cairo and got there in four hours. Had a meal, a couple of drinks, found a bed, slept and made the acquaintance of those animal bed bugs. Saw the Pyramids, climbed them inside and out. Hitch hiked back to our bed in the sand, we organised ourselves and soon had a very comfortable abode, in fact a Palace compared to others. Here we stayed until April.

Photographs taken in the desert by his friend Mike Mair survive from this time. The outside world also intruded as the time when Cecil learned of a friend from Cork who had been killed close by. Their missions took them into Sinai Desert and the Middle Eastern theatre. As needs required, he changed unit often and also found himself at various parts of the North African theatre in Libya, Tripolitania and Tunisia, all the while gaining more experience in flying especially Hurricanes and Spitfires. Promoted to flight sergeant, he also began to experience the loss of fellow pilots – 'their lads' – who crashed on landing, such as Flight Sergeant Symes who was buried in a little cemetery in Zuara (Libya). Describing his unit's tented life in Tobruk in early 1942, Cecil details a 'very free and easy life' with relatively good food – bully beef and fig jam featured – and an outdoor bath – a split oil drum with a fire underneath – from which to watch transports go by; 'What a life.'

Pilot and POW: Cecil in Hitler's Europe

Beginning in June 1943, Cecil was part of RAF No. 73 Squadron stationed at La Sebala outside Tunis, a city adjacent to the war's Mediterranean theatre. There were missions to Malta and later to Monte Carvino near Naples in support of the Allied invasion of Italy. His squadron also operated over Yugoslavia to assist Tito's partisans and he was credited with strafing doors and windows on a German headquarters and five trains, two of them along the Dalmatian coast. He had always wanted to fly single-seater aircraft, remarking to one of his sisters that 'if I get shot down it is only one, [I] don't want to feel I have killed a crew if it was something I did wrong'. On 17 April 1944, he took off in a Spitfire but was shot down by flak (anti-aircraft fire) over Markaska in Yugoslavia and he records in diary being taken as a prisoner of war (POW) by the Germans at 12.20 pm. We still have this letter his mother received from his commander on 24 April stating that '[he] was last seen turning away from the harbour less than 30ft [sic] from the water. Whether or not he was able to escape is not known'. The commander praised Cecil, known to his fellow pilots as 'Mac': 'I cannot speak too highly of Mac. He was a skilful pilot, keen, conscientious and more than willing to participate in any action against the enemy. He was brave and fearless without being foolhardy. Always cheerful, he was a grand companion and was popular with all ranks.' Cecil was not aware when captured that he had just been promoted from being a warrant officer to pilot officer. This added to confusion when Red Cross enquiries were made about his whereabouts; so his family back in Ireland endured three months of waiting before getting assurance that he was alive.

Cecil's captivity took him across Nazi-occupied Europe. First detained in a 'primitive, overcrowded and bug-ridden' civilian prison in Mostar with downed American Liberator bomber pilots for company he was then brought to Belgrade for a preliminary interrogation. Transported by train to Germany, he endured solitary confinement at Dulag Luft camp which the Germans ran as a transit camp for captured airmen at Oberursel, north-west of Frankfurt. Transferred to Hydekrug in Lithuania, there he was incarcerated with about three thousand other POWs arraigned in three compounds, one for Americans and the other two for Commonwealth servicemen. Apart from the strict discipline, he recalled there being adequate food as well as a school, theatre and some organized sports. When news of his promotion to the rank of pilot officer finally came through in July 1944, Cecil moved to an officers' POW camp, Stalag Luft 3 Sagan in Poland, where he stayed until February 1945. The arrival of food parcels and family gifts of cigarettes and small items sent through the Red Cross brightened camp life. In his war log book Cecil kept a record of his and others' waiting game for food parcels. In February 1945, Pat received a letter from him – three months late – in which he referred to the shortages he faced as barracks cook with 'nothing but fresh air inside or outside the camp and all a sea of mud'.

Cecil's account of the last months of his captivity in the spring of 1945 is particularly detailed and heart-rending. With the German Reich shrinking in the face of Allied military advances, Cecil and his comrades were moved from Poland to Stalag 357 Fallingbostel in Saxony where they remained from February to April. With Allied forces closing in further, the German authorities obliged thousands of Allied captives including Cecil to take part in what became known as 'The Big March' when prisoners were marched north-east across the Elbe into a part of northern Germany south of Lübeck. Here, amid the forests and lakes, Allied captives could hear their own side overhead, in the form of daylight flyovers of American bombers and night-time RAF bombers passing on their way to bomb the cities of Hanover and Bremen.

Cecil's diary demonstrates his strong physical constitution even if this trek took its toll emotionally. The march was punitive even if, with Germany's situation desperate by now, some German officers were quietly calculating how they could use these POWs as bargaining chips with the Allies when the end came by disregarding Hitler's instruction that these Allied servicemen be killed rather than freed. Comrades again were key to getting through and Cecil notes carefully the names of the seven others, English and Australian, with whom he marched daily under watchful German eyes. Privations included scavenging from the fields and sleeping in barns or in the open as they marched the 170 kilometres to a dispersal area near Dutzow. From there they marched on to Kugel, reaching it on 1 May 1945. In the field where they stopped a large POW sign and Red Cross flag was displayed as a message to Allied aircrews. Cecil and his comrades knew from bitter experience in these weeks the horror of what we might call 'friendly fire'. During the march, a food stop at Gresse turned to tragedy when RAF Typhoon fighters passed overhead to cheers from the captives. As the British planes peeled away though they proceeded one by one to bomb and fire upon the column of Allied POWs, mistakenly killing between sixty and seventy of their own men that day. For Cecil, himself a Spitfire pilot, witnessing this must have been an unimaginable horror. On 2 May 1945, though, came 'the great moment at last. We are free, the British troops arrived this afternoon'. Cecil celebrated with a 'Liberation Breakfast' next day composed of 'three eggs, bacon, meat roll, fried bread. Fruit duff with cream, bread, butter, Jam [sic]'. VE Day, 8 May, found him in Cosford in England where he drank three pints of beer before he got kitted out and left for Cork where he was reunited with his family on 10 May.

Ambulance driver and witness to war:
Pat in wartime Scotland

Cecil had been flying missions between Egypt and Palestine in 1942 when news caught up with him of a major change in the life of his girlfriend Pat. Informed by his mother of Pat's having been accepted to work as an ambulance driver in Britain, he wrote: 'Well I certainly wish her luck.' It is unclear how this opportunity arose for her but Pat left for Leeds in July 1942 where she joined the AAGB.[3] She was now aged 22 and it was by then nearly two years since Cecil had left Cork. Pat had driven at home but now faced passing a test in a large and unwieldy left-hand drive ambulance but after her second attempt she telegrammed her mother in Cork: 'Accepted as driver. ... Uniform over

£20 send money.' Scotland was home to many hospitals and convalescence homes for injured servicemen; so it was to Aberdeen, not Birmingham as she was first told, that Pat was posted on 26 July 1942. She and other drivers moved from their first hotel lodgings to another, with better food, because of the surveillance of their commanding officer. In Marjorie Baker and Meg Cowan she fast made firm friends.

The ambulances the women drove were the charitable gifts of the American public and in Aberdeen and its environs she drove a series of American vehicles, the Ford 10 (for runs to the train station) and a Chevy for longer journeys. Pat is pictured next to one of 'her' ambulances in one photo (see Figure 3.2). Blue-grey in colour with a red line and a badge of the crossed flags of America and Britain to distinguish the ambulances, there were usually two crew members on board, the driver and another AAGB volunteer to tend to the patients in the back. The destinations included local castles and large houses mobilized as treatment centres. During a blackout her ambulance's bright markings meant she was waved ahead as a guide for forty army lorries. 'There I was beetling along in the middle of the huge convoy,' she wrote. That winter Pat negotiated treacherous driving conditions: 'I drove on the most

FIGURE 3.2 *Pat (Patricia) Fox, driver with American Ambulance Great Britain, Aberdeen, Scotland, c.1943*

awful road, solid ice. I skidded from side to side, despite I was crawling along at 10 miles per hour.' With two seriously injured men in the ambulance, one of whom was the victim of self-harm in the probable hope of discharge, Pat and her comrade Dickie held their nerves when the lights fused five miles from the base, 'crawling back' and 'narrowly missing two buses' using a handheld torch out the window.

What shines through Pat's letters home is her combination of honesty, compassion and strength. Writing home about the German air-raid of 21 April 1943 on Aberdeen, she does not hide her fear:

> I was terrified, we all were. I've never been so near death or injury. One of the incidents was just a bit too close. However we are all safe as are our billets. I finally got back at 4 a.m. having seen dreadful things. We worked all morning and then in shifts. One poor old man I took was very green and shaken. His home had fallen round his ears, sister buried under debris; he was dug out but lost everything. I talked as cheerily as I could and gave him a packet of cigarettes I had. Really you'd think I had saved his life, he broke down and cried, said he never knew anyone could be so kind and what did I do, just cigarettes and a cheery word. There is so little we can do.

In subsequent months she writes of her sorrow at the cases of the injured men. Transporting four young burns victims among plane-crash survivors, she notes of the men that '[it] was their poor faces, hands and necks that got it and I've never seen worse burns. Dressings had to be kept moist with saline. We drove at 20 mph but even that was too fast and they were in agony. … I'd never have thought I could look at such sights a year ago'. Victims of shell-shock had come through 'pure hell' she reasoned, adding that 'the stretcher case was the worst in the hospital, should think he won't recover and goes from one convulsion to another'. Confronted with German POWs on 9 August 1944, Pat found a reserve of sympathy that surprised herself. She wrote:

> You know Mum, despite Red Cross rules etc, I always thought if ever I had a German prisoner as patient I'd give him a bad journey and take as little care as possible. Well I had four stretcher cases and I found I simply had to treat them the same as our boys, one was only nineteen and looked about fifteen. We had terrific publicity, escorts and police. We had one who tried to escape, not with me, thank goodness.

Pat and her peers also fixed mechanical faults in the ambulances but alongside all the work there were moments of release in Aberdeen. Humour helped and Pat enjoyed the wit of some patients like the Cork lad invalided out of Normandy – 'a pure pet' – she visited in September 1944. In an active social life, she and her ambulance colleagues spent time at the officers' clubs of the RAF, Army and Navy, with some of the men there becoming good friends. With them, the women attended the London Philharmonic Orchestra when they came to play in Aberdeen and enjoyed attending touring London theatre productions including a 'wonderful' Noël Coward in a production of his own *Present Laughter*. After a visiting D'Oyly Carte Gilbert and Sullivan production, Pat and friends even dined with some of the leading cast members. Weekly social events included going to the cinema and dances. Some weekends she went fishing for trout and salmon to Deeside with Meg and Marjorie. We still have her fishing rod from these times. There were still options for fine dining even in 1943 when she noted that '[we] had dinner before the show, a pretty good menu for a country at war for 4 years. Clear or tomato soup, Lobster Mayonnaise or Roast Chicken, vegetables, Coffee cream and puree of blackberries, a savoury and coffee. No wonder I'm putting on weight'.

She continued to write often to Cecil during all this time but plans for leave together in London never came off. They kept in contact but gradually his letters became less frequent and she wondered where the relationship was going. Letters got delayed, as happened in wartime, but Pat took solace in news from Cecil in 1943–4 and expressed concern for minor mishaps such as his fall from a lorry. The hard blow came in a letter from her own mother Gertrude in April 1944 to say that Cecil had been shot down. Pat had had a bad feeling in the run-up to this news and felt their future slipping out of reach, she told her mother, before continuing: 'Poor darling, he came through over three years of it, and now to go when he was nearly finished his tour. I'm really too numb to feel anything. But please God missing is so much better than missing believed killed. I've written to the Air Ministry.' Her own mother must have been worried about her during those months as in May 1944, Pat answered her with a flash of the resilience she had learned to live through these times:

Mum, what in the world are you worrying about me for … I found out since I came over here that in this present-day life, and especially in a country at war, one has to become incredibly tough in mind, body and soul. There are plenty of hard knocks for everyone at present, but to make any success of life, one must have the hidden reserve of strength to fall back on, otherwise one goes under. … Perhaps I may be harder on the surface than before, but these days it's got to be like that, otherwise you are no use to yourself or mankind.

So many others with missing or captured loved ones during World War II must have tried to cope in a similar way. The relief, in July 1944, when she received a priority wire from the Air Ministry to say that Cecil was being held as a POW was immense. She wrote home excitedly: 'Never felt so excited before, don't know what I am saying or doing, isn't it just wonderful. Expect to get his address from the Red Cross soon.'

Letters, often delayed, started to come from Cecil again too in late 1944 but, at the start of 1945, there was a twist in the story of the type that World War II separation often produced. Pat became close to an English RAF man, slightly younger than she but with a lot in common with her. Over a few months the relationship deepened and he talked of marriage. Pat's mind was in turmoil as she could not decide what to do. Her friend Marjorie talked to her a lot and told her to wait until she saw Cecil. She was dreading the moment that Cecil would arrive in Aberdeen but that day came on 18 June 1945. Cecil phoned the garage where Pat worked from the railway station immediately upon his arrival, 'So I went straight down. I nearly had to get off the tram I felt so sick. Got to the station and saw him at the other end, we just stood there unable to move or say anything. It was the strangest feeling; I thought I knew for certain what I wanted; now I no longer know.' Over the next few days she saw in Cecil kindness, stability and tolerance. An acquaintance of Pat's who was head of the RAF Military Police in Aberdeen pointed out to her that 'it was grand to meet a man, who had done so much and been through such a lot, [but who] still remained sane and balanced'. Marjorie's advice as a friend was that, beyond any doubt, the one with the finer character was Cecil. And so she made her choice even though she had felt such happiness with the younger man. Over the following months she and Cecil rekindled their love and in September 1945 they married and had a small wedding in Guildford. Cecil's best man was Mike whom Cecil had not seen since North Africa. Her cousins hosted the wedding, and some of Cecil's family came over from Ireland and others living in England joined them for the occasion. Within three years, their married life brought them back to Cork where Cecil secured employment at Irish Steel. The wedding day itself in 1945 had one sad element in that Pat's father died three days before the ceremony and her mother could not come. Even so, Cecil's and Pat's wedding photo shows hope and contentment. And so began their life together after the war.

Notes

1   These two compendiums are entitled 'Sky Storms and Peaceful Harbours: 175709 Fly. Lt. James Cecil McCall' and a second (for Patricia) is entitled 'Khaki to Fur Coat: World War II Letters Home to Ireland: 1942–1945'. Facsimiles of these compendiums may be consulted at Cork City and County Archives, Ireland. All the original documents used in those compendiums and cited in this chapter are in our family's possession.

2 For further insight on the military careers of Irishmen like Cecil, see Steven O'Connor, *Irish Officers in the British Forces, 1922–45* (Basingstoke: Palgrave Macmillan, 2014).

3 For more on this organization, see the website 'American Ambulance Great Britain, 1940–1945' at https://aagb.org.uk/the-organisation/ (accessed 1 March 2020).

4

Educating friends and enemies: An Irishman's experiences in wartime Britain

Patricia Scully

My father John Scully inhabited a dual world, being both Irish and British; born in Dublin in 1924 but growing up in Oxford, England, he was the child of an Irish republican mother and a Moroccan Jewish father. He was called up from medical school in Scotland to serve in the British Army, and his father worked for the British Council in Argentina. Other members of his family died in the Holocaust and worked in the Special Operations Executive. World War II marked the professional and personal lives of all of the above, and in this essay I shall examine more particularly its long-term impact on the lives of my father John and his father Francis Michael. The log book and photo I still have in my possession is a tangible link with John's experience of World War II in the British Army (see Figure 4.1).

The Anglo-Jewish merchant and the Irish republican nurse

In London, in 1923, Nance Scully, an Irish nurse, met and married Francis Abulafia, a young Jewish man from Morocco, North Africa. Their backgrounds were very different. Francis was the eldest son of a Sephardic Jewish family

FIGURE 4.1 *Wartime photo and British Army log book of John Scully*

based in Essaouira-Mogador, who traded in tea on Mincing Lane, the London tea auction centre. His merchant family traded between UK and Indonesia. By the nineteenth century, Essaouira-Mogador was the principal Moroccan port, transporting caravan trade goods between the Africa and Europe, and was established as a major Atlantic commercial centre. Mogador had English schools for its large Jewish population, established by the London-based Anglo-Jewish Association so that the community there was very Europe-focused in keeping with its international trading connections.[1] When Morocco became a French protectorate in 1912 Moroccan Jews were not made eligible for the prized French citizenship, unlike the case of Algerian Jews who had been granted citizenship by means of the Crémieux decree of 1870. This context may explain why Francis (born Joseph Samuel Abulafia) moved to Britain and promptly applied for British citizenship which he was granted in 1923. He became Catholic around the time he wed my grandmother in 1923 and promptly changed his surname to hers by deed poll. He also touchingly took Michael as a middle name in honour of Nance's father.[2]

Nance's family originated in counties Cork and Kerry on the south-west coast of Ireland. Her father had worked at Minard coastguard station on the famously beautiful Dingle peninsula in Kerry, thus involving him and other members of his family in the service of the British state in Ireland either as coastguards or as Royal Navy recruits. Indeed Nance's two brothers, Timothy and John Scully, were in the Royal Navy. The village of Annascaul where they lived also produced a famous Antarctic explorer Tom Crean, also a member of the Royal Navy. Nance was the youngest girl in her family, and trained as a nurse in Cork city – possibly influenced by the loss of her young brother Patrick to tuberculosis in 1917, the same year that her father and mother died. She came back to her home village in Kerry during the War of Independence (1919–21). Though her family had often worked for the British crown, she developed her own political views and she became active locally in the War of Independence helping to shelter Irish Republican Army (IRA) volunteers and treating injuries sustained in local ambushes of crown forces. Her active membership of Cumann na mBan, the Irishwomen's republican paramilitary organization, attests to her commitment to the cause. During the Irish Civil War (1922–3), she was to be on the defeated side of those republicans who fought against the new Irish Free State as a sell-out to Britain.[3]

Making a living as a linguist and educating John

Nance and Francis moved to Dublin so that their child would be born in Ireland. John was born in Dublin on 12 July 1924. The family have said that Francis and Nance lived in Southport and he worked for the *Manchester Guardian*, though I can find no article that appeared under his byline. Settling the family in Oxford, Francis showed a great appetite for learning and new qualifications – first qualifying as a solicitor through the University of Birmingham and then studying ecclesiastical history at Hertford College, Oxford, graduating in 1935. A talented linguist, he also gained a doctorate in letters from a French university at Besançon in 1938. Fluent in French, Spanish, Hebrew, Arabic and Ladino, he taught languages from his Oxford home in the 'Scully Institute' or 'L'Institut Scully' whose tuition offerings included courses in English language and literature, integrating himself into the life of a university town. His wife Nance was a homemaker. She was sometimes known as Paddy in reference to her middle name Patricia, a name I share with her. Every year, she unfurled an Irish tricolour on St Patrick's Day which was her birthday.

John attended primary school at the Dragon School in Oxford, in the same class as the children of J. R. R. Tolkien who was a friend of Francis and Nance, also attending the same Blackfriars Dominican Church. The author gifted a copy of *The Hobbit* to Francis, but John, for some reason, loathed everything to do with the Tolkiens, equating the popular *Hobbit* and *Lord of the Rings* books with Wagner's Ring cycle and things Germanic (which he disliked). Tolkien books were banned in our house when we were kids, with him encouraging us to read better alternatives, as he saw them, such as original Welsh myths and sagas.

In 1929, Francis and Nance bought a small cottage down by the sea near Annascaul in County Kerry. They travelled there from Oxford during the school holidays. John was developing a youthful interest in photography; taking blurry photos from a Brownie box camera and developing the films himself, sticking the photos in albums. His Irish photos captured a range of rural scenes and activities and he enjoyed the outdoor life of Irish summers. For secondary school, John boarded at Ampleforth College in Yorkshire, a prestigious Catholic public school run by Benedictine monks, where he was very happy often not wanting to return home during the vacations, spending his holidays learning photography skills, and sailing with the Sea Scouts, and attending daily office at the monastery. He loved the Yorkshire countryside and the soaring arches of the ruined abbeys, and the hymns sung at school. One of the prefects responsible for discipline who once sternly gave him lines for some misdemeanour was the future abbot of Ampleforth, George Basil Hume, later known as the 'monk cardinal' who overcame his initial reluctance when he was appointed as archbishop of Westminster in 1976, and went on to become a major figure in the Catholic Church and in British public life. Anti-Catholicism still lingered in the 1970s however when my father considered that his being an Irish Catholic (albeit one from a Catholic public school) had led to him being passed over for a job in public health before he got it on the second attempt.

To Scotland and Argentina: A family separated by war

When war broke out in September 1939, John was 15. His parents were back in Oxford, and travel between the UK and Ireland was severely curtailed in 1940; so they were unable to return to Ireland or have Nance's sister Mims visit in Oxford. On 20 March 1942, Francis left Cardiff on board the cargo ship *Port Melbourne* bound for Buenos Aires in Argentina where he was to promote English-language books for the British Council. In September 1942, John went to St Andrews University in Scotland to begin his medical studies though he would have been happier studying engineering. His father's influence was decisive in trying medicine instead. Francis was by then well into his tour of Argentina. Getting there the previous March had involved embarking on a month-long journey. Fluent in Spanish and other languages he might need for South American audiences, Francis appeared to his audiences as British even though he had an Irish name.

It is worth reflecting a little on how other members of the Jewish family in which he had originated fared during World War II. His younger brother Albert Abulafia, who had also become a British subject, joined the Special Operations Executive (SOE) ¯ the outfit of secret agents that Churchill had instructed to 'set [occupied] Europe ablaze' through aid to resistance movements, employing propaganda and acts of sabotage. Like his older brother, Albert was gifted at languages and was put to work as a translator for SOE.[4] Francis and Albert had a younger brother, Meir Abulafia, living in Paris, who died at the Drancy detention camp in the suburbs of Paris. During the German occupation, Drancy was a site where Jews captured in France were detained before deportation to the extermination camps. Overall, 100,000 Sephardic Jews (of Mediterranean and North African origins) perished in the Holocaust, from across Europe including some 85 per cent of Greek Jews, for instance.[5]

Despite paper shortages, the book trade did well in wartime as reading provided a valuable pastime in Britain and further afield. The British Council, which functions still today as a cultural body aimed at disseminating British cultural influence, wanted to expand the wartime readership of British books beyond the English-speaking world and to counteract American publishers' expansion in regions such as South America. This prompted a book-trade initiative called the British Export Scheme (BES) in 1940. It was to promote this scheme that my grandfather Francis travelled to South America in 1942 to act as a permanent representative and type of cultural attaché, financed jointly by the British Council and British publishers. His duties were to set up a central office in Buenos Aires as the British Council's chief representative in Spanish-speaking parts of the American continent and to establish close relations with educational and cultural authorities. From 1944 on, this policy of supplying books that depicted Britain as an exemplary forward-looking social democracy on the cusp of victory which was beginning to implement important domestic reforms was extended to newly liberated portions of Europe. The books chosen catered to a mass audience ranging from illustrated periodicals to 'middlebrow' authors such as J. B. Priestley.[6]

Francis's dangerous journey across a submarine-infested Atlantic meant leaving his wife Nance at home alone in Oxford where she too did her part, acting as a local air-raid warden for the local bomb shelter. She also took in refugees in her home, including one Indian lady (known ever after in the family as 'Auntie') who left with her as a mark of gratitude a beautiful rosewood folding table, inlaid with mother of pearl, a piece of furniture which we still have. From the moment he set sail from Britain, meanwhile, Francis kept a detailed handwritten diary in an exercise book and, from when he began his work in Argentina, compiled an album of photos of relevant newspaper cuttings from his trip. In his diary, starting on 20 March 1942, Francis describes how the *Port Melbourne* moved as part of a deep sea convoy, growing to about forty or so ships, that zig-zagged around British and Irish waters before proceeding to the broad Atlantic, escorted in turn by an armed trawler and then by a naval destroyer and four fighter planes. At one point he thought the convoy was being tailed by German planes, but it was in fact the Royal Air Force (RAF), and he expected to be attacked by German submarines. Such caution was necessitated by the ongoing Battle of the Atlantic; convoys of allied ships were escorted between the Americas and Europe, and were attacked. There were thirty-eight ships sunk in the period between 8 March 1942 and 1 May 1943, an average of about 2.5 ships a month out of a total of 1,168 vessels. They travelled from Cardiff to Milford Haven, also in Wales, and then sailed in fog to Belfast, then back to Bangor, on to the Hebrides off Scotland and finally, instead of making for Halifax, Canada, as planned, they headed south again, past the Atlantic coast of Morocco, and down to Buenos Aires. The route to Buenos Aries was constantly changing, on the advice of the Admiralty. At one point Francis reports that the ship's officers decided not to answer a distress signal from another ship in case they were being lured into an attack. Ignoring a distress call evidently sat uncomfortably with men schooled in the customs and expectations of mutual aid that normally marked life at sea, the incident causing the officers to become very withdrawn and the captain to be absent from breakfast. It evidently weighed on them that the plea for assistance might have been genuine and that maybe a British ship was being attacked and that they had done nothing to help. Francis reports his great loneliness on board the ship and how he was constantly on edge.

For all that, however, Francis's time on board was eventful as those on board formed a tight-knit community with just ten passengers, three of whom were British and seven were from South America. He found a kindred spirit in the captain, and they discussed art, drawing, poetry, French literature and the Church of England, and played draughts with fellow-passenger John Arthur Anderson, who drank lots of beer, and slept well. Francis did not sleep well; he was anxious about attacks from the Germans, and had a painful leg. Francis questioned the crew and described their varying opinions, about whether the ship convoy would be safe, and he listed their responses in a table. He detailed the joy and relief of the officers once the convoy broke up, and their fatigued weary smiles. He described the sea and weather, their food and who sat next to whom at dinner. He ate duckling for dinner on Thursdays and Sundays; it was so warm going through the tropics that one of the passengers, Stierlen, slept on deck in a sheepskin bag.

Francis missed his family and Ireland a lot, imagining on one occasion that he could make out the shape of the maps of Ireland and England in the clouds: 'A strange sight. But the wind came and altered the contours of both clouds. They mingled with others and became indistinguishable.' He kept his watch on Oxford time, to be in tune with what his wife Nance would be doing. He pined for Irish literature, writing that 'I would give anything for an Irish NOVEL [sic]. Not one to be found on board'.

Francis struck up conversation with the Irish sailors on board the ship, noting the similarity of the blue eyes of his son John with Seaman Walsh who had a shamrock and the words 'ERIN' and 'County Wexford' tattooed on his arm. An Irish steward baked him brown soda bread for breakfast, and spoke in Irish to him, which means that he had some knowledge of Irish long before his old age which was when I thought he had learned some. He counselled a sailor from Derry in Northern Ireland on his marriage and debts, relishing the Ulster vernacular which he noted down carefully. Most of all though he thought of his wife and son, reverting to Nance's pet name of Paddy, from Patricia, her middle name, writing wistfully of their seaside haven in County Kerry on the Irish coast and noting elaborate daydreams:

I saw Paddy and John going over the bridge, I saw the day … the days … of our arrival there, and I saw so many other things, other days … days of perfect happiness … how I wish this could be repeated. Perhaps we see things more vividly, more intensely, when we do not see them. I can now see Paddy [his wife Nance], as I saw her yesterday, rising adorable, kind and lovely. I can see her now having tea and John to her left. I can hear what she says and what John says. … I can see him coming to my room twice to say 'Good bye' [sic] before he left for Scotland. [These are] memories to enchant and maintain the anchorage of this soul, where it should be, loneliness.

Yes, and loneliness can be fearful not least amidst this babbling of humanity, here i[on] this ship.

He wonders how he could bring Paddy and John to Buenos Aires, and wrote: '[If] John had a vocation and became a Benedictine, Paddy could have accompanied me.' The ship was totally blacked out at night to avoid detection. As they neared Buenos Aires, they sailed by the site of the major naval battle of the River Plate, near Montevideo, in which, in December 1939, the German ship *Graf Spee* was sunk. Francis and the crew were excited to see the turret of the shipwreck protruding above the sea surface even if the captain held that it was not the said battleship.

In the service of the book trade and the British Council

Francis arrived in Buenos Aires on Thursday, 21 April 1942, and immediately went to the British Embassy. The A.K.C. Corporation gave him an office to work from. He found lodgings at a guesthouse, and was admitted to membership of the 'English Club'. Francis was surprised that his first book customer was an Austrian Jew requesting Catholic prayer books in Spanish. He listed possible booksellers meticulously, received catalogues from London and set up a scheme for sending book reviews to the British Embassy for approval. The supply of English textbooks to schools also interested him. The diary details his first ten days in Buenos Aires but then runs out. We do know that he gave a series of lectures in Buenos Aires in August and September 1942. A newspaper cutting in Spanish stuck in his photo album provides details of what he said and an accompanying photograph shows him speaking as an official British representative with the Union Jack in the background. Described as 'Dr Francis M. Scully, a British intellectual', his immediate purpose is given as '[founding] an entity that facilitates the dissemination of the British book in South America, especially in our country'.

On Wednesday 26 August 1942, Francis was presented at lunch by the Argentine Book Chamber, as the current director in South America of the 'Association of Advertisers of Great Britain and Ireland'. This event was attended by the local VIPs, including the mayor, ministers and a university rector. Francis explained that his mission in South America was to engage Argentinians in English culture and its intellectual values. He gave a prepared speech on the evolution of British culture from the Chaucer era to the present day and reaffirmed the spiritual tradition that united Argentina and Great Britain, which was why Argentina was selected as an ideal location for the British Council to promote British culture. A report in the Argentinian newspaper *La Nacion* from this time quotes him as saying:

[Between] this great country and mine there is not only sympathy and friendship, not only mutual understanding for the diverse and particular manifestations of each one, which are indestructible for being deeply rooted like the roots of the oak, but also ties of community of interests. … What more natural thing then that in our desire to get to know you better we, in turn, would like you to know us more intimately in all the value that we represent in the intellectual, moral and spiritual sphere?

Francis gave his first lecture at the University of Buenos Aires' Faculty of Philosophy and Letters, as part of a cycle of three lectures about 'The Second English Romantic Movement'. This lecture focused on the seven great poets of the early nineteenth century, namely Wordsworth, Coleridge, Scott, Southey, Byron, Shelley and Keats whom he presented with his usual erudition as he did in the remaining two lectures looking again at nineteenth-century poetry and prose writing. At long last, Francis travelled home on board the *Drina* docking in Liverpool on 15 December 1944, having been away for some two years and nine months.

John's national service and a medical career marked by the war

By June 1944, Francis's and Nance's son John, my father, had done two years as a medical student at the University of St Andrews in Scotland. Now required to do his national service, John joined the famous Scots regiment, the Black Watch, at their Perth depot, and after completing various training and assessments he was enrolled as a nursing orderly, and then as a clinical orderly attached to the Royal Army Medical Corps (RAMC). Later he was assigned to the Royal Army Educational Corp (RAEC), and taught English to Polish servicemen stationed at St Andrews and Perth. These Poles were stationed along the eastern seaboard of Scotland and had at first been engaged in building a long chain of coastal defences against prospective invasion. There were about 38,000 such Poles in Scotland by the later stages of the war and while some were building these anti-tank defences on the east coast, still more were training to take part in the Normandy landings of 1944. After 1940, indeed, the Polish Army rebuilt itself in Scotland, after having fought in the Battle for France. John was part of the background support to this big Polish Army effort through his work in the RAEC, which established Army Education Centres, operating in hospitals, prisons and displaced persons' camps. The RAEC sent news-sheet teams with the men involved in the D-Day landings. John's duties included escorting German prisoners of war (POWs) to and from Europe, teaching them English and trying to listen into casual conversations whenever he could to pick up information. My mother said he was also stationed at Bletchley Park, Britain's top secret intelligence centre, but I have found no records for this. He certainly also accompanied German prisoners of war from France to Britain and taught them English in the POW camps. John remained in the RAEC for a further three years after the war ended until 1948. During demobilization, the RAEC aided men returning home from the army to make the transition to civilian occupations, providing pre-release advice and 'formation colleges'.

My father John was already studying to be a doctor before he was called up for national service at the age of 20 in 1944. The war itself left a definite mark on his subsequent medical career. Returning to medical school in 1949 he went to Dublin, the city of his birth, and enrolled as a medical student at Trinity College, Dublin. (To do this, John, as an observant Catholic, had to seek a dispensation from the local bishop to attend the ostensibly Protestant Trinity.[7]) In the aftermath of World War II, Irish university medical faculties in general, and not just Trinity's, benefitted from buoyant demand for medical faculty places from returning American GIs and their equivalents from other Allied nations. There were simply not enough medical school places in their home countries and English-language instruction in Ireland proved attractive.[8] Trinity recruited many such international students and was particularly diverse; those studying alongside John included ex-British servicemen and Polish refugees. While a medical student he joined the reserves of the Irish Defence Forces, serving in them from 1953 to 1955 during which time he was promoted to the rank of lieutenant. By this time, his parents had moved to Dublin and they all lived together again, taking holidays in Kerry as of old. His parents eventually retired to Annascaul where Francis wrote copious correspondence to local newspapers on his typewriter. John continued his photography hobby and photographed local scenes and printed postcards.

By the 1950s, John was a junior doctor doing rotations in various locations around Ireland including in County Galway, where I myself now live and work. He also worked in Belfast in Northern Ireland. In the end though he found he did not fit in in the rural west of Ireland with his southern British accent and he returned to Britain where he worked around the Midlands and in the north of England. He then went to sea working for the Elder Demster Line acting as ship's doctor on merchant vessels operating between Liverpool, the Canaries and Africa. Off duty he indulged his fascination with technology, rigging up different designs of aerials with the radio officer. After they got married, he and his wife (my mother) set up a clinic in Accra, Ghana. Returning to Britain after this African interlude, he left general practice and branched into preventative medicine. Specializing in public health, such as school health screening, in Britain's National Health Service, he advanced in his chosen field ultimately becoming the district community physician for Mid-Staffordshire. Though by now well established, he chose to do further studies at Liverpool University on a specialist subject of his choosing – 'Planned Diet as a Factor in Health'. This topic in fact had a direct link back to World War II in that he studied the public health benefits of improved wartime diets in Britain where the state had intervened through rationing to even out unequal access to good food and the population was kept fit and active in wartime conditions. Closer to home, he produced diet sheets for my mother's friends.

Throughout his medical career in post-war Britain, John remained active in army education as a member of the RAMC, teaching first aid to cadets and examining army personnel on their medical knowledge. Most Saturdays, he would be found at Blackshaw Moor, near Leek, with the army cadets, bringing along my brother when he was old enough, doing firing practice. It had previously been a camp for Polish soldiers and their families from 1946 to 1964. Local Catholic schools and our parish church community included such Poles. John was promoted to the rank of captain in 1973 and attended army camp well into retirement.[9] He would also be inducted as a serving brother in the Order St John of Jerusalem, a working order of chivalry and charitable body best known for providing the St John's Ambulance service in which my father was active. He also adjudicated on first-aid competitions for the Red Cross as well as being on call as a first responder in our area when accidents occurred.

World War II's afterlife and my family's multiple identities

I found out more about my father's and my grandfather's wartime experience when my mother gave me their papers and photos after they died. My father John was a very private person and did not talk much about his war experiences or his family. The war evidently left a mark on him in several ways however. He disliked German and Japanese culture, so much so that he turned off the television when programmes relating to or emanating from those countries came on. He threw out any books we brought in that may have had similar content. We put this phobia down to him having to deal with and treat the injuries of British prisoners of war that were repatriated. Another strain on him was keeping his lifelong involvement with British Army's cadets and the RAMC a secret from his mother who was by now living as a widow in Kerry in Ireland's south-west. Nance, his mother, who as we have seen had been involved in the Irish War of Independence, retained pronounced Irish republican and anti-British views. Thus, when we travelled to Ireland during the winter, my father always had a folding army shovel camouflaged in the car as well as his army sleeping bag in case of snow, but we were warned to keep this tangible evidence of his British Army connections hidden from Nance. By the 1980s, with British Army personnel and others becoming the objects of Provisional IRA car bombs, his army associates issued my father with a mirror on a stick with which to check under his car. Being an Irish citizen working for the British Army he could well have been a potential target. Anti-Irishness within the army itself riled my father, however, and my mother remembers an army dinner they attended where someone had insulted the Irish, prompting my father to remain seated during 'God Save the Queen'. Though undeterred in his British Army work, my father also showed his Irishness in the things and places he showed us. During family holidays in North Wales, he pointed out the location of Frongoch, the internment camp by Lake Bala where Irish rebels from the Easter Rising had been interned in 1916. 'The Troubles' in Northern Ireland cast a shadow on life for the Irish diaspora in the UK. We, children of an Irish doctor, received disparaging comments about being Irish. Despite all this, John's identity, moulded during the war, remained enthusiastically British. He travelled to London for the 'Trooping the Colour' every June and sang along with 'Land of Hope and Glory' when the

Last Night of the Proms was broadcast. A proud moment for him in his job was meeting Queen Elizabeth II. In contrast, to the day she died, his mother Nance remained a staunch Irish republican. When she finally passed away, some local villagers told my parents she should have an Irish tricolour draped on her coffin and a gun salute. I also remember my grandfather Francis, the Moroccan-born Jew who had changed his name and religion early in life and adopted a mixture of Britishness and Irishness into his own identity. Mercifully he escaped the fate of his brother who had put his trust in France only to die at Drancy transit camp. Francis told us he was Spanish, but we did not then understand he meant his family's distant Sephardic origins. He spoke to me in French when I was a child, which embarrassed me because I was not good at languages. When he died and I received his paperwork, I was surprised to find out he was from Morocco, not Spain. He had successfully assimilated into and contributed to British culture. World War II in many ways acted as the fulcrum of the lives of my forbears discussed above. It confirmed them in their hybrid identities as Irish, British, Spanish or Moroccan. Religion mattered too, whether they were Catholics or a Jewish convert to the faith. The ability to speak different languages was paramount in their fitting in where they landed turning them into a family that, notwithstanding the grievous loss of an uncle in the Holocaust, ultimately survived and thrived.

Notes

1 Daniel Schroeter, 'Anglo-Jewry and Essaouira (Mogador), 1860–1900: The Social Implications of Philanthropy', *Transactions & Miscellanies (Jewish Historical Society of England)* 28 (1981): 60–88.

2 The National Archives (Kew), Home Office records, HO 334/96/10292. Nationality and Naturalisation: Abulafia, Joseph Samuel, from Morocco. Resident in London. Certificate A10292 issued 26 July 1923; 'Francis Michael Scully' in *The London Gazette*, 9 October 1925. Available at: https://www. thegazette.co.uk/London/issue/33091/page/6558/data.pdf (accessed 1 July 2020).

3 See chapter on Nancy Scully in Tim Horgan, *Fighting for the Cause: Kerry's Republican Fighters* (Cork: Mercier Press, 2018); Nance's political activities feature in a witness statement given to the Irish Bureau of Military History in 1954 by a local IRA member; WS Ref #: 959, Witness: Patrick Houlihan, Member IRA, Kerry, 1921. Available at: http://www.militaryarchives.ie/collections/online-collections/bureau-of-military-history-1913–1921/reels/bmh/BMH.WS0959.pdf#page=9 (accessed 12 June 2020).

4 The National Archives (Kew), Special Operations Executive personnel files, Albert Abulafia; 1939–1946. HS 9/5/11.

5 Reeva Spector Simon, *The Jews of the Middle East and North Africa: The Impact of World War II* (London: Routledge, 2019).

6 R. J. L. Kingsford, *The Publishers Association, 1896–1946* (Cambridge: Cambridge University Press, 2010). Valerie Holman, 'Carefully Concealed Connections: The Ministry of Information and British Publishing, 1939–1946', *Book History* 8 (2005): 197–226.

7 On the particular place of Trinity College in the life of an emerging independent Ireland, see Tomás Irish, *Trinity in War and Revolution, 1912–1923* (Dublin: Royal Irish Academy, 2015).

8 For an example of such international recruitment at NUI Galway (previously UCG), the university where I now work, see Jackie Uí Chionna, *An Oral History of University College Galway, 1930–1980: A University in Living Memory* (Dublin: Four Courts Press, 2019).

9 Supplement to *The London Gazette*, 19 March 1974. Available at: https://www. thegazette.co.uk/London/issue/46239/supplement/3528/data.pdf (accessed 1 July 2020).

5

The diary of an Italian officer in Nazi concentration camps, 1943–5: The forgotten history of Italian Military Internees

Marina Ansaldo

My grandfather Marcello Consigliere was always a reserved person, with an air of quiet authority about him. He would, on occasion, recount episodes from his life. There were tales of hunting expeditions in the Piedmont countryside, when he pretended not to see a small hare, one too small to get anything to eat out of it and which he had encouraged in the direction of the bushes before his fellow hunters could see it. And there were the tales of the treks up the mountains when he was stationed with the Alpini.[1] What he did not talk about, however, were the two years that he had spent in Nazi concentration camps during World War II. It was not a family secret. There was the diary of his imprisonment – a hand-typed document bound in bright red cloth. I vaguely remember bringing it to school during history class and explaining to my classmates what it was about. I remember reading it at an age when I was too young to understand properly its importance and its implications for my grandfather and for my family. Reading it again for the purpose of writing this chapter, and researching in more detail the history of Italian soldiers in Nazi concentration camps, I have found myself realizing for the first time the complexities of the situation of Italian prisoners during World War II, and the full consequences of his imprisonment on my grandfather's

FIGURE 5.1 *Marcello Consigliere, officer in the Alpini, the Italian Army's mountain infantry corps, c.1940*

life (see Figure 5.1). In the pages that follow I will try to give a sense of the contents of Marcello's diary, with a particular focus on how he describes the precarious predicament of Italian officers in the camps.

As I mentioned, Marcello did not speak about his imprisonment, but he left us the diary. I believe that he put into it all that he thought we needed to know about his experience as a prisoner. The diary is a factual account of his daily life in the camps: the salient events he recorded for each day, the food they were distributed or that he was able to gather, any significant interaction with their captors or with other prisoners, any pressing thoughts or concerns. Interestingly, much of the diary is written in the plural voice ('we') as the description of a collective effort. The diary is, first and foremost, a means of witnessing to the conditions of the Italian officers in Nazi concentration camps and the endurance and courage of those who were able to persevere in the daily fight to remain alive. Moreover, it is a testament to a rare kind of loyalty to one's homeland as these men chose captivity over dishonour. My grandfather's diary is a testament to these people through their small daily gestures of survival, which were in themselves a form of resistance – from the constant food-related hunts and tactics, to the making of cooking hobs out of tin cans, to re-darning the same pairs of worn socks and leisure activities like chess tournaments played with handmade pieces.

A prime example of this spirit of resilience is the preparations Marcello describes for the 1943 Christmas celebrations. Having nothing but ingenuity, Marcello and some of his colleagues were able to improvise a Christmas tree and a nativity scene or crib. My grandfather describes in much more detail, however, their inventive efforts to bake a Christmas cake. In spite of not receiving enough food to eat on a daily basis, he and some friends decided to make the extraordinary effort to keep aside some of their rations leading up to Christmas so that they could celebrate properly (and for once not still feel hungry after a meal). It was quite a remarkable feat for people who were underfed. The recipe, featuring potatoes as the main ingredient, also included eggs, vodka and some coffee; most of the ingredients had been bartered for with wealthier prisoners (who had access to resources that my grandfather and his friends did not), in exchange for some of their daily rations and soap bars.[2] Marcello proudly remarks that the cake required no little effort and ingenuity, not least as they had nothing even resembling an oven. These extraordinary preparations marked out Christmas Day as special allowing Marcello, as he described it, to remember past festivities and faraway loved ones, and to hope to be reunited with them. For that one night he was not hungry, and for the first time in months he had a sound, restful sleep.

From wartime fragments to typewritten memoir

My grandfather wrote the current version of his diary years after the events he describes took place. The first draft was finalized on 10 February 1973 and he completed typing the final version on 12 April 1977. He clearly had the intention all along of keeping a record of the events of those two long years spent in concentration camps. Ever since the day of his imprisonment, he kept a diary of daily occurrences. Initially, he jotted notes on a small notepad that he was able to keep with him. Later on, he started writing on cigarette-rolling papers as this was the form in which paper was more readily available to him. He decided to preserve some of these papers by including them inside the four copies of the diary that he typed out. These notes were often only one sentence or two, which he expanded upon all those years later, when he took on the task of extending the daily entries, typing them out, and including a preface and some additional documents, so that the diary would become accessible to others. This is how he describes that process in the preface:

Today, as I approach the task of developing (succinctly) those notes, I wish I could find there something more about our precarious position, about the constant concerns on our own fate, our uncertain future, the continuous disappointments, the thoughts of our families far away and the utter lack of news from home, some reflections on our lives as prisoners – anything about our moral tribulations. Instead, very little of such things is recorded in the notes. Extremely low spirits, disconcerting news, a dark sense of foreboding: these were daily, constant concerns. There was no need to write down such things because, in essence, these represented nothing new! Instead, worthy of note and, hence, of a sentence in the diary were, for instance, finding a stalk of cabbage in the rubbish; capturing a mouse, after hours of stakeout; obtaining a small increase to your ration – so pressing were our material needs, constantly dissatisfied. This is what brightened a day, distinguishing it from others ... and worthy of note! As I expand these notes, I will endeavour to add something more of our situation and thoughts as prisoners, leaving aside some of the details, today negligible, about our constant obsession: hunger.

Other materials he included in the diary (a testament to his precise and meticulous nature), are his prisoner records, which he was able to find and take home with him following release from the last camp, and a list he prepared with the key details and dates of imprisonment for each of the camps he went through: Kaisersteinsbrück (Austria); Przemyśl (Poland); Dęblin Irena (Poland); Sandbostel (Germany); Wietzendorf Kr. Soltau (Germany); Mühlberg/Elbe (Germany); Spremberg (Germany).[3] The names of the camps were also engraved by Curiale, a friend and fellow prisoner, on Marcello's canteen, which followed him throughout his imprisonment. Curiale completed the engravings on 12 July 1945 and the canteen is now displayed in my parents' sitting room (see Figure 5.2). In the diary, my grandfather describes the frequent transfers between camps in much detail as these always occurred in dire circumstances with his fellow prisoners and he often being locked inside cattle trains for days, with hardly any food and water, leaving the men like 'piles of human flesh'. Marcello published a description of one of these transfers in the March 1970 issue of the Alpini veterans' periodical *Genova Alpina* where he describes the journey between the camps of Przemyśl and Dęblin Irena (both in Poland) between 11 January and 18 January 1944. He describes this as the most harrowing transfer of his imprisonment. The contents of the article match the entries for the corresponding days in the diary. This article is, as far as I am aware, the only part of the diary that has been published to date.[4]

FIGURE 5.2 *Marcello Consigliere's wartime canteen inscribed with places of detention by fellow internee, Curiale*

An Italian army left in the lurch

The diary itself begins with a preface describing the days leading to Marcello's imprisonment. In August 1943 my grandfather was serving in the 104th Regiment of the *Alpini di Marcia Cuneense* as head of its administration office. His regiment had been stationed near the border with Yugoslavia for about seven months where they had been fighting against Yugoslav partisan forces. Italy had been party to the German-led invasion of April 1941 and these hostilities persisted. On 23 August 1943, however, Marcello's regiment received orders to move inland to Egna, near Bolzano, in the Alto Adige region of Italy, where they were to take a rest period. Full of joy at the thought of a break from fighting, they had no idea of what was in store for them. On 25 August they arrived at their destination which was a former school-turned-garrison. Marcello remarks that, from early September, a marked sense of uneasiness grew amongst them. This was partly due to a significant presence of heavily armed German troops in the Alto Adige region where they found themselves and owing to the fact that most of the local population was far from friendly towards the Italian troops, given their troubled history of separatist aspirations in a region only added to Italy after World War I from the old Habsburg Empire.[5] Marcello and his comrades observed a constant flow of German forces southwards as German soldiers began to situate themselves in all prominent locations (crossroads, bridges, mountain passes) with the obvious aim of keeping watch over the Italian soldiers stationed there. Something was clearly afoot. Marcello reports that at around 6 pm on the fateful evening of 8 September 1943 vague and imprecise rumours of an armistice began to circulate. At 7.42 pm Marshal Pietro Badoglio, the Italian head of government, a government that had recently deposed and arrested the dictator Benito Mussolini, broadcast the following radio message:

> The Italian Government, recognizing the impossibility of continuing the uneven fight against the overwhelming enemy forces, and in order to spare further and more severe loss to the Nation, has requested a general armistice from General Eisenhower, commander-in-chief of the Anglo-American Allied forces. This request has been granted. Therefore, all acts of hostility by Italian forces against Anglo-American forces must cease everywhere. They shall, however, react in the case of attacks coming from anywhere else.[6]

This proclamation has been described as marking one of the most tragic moments in Italy's history.[7] It was not preceded, or followed, by any direct order or clarification to the Italian troops and caused a similar degree of confusion amongst soldiers and civilians. Was the war over? Badoglio's vague instruction was received and interpreted differently across the land.[8] Marcello describes the proclamation as cryptic. Elsewhere in Italy historians relate that reactions ranged from disbelief, surprise and joy to confusion and fear as the reality of the situation became clearer.[9] News reporters on the radio described the celebrations that were breaking out across Italy but in the case of Marcello and the rest of the troops stationed at Egna the mood was markedly different. Marcello notes that they sensed imminent danger as they knew that they were in a highly vulnerable position. In fact, the situation was particularly difficult for the troops stationed in the Alto Adige region, where Marcello was, given the large presence of German troops. Historian Elena Agia Rossi states that most of the population in the area immediately sided with the Germans after the announcement of the armistice.[10] Italian troops suddenly found themselves in what was, effectively, enemy territory facing enemy forces with far-superior equipment, weapons and ammunition. The German forces had much clearer instructions: disarm immediately, by any means necessary, all Italian troops.[11]

Stunned, the garrison in Egna assembled, waiting for official instructions from divisional command but to no avail. Their colonel ordered them not to vacate the garrison at any cost and to remain vigilant. Around 2.30 am on 9 September they heard tanks on the move and, before they had the opportunity to react, they were surrounded. A German captain tried to intimidate them through a megaphone and using bad Italian: 'If you don't surrender in three minutes we will open fire.' And so they did. Marcello states that there were only ten officers and fifteen Alpine soldiers at the Egna garrison (the latter mostly recruits and orderlies). They had no cannons, machine guns or even automatic weapons to speak of yet they were facing German tanks. The Germans opened fire, injuring a few men. The Italians responded to the fire as best they could, with muskets and some hand-bombs, fully aware that their efforts were futile. They lasted one hour – during which time they kept trying to obtain orders and instructions from divisional command and other garrisons, by phone and radio, but again there was no answer. They discovered later that the phone cables had been severed by the Germans prior to the attack, but they would never learn why the division command did not return their radio messages. In the end they surrendered, to avoid a pointless massacre. As the Germans took possession of the garrison, Marcello took advantage of a moment of confusion to jump off from a wall at the back of the building and attempt escape, followed by a sergeant and seven Alpine soldiers. They hid in the countryside until noon the following day, making several attempts to escape the area. However, their efforts were in vain, given the very high numbers of well-armed German patrols, ready to shoot on sight. Spotted in a field and ordered to surrender, they decided that resisting would be pointless. They were captured and brought back to the Egna garrison. So began Marcello's long, hard two-year imprisonment.

What made Marcello's predicament, and that of his fellow Italian prisoners, even more difficult was the particular stance that the Germans took towards their former allies. As I mentioned, between 9 and 15 September German forces received very clear instructions on how to deal with the Italian troops they imprisoned. Italian soldiers were to be treated according to their reaction to the request to keep fighting alongside Germany. Those complying would be allowed to keep their weapons and would be treated like German troops. Those refusing to cooperate were to be sent to concentration camps. Those who refused to disarm, openly resisted or attempted to join partisan forces were to receive a different treatment depending on their rank. Officers were to be shot. Soldiers were to be sent to forced labour in eastern Europe.[12] On 20 September Hitler himself clarified that Italian prisoners were to be considered as 'Italian Military Internees' (IMIs) and not as prisoners of war (POWs), which meant that the principles of the Geneva Convention were not to apply to them.[13] These decisions have been regarded as completely arbitrary and criminal.[14] It is estimated that around 810,000 Italian soldiers were imprisoned as a consequence of the armistice.[15] They were immediately requested to surrender and join the German forces – around 94,000 accepted. The rest, over 710,000, were deported as a consequence of their refusal.[16] Soldiers were sent to forced labour, and officers were kept in the camps.[17] Marcello was amongst them.

Paying the price for keeping your word

On his arrival at his first camp at Kaisersteinsbrück (Austria) on 12 September Marcello learnt of his new official designation as an IMI by means of a public notice affixed to the barrack's door. This is how he describes its contents:

> We are not considered prisoners of war, because our two Nations are allies, but we are Military Internees … as if we were guests of the Great Reich! And, as such, we are not to be treated as prisoners of war. Acting in such a way the Germans would like the World to believe that we are treated with a certain respect, not as prisoners. The harsh reality, in fact, is quite different: we are denied the assistance of the International Red Cross, of the Vatican, and of any other body of succour. Furthermore, the Germans do not consider the Geneva Convention to apply to us. … In essence, they give us as little as they can, and much less than what is given to the other prisoners who, additionally, have access to several other aids. Nobody can intervene on our behalf.

Marcello left that first camp the following day and arrived at Przemyśl (Poland) on 20 September. Gathered together two days later, the men got an official announcement (in Italian) about their new status, a statement which Marcello took care to write down in shorthand. Italian officers were to be given the opportunity to volunteer to fight in Italy for Mussolini and his newly established (and pro-German) Italian Social Republic. The Germans had sprung the briefly deposed dictator from arrest to head this new regime.[18] Marcello and his peers were informed that many non-commissioned officers and soldiers had already joined up to serve Mussolini and, as a further sweetener, the German commander held out the prospect that officers who now changed sides would, as far as possible, be placed with the men they had up to recently commanded. If they joined, they were committing to keep fighting for Mussolini until the end of the war. Crucially, the newly captured Italians were forcibly reminded of how the legal government of the king and of Badoglio had led them down badly and effectively thrown away its own legitimacy: 'This Government has released all Officers from their oath, following the surrender and flight of the King who, with such actions, has left the Nation at the mercy of the Enemy, and has plunged it into shame and misery.'[19] Those who refused to join Mussolini would remain imprisoned in the camp and he would decide the fates of such officers. Gatherings of any nature amongst themselves were strictly forbidden, and they were warned that this would be enforced by German soldiers. Marcello reports that, to the majority of them, this proposition was simply unacceptable. This is how he expresses this crucial sentiment, that will see himself, with many others, choosing to remain as prisoners in the Nazi camps rather than breaking their oaths: 'They cannot release us from an oath with a couple of words.'

On 1 October, Marcello reports that there were many discussions among themselves about the merits of joining the Italian Social Republic. Some were unsure but he was clear in his mind: 'I have no doubts: I took an oath to the King, I am not at all released from it, and I must abide by it.' He reports that those considering joining did not do so out of principle but mostly because they could not withstand the physical and psychological tribulations and hunger of their new condition as prisoners. Italian officers were asked to side with the German forces again and again but Marcello and most of the IMIs did not yield. He never at any point expresses doubt in the pages of the diary – his oath would stand. The record shows that the vast majority of IMIs (between 600,000 and 650,000) refused to join the Italian Social Republic and thus remained imprisoned, all the more remarkable considering that the chance to free yourself by changing sides remained a live option during their long captivity.[20] These IMIs are aptly described by the Italian journalist and writer Giovanni Guareschi (who was among them, and is often quoted in Marcello's diary) as the 'volunteers of the wire fence'.[21] Their refusal has been described as an act of resistance, without weapons, and the first mass rejection of Italian Fascism.[22]

Marcello extended refusal to comply with his captors' wishes on the matter of forcing officers to work. On 23 January 1945 it was officially announced that all Italian officers would be put to work, another breach of international norms as officer-prisoners were normally exempt from the obligation to work. Requested in February to fill out a form to declare the preferred type of employment, Marcello balked: 'I decide immediately: I submit a blank form. I will calmly await the reactions from the Germans, and decide to remain firm in my decision.' On 26 February Marcello and his fellow IMIs in the camp at Mühlberg/Elbe (Germany) were advised by the ranking Italian officers among them to prepare a declaration attesting that they were being forced to work against their will, a document that would be countersigned by Colonel Bruno Toscano, the most senior Italian officer in the camp, if and when they were made to do forced labour. Clearly Marcello was not alone in feeling that these requests were unacceptable and ought to be opposed at all costs.

By then the war was nearing its end and the Germans' situation turned more desperate. As it happened, the Germans never got around to sending Marcello to work: in fact, the factory they had been destined for was destroyed by Allied bombs. But even as the Germans realized that defeat was inevitable, Italian IMIs had special treatment reserved for them. On 24 April Marcello learned from a well-trusted source that, two evenings before, SS Supreme Command in Berlin had issued the commander of their camp with orders to kill all three hundred Italian officers present – orders which the commander, an Austrian not named by my grandfather, decided to ignore. Marcello wrote that he and the other 299 officers present in Mühlberg/Elbe owed their lives to this man. My grandfather was aware that this order was not unique to their camp and that many Italian officers and men were killed as a result. Composing his memoir in the 1970s, he stated that it worried him that many of these incidents had passed unrecorded. For his part, therefore, he recorded the following executions citing figures which, meticulous as ever, he states he had verified as accurate. His list included the following:

- Sebaldushof labour camp in Treuenbrietz: 140 IMIs murdered on 23 April 1945

- Radeberg: 10 officers who had been sent to forced labour were shot dead on 18 April 1945

- Smideberg: 5 Italian officers shot dead on 13 April 1945[23]

He also noted rumours of the SS killing several others. To Marcello's mind, the rationale for these massacres was to punish the IMIs for their decision to resist. A German non-commissioned officer (NCO) told a friend of Marcello's that 'you were very lucky, you Italians who refused to join either the armed forces or forced labour. If we had won the war none of you would have returned alive to your Homeland'.

IMIs and national embarrassment

Marcello and the other IMIs who did return home owed their survival both to their own sheer determination and to a significant dose of luck. Many others were not so fortunate.[24] Even after returning home, though, IMIs had new challenges to face. Prior to conducting research for this chapter, I had not realized that Marcello was far from the only Italian prisoner in German concentration camps in World War II who, having returned home, spoke little about those hard times. This was not only due to difficult memories which

I had always assumed. As well as that, IMIs had particular difficulties in making themselves heard in post-war Italy.[25] I never knew that my grandfather, having had the courage and moral rectitude to stand fast by his oath to king and country (which had earned for him two hard years of imprisonment), went home to a nation that did not proclaim IMIs as heroes, but, instead, kept them on the sidelines, as a quiet source of embarrassment to government and society. Their existence was a stark reminder of how poorly the Italian government had handled the armistice and its aftermath. For the political right, the IMIs were deserters. For the left, they were soldiers of a defunct and unloved regime.[26] In sum, the IMIs were for a long time not spoken of and the first official studies on them were carried out by German scholars.[27] It is only in the last decade or two that more focus has been placed on them by Italian historians. In fact, a conference on 'Gli Schiavi di Hitler' (Hitler's Slaves) took place in Genoa on 21 February 2020 (whilst I was writing this chapter) at which Orlando Materassi, from the *Associazione Nazionale ex Internati* (National Association of Former Internees), said that there is still work to be done to bring to light fully the history of the IMIs, a subject still overlooked in the Italian school history curriculum and still little known to the Italian public. The historians present agreed. Now, with the last surviving internees fading away, it is more important than ever that we remember.

Memory and the gift of resilience

The diary itself contains an implicit message about the importance of memory. As I was reading the diary again in preparation for writing this chapter, I found a clipping from a magazine, sellotaped to the back of one of the diary's pages, in a fashion similar to how my grandfather had preserved his own original handwritten notes. The clipping in question is a letter from a reader to the editor of *Confidenze* magazine, published in July 1978, just over a year after Marcello finished typing up the diary. The title of the article is 'My Grandfather's Diary'. The reader recounted having found their deceased grandfather's diary about his imprisonment during World War I and wondered what to do with it. Finding this press cutting as I prepared this chapter, similar questions were also going through my mind. The editor of the magazine answered that the diary should be preserved, and treated with reverence, preserving and passing on the memory to the next generation. Ultimately, he concluded, the memories of our parents and grandparents are part of what makes us who we are. My grandfather's act of preserving that article in his own diary leaves a clear message for me and my family, I consider. Family history ought to be preserved, and I would like to think that Marcello would approve of my writing this chapter. I now understand better my grandfather and his silences. His example of stoic loyalty to one's ideals I shall carry with me always. His message of resilience in the face of life's adversities is stated explicitly in his dedication of the diary to my mother, with the following words: 'To Luisa, so that she may know and think upon what happened to her father, during two long and hard years of imprisonment, and realise that one must always react in the face of life's adversities. Who, in Germany, of sound body, allowed themselves to be overwhelmed in spirit, never saw the Homeland again.'

My mother recalls receiving a copy of the diary from Marcello at a difficult time when she had been quietly dealing with depression – to her it was a strong message from her taciturn but much-respected and loved father that she ought to react, and stand on her own feet again. It is a message we can all use. Now and again, at times of crisis in my life, I reflect upon what my grandfather had to face, and the dignity and courage with which he did so, and I hope that I can muster a fraction of that strength to enable me to face the smaller crises of our time.

This is how Marcello chose to conclude the diary, and it is only appropriate to do the same here:

> Suffering, deprivations, uncertainties, fear and hunger … all was endured in the name of two fundamental ideals:
> - The constant thoughts of ITALY and FAMILY, and the hope, never surrendered, to see them again
> - The solemn and irrevocable oath of loyalty to the HOMELAND!
> The former I.M.I (*Internato Militare Italiano*)

Matriculation number: 138543/ XVII A

Notes

1 The Alpini are the special mountain infantry units of the Italian Army.
2 These 'wealthier' prisoners were Italians who had decided to join the Italian Social Republic and were in consequence awaiting release. This question of difference in status among Italian prisoners recurs later in the chapter.
3 Marcello indicates in this list the designation of each camp – mostly *stalag* (camps for enlisted personnel who were prisoners of war) or *oflag* (camps for officers prisoners of war). Marcello was in the final two camps listed after the area had been liberated by the Red Army. The camps were for military allies, under Russian supervision. Although, technically, they were no longer prisoners Marcello describes in detail the perils of these places.

4 Marcello Consigliere, 'Ricordi di prigionia del Col. Consigliere', *Genova Alpina: Mensile per gli alpini della Liguria* 2, no. 3 (1970): 10–11. Available at: http://www.alpinigenova.it/genova-alpina-nuova/genova-alpina-1970/ (accessed 20 March 2020).

5 Mario Bernardo, *Il Momento buono: Il movimento garibaldino bellunese nella lotta di liberazione del Veneto* (Rome: Ideologie, 1969), 23–5.

6 My translation. See 'Badoglio annuncia l'armistizio dell'Italia', *La Repubblica*, 7 September 2013. Available at: https://video.repubblica.it/spettacoli-e-cultura/badoglio-annuncia-l-armistizio-dell-italia/139334 (accessed 22 February 2020).

7 Elena Aga Rossi, *Una nazione allo sbando: 8 Settembre 1943* (Bologna: Società Editrice il Mulino, 2003), 25.

8 Rossi, *Una nazione allo sbando*, especially 135–49.

9 Rossi, *Una nazione allo sbando*, 135.

10 Bernardo, *Il Momento buono*, 23–5.

11 Gerhard Schreiber, *I militari Italiani Internati nei Campi di Concentramento del Terzo Reich, 1943–1945* (Rome: Ufficio storico, Stato maggiore dell'esercito, 1992), 137.

12 Rossi, *Una nazione allo sbando*, 136–7.

13 Schreiber, *I militari Italiani Internati*, 122.

14 Schreiber, *I militari Italiani Internati*, 122, 138.

15 Mario Avagliano and Marco Palmieri, *I Militari Italiani nei Lagher Nazisti: una resistenza senz'armi, 1943–1945* (Bologna: Società Editrice il Mulino, 2020), Kindle ed, 'Introduzione'.

16 Marco Palmieri, presentation at historical conference entitled 'Gli Schiavi di Hitler', 21 February 2020 held at Palazzo Tursi, Genoa, an intiative of the Centro Studi Schiavi di Hitler. Further details available at: http://www.schiavidihitler.org (accessed 30 March 2020).

17 Palmieri, presentation, 21 February 2020.

18 The Italian Social Republic (September 1943–April 1945) was a new regime founded after the armistice. It was desired by Nazi Germany and led by Benito Mussolini, with the purpose of managing Italian territories under Nazi control after the armistice. The Italian government did not recognize the Italian Social Republic as a legitimate state.

19 The oath referred to that taken by all members of the Italian Army of all ranks. The version which IMIs had taken (in effect since 1929) translates as follows: 'I swear to be loyal to His Majesty the King and his Royal Successors, to observe loyally the Statute and the other laws of the State and to fulfil all the duties of my State, with the sole purpose of the inseparable good of King and Homeland' (my translation), *Regolamento di disciplina militare* (1929). Available at: http://www.regioesercito.it/regioesercito/redoc/manumil1.htm (accessed 20 March 2020).

20 Avagliano and Palmieri, *I Militari Italiani nei Lagher Nazisti*, 'Introduzione'.

21 Giovannino Guareschi, 'Occhio segreto nel lager', *Oggi*, 19 March 1946, 9.

22 Palmieri, presentation, 21 February 2020.

23 For similar episodes of Germans murdering Italians at the end of the war, see Avagliano and Palmieri, *I Militari Italiani nei Lagher Nazisti*, 'Eccidi e Marce della Morte'.

24 It is estimated that at least 50,834 IMIs died in the camps; Avagliano and Palmieri, *I Militari Italiani nei Lagher Nazisti*, 'Introduzione'.

25 Palmieri, presentation, 21 February 2020.

26 Orlando Materassi, presentation at historical conference entitled 'Gli Schiavi di Hitler', 21 February 2020 held at Palazzo Tursi, Genoa, an intiative of the Centro Studi Schiavi di Hitler. Further details available at: http://www.schiavidihitler.org (accessed 30 March 2020).

27 On this point, see again Avagliano and Palmieri, *I Militari Italiani nei Lagher Nazisti*, 'Introduzione'.

6

Behind enemy lines: The story of an American soldier and the Italian family who saved him

*Colleen Maloney Williamson
and Maureen Maloney*

Obituary – Thomas Joyce Maloney

87, died peacefully in his sleep on September 20, 2010 in Upper St. Clair. A decorated World War II veteran, Tom served as a Sergeant in the Army Air Corps. In February of 1945, his plane was shot down over Condino, Italy where a local family, the Pellizzaris, saved his life by hiding him from the Nazis and the Fascists until the end of the war. In 1955, Tom opened the first in a chain of Hallmark greeting card stores in Downtown Pittsburgh – The Card Centers. Along with his wife and family, Tom owned and managed the business until they closed in 2005. An avid sports fan and sportsman he enjoyed playing golf at Alcoma Golf Club and handball at various sports clubs around town. A devout Catholic, he attended daily mass and had a special devotion to the Blessed Mother. Tom leaves a legacy of optimism and generosity to his many employees, customers, dear friends and beloved family. He was greatly loved and will be dearly missed by his wife of 62 years Mary Dee Lyden Maloney; his children, Colleen (Ed) Williamson, Tim Maloney, Kathy (Dan) Beckovich, Maureen Maloney, Patty (Matt Knoblock) Maloney; his grandchildren, Brian, Kate, Colin and P.J. Williamson, Matthew Beckovich, Keri Nugent and Mary Knoblock; and by his many devoted nieces, nephews and extended family.[1]

Like many American veterans from World War II, Dad rarely spoke of his combat memories. We heard vague details of what happened: plane shot down, frozen feet, the pair of cousins who rescued him. When he passed away in 2010, we siblings realized how little we knew about this part of Dad's life and began talking about going to Italy ourselves to see the place where he was shot down. We made the trip in 2019 and realized how deeply our family history was intertwined with the Condino families that rescued and hid Dad. The following account is the combination of our family stories, newspaper and book accounts, and anecdotes from Italy by local historians, friends and the children of the cousins who saved him.

Thomas Joyce Maloney was born on 11 December 1922 in Pittsburgh, Pennsylvania, the youngest child of a prosperous, devout Catholic family. Dad was handsome, with copper-coloured hair, blue eyes and a contagious smile. He was fun-loving and enjoyed making a show of himself, always laughing at the results. In 1941 Dad was a student at the University of Pittsburgh, where he met our mother. Thanks to a fateful alphabetical order seating in biology class, Mary Dee Lyden and Tom Maloney were assigned to be laboratory partners. During a dissection lab, Dad tried to impress Mom by choosing the fattest frog he could find, only to be dismayed to find that the frog was fat because of a glut of eggs inside. On 7 December 1941 Mom and Dad were attending mass at Sacred Heart Church when they heard the news of the bombing of Pearl Harbor.

Our father's war

Dad enlisted in the US Army on his twentieth birthday in December 1942 and reported for duty on 17 July 1943. When the opportunity arose, he joined the Army Air Corps, predecessor of the US Air Force. From July 1943 to December 1944 he trained to be a radio operator, mechanic and gunner in South Dakota and Arizona. On 31 December 1944 Corporal Thomas J. Maloney deployed to the European African Middle Eastern Theatre of Operations (EAMETO). He arrived at the Solenzara Airdrome, Corsica, on 19 January 1945, as a member of the 12th Air Force, 57th Bombardment Wing, 447th Bomb Squadron, 321st Bombardment Group.[2] Dad became part of the Battle of the Brenner, a plan to impede the movement of German troops and supplies to and from Italy.[3] He participated in six missions.[4] On 6 February 1945 he embarked on his sixth mission. The assignment was to bomb the Rovereto Marshalling Yard and the Crema Rail Bridge in northern Italy. Dad's plane, Superstitious Aloysius, was one of sixteen B-25J bombers flying in formation over the Alps towards the target. Just south of Rovereto, Dad's plane and two others were downed by Nazi anti-aircraft fire. One plane crashed into Mount Brugnolo and another into a farm in Torrebelvicino.[5]

The six crew members from Dad's plane parachuted out of it before it crashed into the San Gregorio monastery chapel. Five landed in the valley near the town of Condino and were immediately captured. Dad landed above the town on Mount Rango. It was very cold and the fresh snow was deep. In what must have been desperation, he eventually turned himself in to German soldiers as his feet succumbed to deep frostbite. A local doctor was called in to examine his feet and asked Dad where he was from. He answered, 'Pittsburgh, Pennsylvania.' The doctor, who knew something of the city, asked him an obscure question about Pittsburgh that Dad was able to answer correctly. This was a test to see if he was an infiltrator. Having passed the test, the doctor told Dad that the Germans would kill him because of the poor condition of his feet. The doctor said he would set up a rescue. Partisans came and broke him out. They took him to the location close to where he surrendered to the Germans and told him they would be back for him.

The partisans never returned, however. For three days Dad wandered the mountain, hungry and cold, searching for the Swiss border.[6] He used up all his provisions and even burned a few dollars from his pocket for warmth. By the time he found a grotto to the Blessed Mother, he was desperate. That day, cousins Beppino and Fulvio Pellizzari, young men in their twenties from Condino, climbed Mount Rango looking for crew members' silk parachutes to repurpose into shirts. They were dressed in German uniform jackets as Italian men had been ordered to. When they came to the hill dedicated to the Madonna, Dad heard the cousins approaching. As they neared, he stepped from behind a tree into their path, hands holding his rosary high, and surrendered. Through gestures and acting, the cousins communicated they were not soldiers and knew he was from the plane that crashed into the monastery. Dad later recounted, 'I was here to pray and when I saw Fulvio and Beppino I pulled out the rosary as a sign of peace.'[7] Dad had a high fever, his feet were frozen and he was exhausted.[8] The cousins offered him grappa, a strong Italian drink, to warm him. In his starving, weakened condition Dad

FIGURE 6.1 *Fulvio Pellizzari, Thomas Joyce Maloney and Beppino Pellizzari, 1945*

became drunk and was unable to walk. The cousins took turns carrying Dad down the mountain on their backs through the deep snow (see Figure 6.1). They hid Dad at a farm close to Condino where he was fed warm soup. The cousins went to tell the story to their parents.[9]

The mountain town of Condino had been entrenched in war for five years and it was winter. The people had just enough to survive. And Dad's plane destroyed the chapel above their town, killing two friars. Despite these circumstances, Beppino and Fulvio quickly moved Dad to the home of Beppino's parents, Giuseppe and Angelina Pellizzari. Dad was scared. On his knees he begged Angelina, 'No Germans, I'm going to die! No, mutti, no Germans I die!'[10] He emptied his pockets and Angelina saw the rosary, prompting her decision. She said, 'He can stay.' The experience solidified his lifelong devotion to Mary. The Pellizzari family hid him for the next two months and treated him as a son.[11] When he arrived at the Pellizzaris' home, Dad was very sick. His fever was high and his frozen foot was close to gangrene. Hiding Dad was dangerous. The Germans patrolled the area looking for the escaped American soldier and would not hesitate to shoot anyone discovered hiding him. It was impossible to get medicine. So Aunt Santina and Mama Angelina used an old treatment of boiled water with salt and fir resin on Dad's feet. His fever diminished and his feet began to recover.

The family let no one into the house for fear of being discovered and shot. There were other brave citizens, however, who helped during Dad's stay. To find out how to treat Dad's feet, Giulietta Dorna, the mother of the cousins' friend, chatted with the pharmacist about how frozen feet had been cared for in World War I and took this information about the salt and resin treatment back to Aunt Santina and Mama Angelina. Salt was rare and Angelina, who had many cows, used the salt meant for the cows to treat Dad's feet. Resin was readily available from fir trees.[12] The elementary teacher, Vittoria Poletti, sent her daughter with a first-grade book and instructions on how to help Dad learn some Italian so he could communicate more easily.[13] Fulvio's family sent flour, cheese and anything else they had to help.[14] Santina's daughter, 12-year-old Fernanda Quadrita, saw Dad every day, against her mother's wishes. 'Every free moment I went to visit him and for this reason we became very good friends.'[15] When he was hidden, she brought him food, talked, visited and prayed with him, 'sometimes the Hail Mary and other times the whole Rosary'.[16]

A small outpost of German soldiers was located in the village to control the surrounding area.[17] The peril to the Pellizzaris and the Condino community cannot be overemphasized. Time and again they protected Dad. If the Italians had advance notice of German checks, they hid Dad, but there were times when danger unexpectedly showed its face. One day German soldiers assembled the local citizens. Dad dressed in a woman's coat with a scarf wrapped around his head and face. Red hair was common in the area, but Dad's fair complexion was not. He was placed in the centre of the group, blocking him from view, and was given a baby to hold. When the Germans came along, he lifted the baby to his face as if to warm the baby with his breath. The soldiers did not notice him. Another time, Dad was walking with a group when they came upon an unexpected checkpoint. When they realized the situation, the group held back and waited until the guard changed and a person known to them was in his place. A young woman linked arms with Dad. He held hands with her children and they moved through the checkpoint as a family.

Near the end of April 1945 the Germans were retreating north from the efforts of the partisans and the Americans. One German unit stopped in Condino, but Dad could not be found to be warned. The family thought he was walking on Mount Rango. Beppino ran in search of Dad, but could not find him. Later, Dad told Beppino, 'I saw you run. I called you with rocks but you did not understand.' The next day, Dad was given peasant clothes and sent to the mountains where he hid until the Germans left.[18] On 24 April American forces arrived in Condino. Everyone ran out into the streets, embracing each other and shouting with joy. When the Americans discovered Dad, there was a great party. The soldiers passed out chocolate, cigarettes and food. Dad started off with the soldiers, but ran back a few minutes later.[19] He stayed with the Pellizzaris a few more days until the American soldiers returned, gave more food to the family and said Dad had to return with them or he would be considered AWOL (Absent Without Leave). Before he left, a picture was taken with the whole family.[20]

In February 1945, Dad's family back in Pittsburgh was advised that he was missing in action. Just after VE Day, they joyfully received the news that he had returned to the Air Force. A few days later they received the first letter from him:

Dear Mom and Dad
Well here I am in [deleted by military authorities] and the place isn't too bad. In fact it's ok. I haven't received any mail from you as yet but hope to get it soon –
Don't worry about me because this place is ok and I should be home in about July so we'll have a lot of time together – I miss you all an awful lot and want to hear from you pretty often – I'll write as much as possible too –
Have you heard from Fran [his older brother] lately? I guess he'll be home soon – It's not going to last long over here so I'll be home too –
I hope everyone is ok and don't worry about me because I'm fine and the food is pretty good so all I need is your prayers – Write soon.
                    Your loving Son
                    Joyce

Every few days they received another letter. Dad departed Europe on 1 June 1945 and arrived in the United States on 9 June. He spent time in San Antonio, Texas, at the District Army Air Forces Personnel Distribution Command. He was awarded the rank of Staff Sargent on 19 August. He received the following awards and citations: Good Conduct Medal, Purple Heart, Air Medal and European African Middle Eastern Campaign Medal with four Bronze Service Stars. He was honourably discharged on 27 October 1945.[21]

Discovering our father's past

As children we knew that Dad had been a soldier in World War II, that his plane had been shot down and that his life had been saved by a family. Even as we moved into adulthood, Dad never shared the story of his rescue. And, in the way children never consider their parents' lives prior to becoming parents, it was not something we thought to ask about. That changed in 1987. Fernanda Quadrita, Dad's 12-year-old friend in 1945, travelled to nearby Ohio for a family wedding. At the wedding she asked guests from Pittsburgh if they knew Tom Maloney. One of the guests said she did not know him but volunteered to call every Tom Maloney in the Pittsburgh phone book to see if she could find him. One morning the phone rang and Mom answered it.

> 'Is this the home of Tom Maloney?' the woman on the phone asked.
> 'Yes,' Mom answered.
> 'Was he in northern Italy during the War?'
> 'Yes,' Mom replied.
> 'Was he helped by a family named Pellizzari?'
> 'Yes.'
> 'Is he still alive?'
> 'Yes, he is sitting here eating his cereal.'

The woman relayed that Fernanda was in the area for a wedding and would be flying out of the Pittsburgh airport later that day to return to Italy. Mom and Dad drove to the airport to meet her. They visited for a short while and invited Fernanda to return to Pittsburgh. The next summer, Fernanda and her nephew came to stay with Mom and Dad. The nephew translated for them but they also reverted to their methods of communication from all those years ago. When Fernanda left, Dad promised to return to Condino.

In October 1990 Mom and Dad travelled to Condino. Fernanda met them at the train station in Trento, along with relatives of his rescuers, Beppino and Fulvio, who had passed away some years previously. Over the next few days, Dad visited Mount Rango, the site of his rescue; the rebuilt San Gregorio chapel; the tombs of Beppino and Fulvio; and the village. The people of Condino celebrated Dad's return with a banquet.[22] When Mom and Dad returned they brought local Italian newspaper reports of their visit. With the translated articles we first started to understand the story of Dad's crash and rescue. We learned of the joy of Beppino's and Fulvio's children and grandchildren – and the entire village – that celebrated his return. 'All the people in Condino know today of his adventure because the case of the pilot saved has been written in the history of the country.'[23]

After Mom and Dad passed away, our sibling quintet resolved to visit Condino. In early 2019 we booked flights and contacted the Pellizzari family hoping to meet them, see Fernanda and visit the place where Dad had been shot down. We were not expecting the welcome we received and the stories we heard. We arrived at our accommodations in Ponte Caffaro at the top of Lake Idro on a Friday night. On Saturday morning Beppino's daughter, Mariangela, her cousin, Luciana and Beppino's granddaughter, Eleanora, came to meet us. Eleanora translated our conversations and Luciana showed us a translation app we could use to converse. We spent time learning the family tree of Beppino and Fulvio. We made plans for Mariangela to come later and lead us to the meeting place in Condino.

Condino is about 16 kilometres north of Ponte Caffaro in a narrow valley of the Alps with towering mountains on each side. These are the same mountains Dad saw, beautiful to us but frightening to him. We arrived outside the village hall to a crowd of about fifty, including Pellizzari family members, friends and local historians. To our surprise, they applauded our arrival as we got out of the car. Each person greeted us. We met Enrica, the baby Dad held to his face to hide his identity during a raid. We met Fernanda's daughter, Franca. We met other family members and friends whose lives had been marked by Dad's crash and rescue. The outpouring of love and excitement was moving.

After this welcome, we all moved inside to the village council chamber, a beautiful room with murals telling the history of Condino, including Dad's plane crashing into the chapel. The mayor, Claudio Pucci, and his wife, Chiara, gave a moving welcome in Italian and English, celebrating the history of February 1945. They told the story of the crash, remembering the two friars who perished, the ten others who were injured and the flight crew of Dad's plane. They paid tribute to those who had protected Dad: Beppino and Fulvio Pellizzari, Giuseppe and Angelina Pellizzari, Giuseppe's sister Santina, Fulvio's wife Elise and Beppino's sisters. 'None of them panicked; on the contrary everyone chose, risking his or her or their relatives' lives, to hide, take care of and nourish young Thomas Maloney for some months. These are extraordinary deeds of worth and human solidarity.'[24] We thought that the Italians who had rescued Dad did so because they were part of the Resistance, but we learned they were not. The Pellizzari family and the village of Condino had saved Dad because it was the right thing to do.

After the speech, everyone walked through the old part of Condino, past the home where Dad had been cared for and hidden, to the Condino Alpine Group lodge. They presented us with the flag of the group and showed us a display that included a piece of the tail of Superstitious Aloysius, along with a model of a B-25J and many US Army documents pertaining to the crash. This visit was followed by a delicious pasta dinner. After dinner we heard stories from many of the people gathered, including the checkpoint story. Luciana and her family had been planning this dinner from the moment our letter arrived in May. This opportunity to talk to and share stories gave us a new perspective of how one event can change the course of many lives.

The final stop of the evening was at the community centre to watch a documentary, *An American from the Sky*, created for our visit by Claudio Rosa. The movie was shown twice, narrated in English and then in Italian. It included accounts from local historians and residents describing their family stories about the crash. Footage was included from Dad's and Mom's visit in 1990, including a brief moment of Dad's infectious laughter that we have missed every day since he passed away, a sound so familiar and yet an unexpected reminder of loss, laying bare the hole in our hearts that never quite closes when you lose someone you love. We ended the evening accepting Luciana's invitation to her home to taste homemade walnut liqueur with her husband and brother. The next day, Mariangela hosted a Pellizzari family party on Mount Rango at the barn where Dad had been hidden. The barn has been converted to three family summer retreats. The descendants of Beppino and Fulvio and some local historians were at the celebration. Mariangela and her family treated us to traditional northern Italian food, with each dish prepared by a different person. The feast included potato polenta, pork in tomato sauce, sausages, chicken, cakes and wine. We talked, answered questions and were interviewed by the historians about our understanding of Dad's wartime experience (see Figure 6.2). On our final day in Condino, Franca took us to see Fernanda, who now lives in a nursing home. It was a wonderful visit. Fernanda has memory problems but she knew we were Dad's children. She kept repeating, 'Tom's children. Tom had five children.' Then she would point to Tim, the only brother among us five, and say, 'He is little Tom. He looks like Tom.'

FIGURE 6.2 *Maloney and Pellizzari descendants at Mount Rango celebration, 2019*

In Condino's history, the final chapter of Dad's story is the rebuilding of the monastery chapel. Our final chapter in Condino was a visit with many of our new friends to the monastery and chapel. We saw where the plane crashed into the altar of the chapel. The impact was so loud and powerful that it blew out the windows of the chapel. Black soot from the ensuing fire covered everything.[25] After the crash the townspeople found that the Blessed Mother statue had fallen, but had only suffered a few dents. The statue was removed to another church until the monastery was repaired. After the tour we said farewell to our new friends and family.[26]

The three days in Condino was an outpouring of love and friendship, planned from the time they received our letter. Luciana, Mariangela and Franca planned events that celebrated the connections between their family, the community of Condino and our family. We learned details that filled in our rough sketch of Dad's story. While Dad's crash changed the trajectory of the lives of the Condino townspeople, their selflessness made our lives possible. That one brave and noble act of the Pellizzarris and the community of Condino to save our Dad resulted in the birth of our generation, our children's generation, our grandchildren's generation and all the generations to come. That act of kindness can never be repaid.

The transmission of values

Discovering Dad's story deepens our understanding of what he valued and how he lived his life. His values were evident to us through his actions, but knowing more about this significant event in his history adds another layer to our understanding. Like the Pellizzaris and the people of Condino, he always tried to do the right thing in every situation. Sometimes this meant taking risks. He joined the Air Force even though his older brother was already serving as a soldier in the Pacific, exempting Dad from conscription. After escaping from the Germans in Italy, he risked his life showing himself to Beppino and Fulvio. In 1955, he started his own business as a better way to provide for his family. He left a secure job and established one of the first chains of greeting card stores in the country in downtown Pittsburgh. This was truly a family business and he made sure we knew we were an important part of it. Many Sundays, Dad would pile us into the car and take us to the store to reorganize or stock merchandise. Our 'pay' was a cheeseburger and a milkshake from the drug store. Each of us had our first job working at the stores. Many of our cousins and friends had the same opportunity. Like the family in Condino, his risk provided an opportunity for us to learn to work together.

Dad was generous. In Condino he saw how people can share even though they had very little. He was aware of the townspeople's meagre provisions and the sacrifice they made to feed him. When he first returned from war, he could not eat steak and rich foods. Throughout his life we always saw Dad give help to anyone who needed it, almost as if he was paying forward the debt he owed to the townspeople of Condino for saving his life. He contributed regularly to his parish and charities. Our parents regularly donated goods from their stores to local church festivals. He was a good employer to the people who worked for him, helping to send their children to camp, supporting them in times of sorrow and setting up a profit-sharing plan for long-time employees. Dad had a soft spot in his heart for the homeless, perhaps, as we know now, because of his time without a home at the mercy of others in Condino. He kept $1 bills in one pocket and $5 bills in another. He gave a dollar to the homeless people he did not know and five dollars to those he knew. He was generous with his children as well, helping each of us buy our first house.

Dad had a lifetime devotion to the Blessed Mother, another figure who did what was right when faced with difficult circumstances. As a boy he helped build and maintain a grotto dedicated to Mary on his parish church grounds. As a result of his devotion he was permitted to serve mass at a young age. Providence solidified this devotion when he encountered the statue of Mary in Condino. At the end of the war he sent home a grotto statue of Mary to his parents. Throughout his life, he prayed the rosary every day and attended daily mass. He supported and participated in the Rosary March in Pittsburgh each year. He and Mom made pilgrimages to Marian shrines around the world: Fatima, Lourdes, Medjugorje and Kazan.

Family was most important to Dad. He grew up in a close-knit and loving family. His second family, the Pellizzaris, welcomed him and protected him as a son. Both families were models for the love, kindness and protection he showed to others in his life. He loved being a dad. Mom and Dad were partners in business and in family. After he opened the card stores, Mom worked on Saturdays and Dad stayed home with us. We had many adventures playing, watching football and baking layer cakes in pie pans. He attended our games, plays and extracurricular activities and helped with our many projects. Dad was a loving son and brother. If we were not at the store, we were visiting our grandparents, aunts, uncles and cousins. Organizing family parties and reunions were regular events throughout our lives. Dad could not attend the last Maloney family reunion in 2010 due to his declining health; so at the end of the party all the cousins and their children gathered in the lobby of his building to celebrate him, a great showing of love and respect.

Doing what was right – for himself, his family and others in need – was the through line of Dad's life. The wartime experiences Dad shared with the Pellizzaris and the town of Condino fortified his resolve to live his life with integrity. He modelled these values for us. His experiences in Condino shaped his life and in turn ours.

Notes

Thanks to Katharine Williamson for her contributions and comments that added much to the contents and delivery of this chapter.

1 Thomas Joyce Maloney, Obituary, *Pittsburgh Post Gazette*, 23 and 24 September 2010. Retrieved from https://www.legacy.com/obituaries/postgazette/obituary.aspx?pid=145566448 (accessed 1 February 2020).

2 *Transcript of Military Record*, Department of the Army, United States of America (Washington DC, 1950).

3 *The Battle of the Brenner – 57th Bomb Wing*, Digital Aviation Library (2019). Available at: https://www.aviation-library.org/the-battle-of-the-brenner (accessed 22 February 2020).

4 J. Fitzgerald, n.d., *12th Air Force, 57th Bombardment Wing (M), 321st Bombardment Group M History: January 1945*. Available at: http://57thbombwing.com/321stHistory/321_BG_1945-01.pdf and J. Fitzgerald, n.d., *12th Air Force, 57th Bombardment Wing (M), 321st Bombardment Group M History: February 1945*. Available at: http://57thbombwing.com/321stHistory/321_BG_1945-02.pdf (both accessed 22 February 2020).

5 Antonella Previdi, *La storia del 'Maybe': il bombardiere B-25J Mitchell caduto il 6 febbraio 1945 sul Monte Brugnolo tra la Valle di Gresta ed Arco* (Nago-Torbole, Trentino: Associazione Culturale Benach, 2014), 123.

6 Claudio Pucci, *Il Convento Di Condino 1945–1949: La Ricostruzione* (Condino, Trentino: Biblioteca Comunale Di Condino, 2011), 40.

7 Pucci, *Il Convento Di Condino*, 40.

8 G. Beltrami, 'Il ritorno di Tom, l'aviatore', *L'Adige*, 19 October 1990.

9 Pucci, *Il Convento Di Condino*, 40.

10 Beltrami, 'Il ritorno di Tom'.

11 Pucci, *Il Convento Di Condino*, 41.

12 Pucci, *Il Convento Di Condino*, 41.

13 Pucci, *Il Convento Di Condino*, 42.

14 Pucci, *Il Convento Di Condino*, 42.

15 Claudio Rosa (Director), *Tom Maloney in Condino, an American from the Sky* (Motion Picture) (Italy, 2019).

16 Rosa, *Tom Maloney in Condino*.

17 Pucci, *Il Convento Di Condino*, 39.

18 G. Beltrami, 'Una festa commovente per l'amico americano', *L'Adige*, 25 October 1990.

19 Pucci, *Il Convento Di Condino*, 43.

20 Rosa, *Tom Maloney in Condino*.

21 *Transcript of Military Record*, Department of the Army, United States of America (Washington, DC, 1950).

22 Rosa, *Tom Maloney in Condino*.

23 Beltrami, 'Il ritorno di Tom'.

24 Claudio Pucci, 'Welcome to the Relatives of Thomas Joyce Maloney', *Commune di Borgo Chiese*, Trentino, Italy, 6 July 2019.

25 Rosa, *Tom Maloney in Condino*.

26 Pucci, *Il Convento Di Condino*, 34.

7

From El Alamein to Bergen-Belsen: An Irish dental officer's war

Ciara Boylan

My grandfather, J. J. 'Jimmy' McNamara, was born in Co. Clare in the west of Ireland on 23 July 1911. After qualifying as a dentist in 1937, he joined the British Army, serving as an officer in the Army Dental Corps (ADC) throughout the war. Between 1940 and 1943 he was posted to North Africa as part of the Middle East Command taking part in the Western Desert campaign. In 1944 he was sent to northern Europe with the British Liberation Army after D-Day. He was recalled from Ireland after VE Day, 8 May 1945, and sent to Bergen-Belsen concentration camp to help with the task of quantifying the dead from dental remains and attended the Belsen trial.

What follows is an attempt to recount and reflect upon Jimmy's war, drawing on the official record of his army service, a personal archive of letters he sent to my grandmother and family memories shared by his four children and son-in-law (see Figure 7.1). All of these sources have their limitations. The official record is accurate but sparse. His letters to my grandmother are abundant, but necessarily evasive on many details owing to the repressive influence of army censorship. The family memories of Jimmy's war, like all second-hand memories, must be treated with due caution. Nonetheless it is these family memories that have provided the richest insight into my grandfather's experiences, and these vignettes form the basis of the account below.[1]

FIGURE 7.1 *Kathleen McNamara, Ciara Boylan and Jimmy McNamara, c.1986*

Like so many of his generation of war veterans, my grandfather rarely spoke about the war in the decades afterwards (he died in 2003), and, when he did, it was invariably after imbibing a few glasses of Jameson whiskey, after which (and I can attest to this from childhood memory) his elocution was less than distinct. So much of what he said on these occasions was therefore missed by his listeners. When asked about the war at other times, he would answer but did not elaborate. As such, Jimmy's memories were never formally recorded, and those that his family recall were collected in a haphazard and accidental way, often with ears strained and patience tried.

Jimmy's recollections were also recounted at a considerable temporal distance from the events described. Aside from the almost inevitable degradation of memory associated with the passage of time, the inescapable mediating influence of the life that has been lived in the meantime – both the way things 'turned out' for the individual as well as the way society 'turned out' – must be acknowledged. The second-hand memories of the succeeding generation that I have drawn on – their memories of Jimmy's memories – have themselves been sifted through all manner of unavoidable filters from the corrosive effects of time on memory to their personal relationship with Jimmy and their world views. The best one can do is approach this store of narrative with an awareness of the valuable, but often antagonistic, relationship between history and memory.

Becoming an officer

Jimmy was the second of six children from a small farm in the townland of Ballymakea, Mullagh, Co. Clare. While the farm income was modest, Jimmy's mother worked as a primary schoolteacher and it was probably this additional income that funded the children's education. Jimmy and his older brother, P. J., were sent to St Mary's College, a boarding school in Galway City, and subsequently undertook degrees at the Royal College of Surgeons in Ireland where Jimmy studied dentistry, qualifying in 1937.[2] Dentistry was perhaps not a divine calling for Jimmy, and he likely chose it to differentiate himself from his brother, P. J., only eleven months his senior, who was studying medicine.

Both Jimmy and P. J. excelled at sports in school and university and Jimmy's passion for sport was an enduring one. He was an especially gifted track-and-field athlete and was given Olympic trials in 1932 for the 400 metre hurdles.[3] One particular anecdote from Jimmy's sporting career gives a glimpse into his character. At an intervarsity games he was competing in the high jump and, with his nearest competitor eliminated, cleared the bar at 6 foot, then an Irish record. Examining the wooden bar, Jimmy noted that it had sagged somewhat in the wet conditions and refused to accept the record despite the umpires' decision. This integrity was central to his character. He loathed dishonesty or deception of any kind and hated boasting or conceit. Incidentally, this included the practice of army officers rushing back to their tents to commit their own part in a particular engagement to paper, effectively notetaking for their memoirs, as he hated the idea of officers exaggerating and valourizing their participation.

Immediately after graduation, again influenced by his older brother, Jimmy emigrated to England to enlist in the British Army. P. J. joined the Royal Air Force (RAF) as a doctor and Jimmy joined the ADC. He was appointed to a short-service commission as a lieutenant on 10 September 1937.[4] Jimmy's decision to enlist in the British Army was motivated fundamentally by the lack of job opportunities in 1930s Ireland, a period of severe economic depression, as well as a desire for adventure. As Steven O'Connor's research on Irish officers in the British Army has shown, these motives were typical.[5] It is estimated that about sixty thousand Irish citizens from the Irish Free State served in the British armed forces during the war and that perhaps eight thousand of these were officers.[6]

The ADC was established in 1921 in response to the recognized need for dedicated dental provision within the armed forces in order to limit the wastage of otherwise-fit soldiers because of dental problems.[7] For the first time a comprehensive and continuous scheme of dental treatment became available to the solider throughout his career. In 1938 the ADC comprised 162 dental officers, 40 dental mechanics and 170 dental clerk-orderlies, one of whom was allotted to each officer.[8] Jimmy passed his ADC and Royal Army Medical Corps examinations in October and November 1938 and on 30 November 1938 was promoted to the rank of captain. The range of training that was offered to officers during the war included anaesthesia, dental prosthetics and maxillofacial surgery, delivered at the ADC School of Instruction in Aldershot. Given that my grandfather was skilled in all these procedures, it is reasonable to assume that he received formal training in these areas. The ADC expanded rapidly during World War II in terms of personnel and the number of dental centres and throughout the war members of the ADC were attached to field ambulances, casualty clearing-stations and general hospitals, while mobile dental units also accompanied troops in the field.

In the first year of his career, before hostilities were declared, he provided routine dental care for military personnel and their families at Catterick and Chatham army bases. The most important event of his pre-war life, however, was his first encounter with my grandmother, Kathleen Joyce, at a dance in London's Grosvenor Hotel on St Patrick's Day 1939, organized by the National University of Ireland's London Club. My grandmother, from the village of Kilconnell in Co. Galway, was teaching in a school outside London at the time, but returned to Ireland soon after their meeting, when war became imminent. That night they began a six-year courtship conducted almost entirely through correspondence. There is a sense from what he wrote to my grandmother that her letters helped to sustain him in some way through the mixture of tedium and trauma that made up the war experience of many army personnel. He is eager for news about her life and about horse racing, he asks for newspapers and photographs, and receives books and a much-admired pair of corduroy trousers. One can also detect an anxiety that my grandmother might go cold, prompted by the very real possibility that she could abandon him for somebody much more conveniently close to home. This did not happen, and they married in August 1945, having met in person on only one occasion in the intervening years (see Figure 7.2).

A dentist at war

Jimmy spent some months at the outset of the war stationed at Omagh in Northern Ireland, before embarking for Palestine on 29 November 1939.

FIGURE 7.2 *Kathleen Joyce and Jimmy McNamara on their wedding day, August 1945*

This marked the beginning of over four years in the Middle East and North Africa, during which he moved between general hospitals, dental centres and POW camps across Palestine and Egypt. After his return to Europe at the end of 1943, he was stationed at dental centres in Kent and Surrey during the first half of 1944, before embarking for mainland Europe on 25 July 1944, six weeks after D-Day. He followed the path of the British Army of Liberation through France, including a bombed-out Caen, and into Belgium in 1944/1945.[9] Table 7.1 shows his known overseas postings and locations.

As a dental officer, my grandfather had three core duties: passing soldiers as dentally fit for the field, treating soldiers for dental problems and facial injuries, and identifying remains from dental records. Sometimes these roles overlapped; he described the experience of having cleared a young soldier as fit and, soon afterwards, sometimes within twenty-four hours, having to establish his identity using his dental records – the last feasible method of identification for some of the bodies that returned from the front. Having undertaken specialist training in maxillofacial surgery, Jimmy performed procedures on facial wounds, particularly the repair of shattered jaws. He became very skilled at this branch of reconstructive surgery and after the war

TABLE 7.1 Known Overseas Postings and Locations of Jimmy McNamara, Dental Officer

Date	Posting	Location
November 1939	Military Hospital	Haifa, Palestine
July 1940	No. 60, General Hospital	Sarafand al-Amar, Palestine
November 1940	No. 60, General Hospital	Jerusalem
March 1941	No. 27, General Hospital	Geneifa, Egypt
1 September 1941	No. 27, General Hospital	Geneifa, Egypt
25 September 1941	No. 13, Dental Centre	Unknown, Egypt
May 1942	No. 306, POW Camp	Fayid, Egypt
July 1943	No. 13, Dental Centre	Unknown, Egypt
September 1943	No. 40, Dental Centre	Unknown
July 1944	No. 213, Field Dental Centre	France
April 1945	No. 213, Field Dental Centre	Belgium

regularly performed surgical procedures at the Regional Hospital in Galway, in whose town centre he had started a private dental practice. In recognition of his work in dental surgery and forensics he was awarded a fellowship by the Royal College of Surgeons in Ireland in 1963, one of the first group of fellowships awarded by the newly established Faculty of Dentistry.[10]

Dealing with dental infection in the field was a serious issue in the pre-antibiotic era, since a dental abscess could lead to septicaemia and even death. Jimmy's first encounter with penicillin, the antibiotic wonder drug that revolutionized medicine, was in North Africa. Although penicillin had been first discovered in 1928, production of the drug was ramped up during the war, spearheaded by the US military, particularly during 1943.[11] Jimmy was treating a patient with a particularly bad tooth abscess that required immediate extraction of the tooth under general anaesthesia to avoid the threat of septicaemia. Using an anaesthetic was not without risk, as any period of anaesthesia in excess of about fifteen minutes risked patient mortality, mostly from cardiac complications. In addition, the infection was so extensive that extraction threatened the viability of the jaw. Jimmy and a colleague were conferring on the risks involved when an American doctor overheard them and asked to see the patient, whose disfigured jaw had swollen alarmingly to about the size of a tennis ball and who was writhing in pain. The doctor offered them penicillin. Thinking they had little to lose, Jimmy administered what would be considered a very modest dose by today's standards. He went to check on the soldier the following morning to find him asleep with the abscess almost completely dissipated.

He also provided dental care for prisoners in POW camps. He referred to a two-week spell of this work in early 1941, writing to my grandmother that he 'got tired very quickly because if you did this well they absolutely stormed the place, and the queue was getting bigger so I gave up'.[12] From May to September 1942 he was attached to No. 306 POW camp located at Fayid in Egypt, one of ten POW camps established by the British in the Suez Canal region to house German, Austrian and Italian prisoners of war. So crowded were the camps at this point in the war, just before the Second Battle of El Alamein, that Jimmy remembered having to dredge a canal in the desert to provide water to meet the dental and medical needs of the camp. He also remembered having to turn away British Army officers who were seeking him out for routine, sometimes even cosmetic, dental treatment. Frustrated by the fact that the prisoner population included dental officers and orderlies who were sitting idle while he and his colleagues were overworked, he mounted a persistent campaign with his superior officers to allow him to make use of this expertise. While he was initially met with strong resistance, he ultimately persuaded them to allow him to put enemy dental personnel to work in treating their fellow prisoners. This was far better than having these men 'sitting on their arses in the sand', as he memorably put it to my father. He was clearly proud of this victory against what he referred to as the 'stupidity of the military mentality'. He became friends with one Italian dental technician whose skill he regarded highly and who painted a likeness of my grandmother from a photograph.

Medical and dental personnel did not, of course, see action themselves. Rather they witnessed the carnage of major manoeuvres and battles from behind the lines. On this my grandfather was largely silent. He did, however, describe witnessing a military firing squad. He recalled a Scottish military police officer who had come up through the ranks and was, as such, resented by many of the Sandhurst officer class. A braggart by nature, his bravado was exacerbated by his social isolation and he came into the mess on one occasion boasting about the morning's firing squad – which my grandfather felt he did at least in part to repulse the genteel sensitivities of the officers. Jimmy, wanting to call his bluff, asked whether he could attend the next scheduled firing squad and prevailed on his commanding officer for permission. He arrived at 6 am on the allotted morning and witnessed the stark efficiency with which the death penalty was carried out in the field. According to his son, Jimmy remembered some going solemnly to their deaths, some protesting their innocence and others crying for their mothers. In British law, capital punishment for all offences in the field had been outlawed in 1930 with the exception of mutiny and treachery.[13] During the war three soldiers were executed for mutiny, one for treachery and thirty-six for murder.[14] It is therefore likely that those facing the death penalty were enemy prisoners of war as this was known to have happened in Allied-run camps.[15] They may have been escapees or may have committed a capital crime such as murder within the camp. His son asked him how he felt at that moment as an observer. He replied that you could not betray any emotion, although you could not help but feel that at least some of these men were undeserving. Nonetheless, he agreed in principle with the use of the death penalty in the field where it was necessary, as in the case of mutiny, which could severely damage esprit de corps, or the passing on of intelligence, which could result in lost battles and increased casualties.

Jimmy's war was not without its lighter moments. His letters to my grandmother mention rounds of golf in Alexandria, swimming in the Suez Canal and games of tennis in the desert. There was also coarse and game fishing and duck shooting on the Nile. These were, of course, officers' pursuits and ones Jimmy thoroughly enjoyed. Despite coming from a small farm in the west of Ireland, he mixed comfortably with members of the British upper class, making lifelong friends with George Travers Fullerton-Carnegie, a distant relative of Queen Elizabeth and the Queen Mother. One luxury he was afforded was particularly gratifying to him as a horseman. Although the British Army had mechanized most cavalry regiments, replacing horses with armoured cars, British troops in the Mediterranean theatres of war, particularly Palestine and Italy, maintained the use of horses for transport and other support purposes. Being close to his commanding officer, Lt. Col. Alexander Duggan, an Irishman from Bray in Co. Wicklow, he was given permission to ride out in the mornings during a quiescent period of the war in Palestine.

While in Egypt, he tried to get to Cairo as much as possible, a welcome relief from the desert and the 'miles and miles of sand on every side' as he described it to my grandmother, adding that 'after this episode I shall never again want to see sand'.[16] He wrote about acclimatizing to the heat in Palestine, an experience which he felt stood to him when he was moved to the more intense cauldron of the Egyptian desert. In northern Europe in early 1945, he complained about the fierce cold, but again there was entertainment. He wrote from Belgium about rounds of golf at Waterloo and days at the races in

Brussels, and years later enjoyed recounting his stories of bartering medicines, chocolate and sundry items with Belgian farmers in exchange for eggs.

One anecdote stands out from his period in North Africa. Though details are hazy, it seems that when Jimmy was in Cairo he befriended a local businessman who had a rare copy of T. E. Lawrence's unpublished second book, *The Mint*. This was an autobiographical account of the period after World War I, when Lawrence enlisted in the RAF as an ordinary aircraftman under an assumed name. It seems this prized possession was kept in a safe room under lock and key at this wealthy acquaintance's house, and my grandfather was apparently admitted over the course of a number of days to read it. The original manuscript dates from 1928, and Lawrence ordered the work not to be published until 1950. However, it was sold to an American collector, and, in order to protect US copyright of the work, a limited edition of no more than fifty copies of the manuscript was published in New York in 1936. Ten of these went on sale at the prohibitive price of half a million dollars. It is not clear what version of the book Jimmy was granted access to, but he valued the chance to read the work, regarding it as a great privilege, notwithstanding the unusual and clandestine circumstances in which he read it.

Jimmy's patriotism as an Irishman and his experience as a British Army officer apparently sat comfortably side by side. The experience of Irish officers in the British Army seems to have been largely positive, with little evidence of any active discrimination.[17] Rather, in its efforts to maintain morale amongst the troops, the army made efforts to acknowledge and celebrate Irishness throughout the ranks, while the practice of the Catholic faith was actively encouraged. Jimmy's letters to my grandmother make clear the ways in which Irishness was accommodated within the officer ranks. In a letter from March 1941 from the general hospital at Geneifa in Egypt, he laments that he did not receive the shamrock she had sent 'in time to display my national emblem on our national holiday'.[18] In the same letter he described being asked to translate menus into the Irish language for an officers' guest dinner. He and a fellow Irishman, neither of whom had a solid grasp of Irish, resorted to a 'very nice blend of swear words and snappy phrases' on the basis that nobody would be able to translate them.[19]

Jimmy would not have tolerated any insult about being Irish and indeed only one negative anecdote has been passed down, remembered by his eldest son. At some point during the North African campaign an accomplished older general – an elder statesman type – was sent out on a kind of motivational speaking tour to respond to concerns that some officers were expressing something worryingly akin to admiration for General Rommel's military prowess. This man was presumably supposed to remind officers of the noble lineage of British militarism and its global superiority. At any rate, during an after-dinner speech the general made an anti-Irish jibe, upon which Jimmy, against all military protocol, pushed back his chair and made for the door in protest. He described this as the longest walk of his life. His relief was considerable when he heard other chairs scraping the floor and realized that some fellow officers were joining him in his walkout. He escaped without reprimand and indeed made up with the general afterwards.

Most of the Irish people who served in the British armed forces during World War II encountered indifference rather than hostility on their return home.[20] The very significant Irish contribution to the British war effort did not conform to the state narrative of Irish neutrality; so for the most part what greeted former British Army personnel was a decades-long silence.[21] Jimmy, for his part, was grateful to the British Army for giving him a career opportunity and was proud of his service. He never attempted to conceal his time as an officer and was proudly known as 'the major' at the County Club in Galway City where he socialized.

Counting the dead in Bergen-Belsen

It is not known where Jimmy was on VE Day but his Record of Service Book notes a nine-day period of leave starting on 3 May. By 2 June he was back in Belgium with No. 213 Field Dental Centre. On 11 August he was given further leave, during which he returned to Ireland and married my grandmother, Kathleen, in Dublin. The next set of dates in his Record of Service Book shows that he disembarked at Dover on 9 October 1945 and was demobbed on 11 October. It was therefore in this period between his leave in August and his demobilization in October that my grandfather was sent to Bergen-Belsen concentration camp.

Belsen was liberated by British forces on 15 April 1945 where they met scenes of unimaginable horror. Inside they found about sixty thousand emaciated men, women and children without access to sanitation, running water or food. More than thirteen thousand corpses at various stages of decomposition lay unburied around the camp.[22] British Army personnel mounted a humanitarian and medical relief effort. They also began investigating the crimes committed at Bergen-Belsen. My grandfather rarely spoke about this episode. My mother remembers him telling her that he was sent to Belsen to identify remains from dental records. My uncle, however, believes he was tasked with helping to quantify the dead and make a best estimation of the numbers who died in the camp. According to my uncle, Jimmy was back home in Ireland in my grandmother's home place of Kilconnell surrounded by his army trunks when he was recalled to mainland Europe unexpectedly. Very little was discussed en route. Only upon arriving at the camp were he and a group of medics and dentists briefed on what had taken place and the work they would be undertaking. They were told to prepare themselves; they were about to witness the aftermath of unspeakable acts of inhumanity. Jimmy referred to examining dental remains recovered from the 'ovens', by which he was undoubtedly referring to the Belsen crematorium. Those are the only details remembered by Jimmy's children.

The postscript to this episode and to Jimmy's war was his attendance at the Belsen trial, where those who ran the camp were tried between September and November 1945 at Lüneburg, which falls within the time period that he was back on the Continent. It is not clear if he attended in an official capacity or as an observer, but he mentioned being escorted to a designated seat every morning. At Lüneburg it is known that British personnel serving in the occupation zone watched from the public gallery.[23] The family do not know anything more about his attendance. He made one observation, which appears to relate to the Nuremberg trials. Notwithstanding the horrific nature of the crimes committed, he disapproved of the manner in which the Nazi officers were presented to the courts. Some were permitted to wear their own uniforms; others were deliberately given ill-fitting uniforms. Some had neither braces nor belts and had to shuffle into the court, holding up their trousers, in as ignominious and unflattering a manner as possible. Those who used false teeth had them removed. The idea was to humiliate them, to show the world that they were anything but the 'master race'. In Jimmy's view the victors should have observed the strict impartiality of a fair criminal trial. This tactic of presenting Nazi officers to the court and the world's media in this manner, despite their heinous crimes, eroded some of the moral authority of the court, he believed.

Bearing first-hand witness to the darkest act of Nazism must have provoked unnameable emotions in all of those who saw inside the concentration and death camps after they were liberated. It is almost impossible that this experience did not leave some mark on my grandfather, but it is also a futile exercise to surmise when he remained silent on the topic. In 1958 a KLM flight crashed off the west coast of Ireland killing all ninety-nine passengers and crew on board. The bodies were brought to the docks in Galway. My uncle Don remembers the makeshift screens made from the hanging sails of hookers, reminding him of shrouds, and the people's macabre interest as they tried to get a look behind them. The remains of the victims had been netted by the trawlers and brought ashore at the docks, from where they were taken to the morgue and then to the pathology department at the hospital, where Jimmy and the professor of pathology, Johnny Kennedy, tried to identify them. Don was 9 years old at the time. He remembers walking with Jimmy, who was in a low mood, and asking him whether he had been to the docks and the morgue. Yes, he answered, simply adding, 'It brings so many bloody things back.'

Family history and national history

For most Irish people, World War II was 'the Emergency', coloured by the policy, and propaganda, of neutrality.[24] Unlike most of the rest of Europe, in Ireland World War II was not the defining event of the twentieth century and did not significantly shape Irish national identity. There is no 'fight them on the beaches'[25] nostalgia to be used (and abused) by politicians, no troublesome Vichy legacy to be confronted, no GI heroism on the Normandy coast. It is possibly for this reason that our family did not talk much about Jimmy's experiences. They were interesting, certainly, but they were his as an individual and not part of the broader national story, which is often the natural reference point for family histories.

I loved history as a child and followed this interest through an undergraduate degree at NUI Galway and ultimately a doctorate in Irish history at the University of Oxford. I remember feeling vaguely embarrassed by my grandfather's participation in the war as a member of the British Army and did not like admitting it to other Irish people. I could not shake off the nagging sense that my grandfather had somehow sullied his Irishness by wearing a British uniform. My discomfort was telling me that my family history had failed the test of Irishness. There was a conflict at play here. My exposure to academic history taught me that my grandfather's experiences were common and were precisely the kind of nuanced story that the historian was duty-bound to bring into the light and explore. The increased scholarly attention paid over the past two decades to Irish participation in the two world wars began the process of rehabilitating the experiences of Irishmen and Irishwomen, which had been effectively repressed within the official historical narrative sanctioned by the Irish state. Ultimately, however, I learned that it is only when stories are publicly shared that they become integrated into the national narrative and we come to a more nuanced understanding of our past. Academic history opens the door, but the rest of us have to walk through it.

When I was working at the National Library of Ireland in 2012, we held a World War I Family History Roadshow as part of a wider European project.[26] The library asked members of the public to bring in memorabilia related to World War I which we would then digitize. Unsure of what the response would be, we opened the doors that morning and were greeted with a line of people carrying medals, photographs, letters, diaries, discharge papers, keepsakes and much more besides. After decades of silence on the participation of Irishmen and women in the war, their pent-up desire to tell their family stories was almost palpable. I sat down with people who showed me artefacts and archives and told me their family stories, which I later wrote up to accompany the digitized images of their memorabilia. Hearing the stories of young men lost at Gallipoli and the Somme, of heartbroken mothers who stowed away letters in tins and stayed silent, of returned soldiers with shellshock, damaged lungs and limited prospects, I was struck by how cruel it was that these families were not permitted to acknowledge the lives and careers of their relatives. On a personal level, I began to fully understand my grandfather's decision to emigrate and follow an opportunity that promised financial independence, experience and adventure. More fundamentally, I realized that the retired British Army major who raised the tricolour on a flagpole outside the house every St Patrick's Day with fresh shamrock in his lapel was not a conundrum; his was a very Irish case.

Doing family history is fraught with hazards. The emotional attachment to the subject can provoke unjustified sympathy in the family historian at one end of the spectrum and everything from anger, disappointment and shame at the other end. However, the strong empathic connection with a historical subject who is a member of your family has advantages, not least of which is the enhanced ability to live history through them. Jimmy's story is one example of the extraordinary experiences of the generation who were caught up in the conflagration of 1939–45. Writing it has brought to mind the resilience of people whose lives were shaped by the kind of world-altering upheaval and conflict that subsequent generations must continually recommit to avoid. In the middle of a global pandemic, it is that resilience that inevitably resonates – an echo that becomes a prayer.

Notes

1 I am very grateful to Jimmy's four children Noeleen, Don, Brian and Marianne and his son-in-law Tom for generously sharing their recollections of his war experiences with me.

2 *The Irish Press*, 1 May 1937.

3 One nice anecdote here was that Jimmy was competing against Bob Tisdale at these trials and, recognizing Tisdale as a singular athlete and serious medal hope, gave him his superior running shoes. Tisdale qualified and went on to win gold at the 1932 Los Angeles Olympics later that summer in a world-record time.

4 Details of Jimmy's promotions and movements are contained in his Officer's Record of Service Book.

5 Steven O'Connor, *Irish Officers in the British Forces, 1922–45* (Basingstoke: Palgrave Macmillan, 2014); Steven O'Connor, 'Why Did They Fight for Britain? Irish Recruits to the British Forces, 1939–45', *Études Irlandaises* 40, no. 1 (2015): 59–70.

6 O'Connor, *Irish Officers*, 39.

7   'History of the Royal Army Dental Corps' (n.d.), The Museum of Military History. Available at: https://museumofmilitarymedicine.org.uk/about/corps-history/history-of-the-royal-army-dental-corps/ (accessed 15 March 2020); 'Royal Army Dental Corps' (n.d.), National Army Museum. Available at: https://www.nam.ac.uk/explore/royal-army-dental-corps (accessed 15 March 2020).

8   Major S. H. Woods, 'An Outline of Dentistry in the British Army, 1626–1938', *Proceedings of the Royal Society of Medicine* 32, no. 2 (1938): 111. Available at: https://www.ncbi.nlm.nih.gov/pmc/articles/PMC1997333/?page=13 (accessed 2 April 2020).

9   My mother sent the letter to the mayor of Caen who placed it in the city archives.

10 *Sunday Independent*, 17 November 1963.

11 Robert Gaynes, 'The Discovery of Penicillin – New Insights after More than 75 Years of Clinical Use', *Emerging Infectious Diseases* 23, no. 5 (2017): 849–53; John Patrick, 'The Search for Synthetic Penicillin during World War II', *The British Journal for the History of Science* 16, no. 2 (1983): 154–90.

12 Jimmy McNamara to Kathleen Joyce, 22 March 1941, private archive.

13 David French, *Raising Churchill's Army: The British Army and the War against Germany, 1919–1945* (Oxford: Oxford University Press, 2001).

14 John Peaty, 'Haig and Military Discipline,' in *Haig: A Reappraisal 80 Years On*, ed. Brian Boyd and Nigel Cave (Barnsley: Pen & Sword Military, 1999), 196–222.

15 Alexander Gillespie, *A History of the Laws of War*, Vol. 1: *The Customs and Laws of War with Regards to Combatants and Captives* (Oxford: Hart Publishing, 2011), 190.

16 Jimmy McNamara to Kathleen Joyce, 22 March 1941, private archive.

17 O'Connor, *Irish Officers*.

18 Jimmy McNamara to Kathleen Joyce, 22 March, 1941, private archive.

19 Jimmy McNamara to Kathleen Joyce, 22 March, 1941, private archive.

20 O'Connor, *Irish Officers*.

21 Brian Girvin, 'The Forgotten Volunteers of World War II', *History Ireland* 6, no. 1 (1998). Available at: https://www.historyireland.com/20th-century-contemporary-history/the-forgotten-volunteers-of-world-war-ii/ (accessed 20 April 2020).

22 Joanne Reilly, *Belsen: The Liberation of a Concentration Camp* (London: Routledge, 1998).

23 'The Liberation of Belsen', National Army Museum. Available at: https://www.nam.ac.uk/explore/liberation-belsen (accessed 31 March 2020).

24 Brian Girvin, *The Emergency: Neutral Ireland 1939–45* (London: Macmillan, 2006); Clair Willis, *That Neutral Island: A Cultural History of Ireland during the Second World War* (Cambridge: Belknap Press, 2007).

25 W. S. Churchill, 'We Shall Fight on the Beaches', House of Commons, 4 June 1940. Available at: https://winstonchurchill.org/resources/speeches/1940-the-finest-hour/we-shall-fight-on-the-beaches/ (accessed 1 March 2020).

26 'Europeana 1914–1918'. Available at: https://www.europeana.eu/en/collections/topic/83-1914-1918 (accessed 20 April 2020).

8

Recording the war in Connemara: A Guianese sailor in the eastern Mediterranean

Cormac Ó Loideáin

'**D**on't contaminate the mayonnaise' is a catchphrase my family and I fondly associate with my great-uncle and World War II veteran, Manny dos Santos. Even to this day, the phrase instantly evokes fond childhood memories of picnicking by the sea with my father's aunt, Mary, and her husband, Manny, some three decades ago. The couple used to come from California each year to visit my family in Connemara in the west of Ireland. Indeed the arrival of the 'Yanks', as we called them, heralded in the summer months. My cousins and I eagerly awaited the many day trips and picnics with them along the Atlantic coast. Each outing saw the contents of a big red cooler box, picnic condiments, crisps, treats, soft drinks and a flask of tea, unpacked onto a large blanket. Sandwiches were made with military efficiency under the watchful eye of Manny who made sure the knife used to spread peanut butter and jelly was not used to spread the mayonnaise.

I suspect my father's family found it curious that this kind and playful man, who spoke with a soft Caribbean lilt, was married to their aunt Mary, who had emigrated to America from a small Irish-speaking community in the west of Ireland in the 1950s. We certainly never suspected he had a military past and might never have been aware of it, had my father not decided in 1998 to interview Manny about his early life in British Guiana, using a home video camera (see Figure 8.1). Manny's military adventures emerged soon

FIGURE 8.1 *Manny dos Santos in Aillwee Caves, Ireland, 1990s*

in this interview, when he got to the last few months of World War II. He revealed that, as an adventurous 20-year-old in Georgetown, the capital of British Guiana, he had enlisted in the British Royal Navy in November 1944. His own children knew little of his wartime activities – his daughter, Bella, said that he spoke little of it at home – and learned much when my father showed them the recording of the interview. While, given its unplanned and informal nature, the interview left many stones unturned, the nuggets of information contained therein have allowed me to explore this fascinating episode in our extended family's history. His official Royal Navy record and the broader naval history of World War II both corroborate his story and reveal what he left out.[1]

Manny's wartime experiences

Emmanuel Peter dos Santos was born in British Guiana in 1924, the grandson of Portuguese emigrants from Madeira. Manny had a relatively privileged childhood compared to most people at the time in Georgetown. Manny's father, Antonio dos Santos, owned a soft drinks factory as well as various other properties in the area. Every Sunday, Manny cycled to his father's properties to collect rent from the tenants. In later years, Manny would rarely speak openly about his upbringing. By all accounts, he had a difficult childhood. Conversations with his daughter, Bella, revealed that his relationship with his father, a strict disciplinarian, had been fraught. Manny and his seven siblings would often seek comfort from their mother, Isabella Marie Elaine, with whom he had a very close relationship. Tragically, she died following a long illness in 1944. It is possible that her death and his fractious relationship with his father encouraged Manny to enlist in the British Royal Navy as a means of gaining independence, although, in the absence of his own testimony on this matter, we can only speculate.

We do know, however, that the war had a major impact on British Guiana. As a colony of the British Empire, it was very much involved in the Allied war effort from the very beginning. Two-thirds of all Allied aircraft were manufactured using aluminium produced from Guianese bauxite. In addition to providing crucial raw material for the war effort, British Guiana also provided a strategic site for a US military airfield. Atkinson Field, located on the east bank of the Demerara river, south of Georgetown, was leased to the American military as part of an arrangement negotiated between the UK and the United States at the beginning of the war to procure fifty World War I era destroyers. The war also shaped the lives of the people of British Guiana. The Defence of the Realm Act, which introduced the regulation of prices, rationing and censorship, came into effect throughout the Caribbean region in 1939. Along with Manny, a number of Guianese men and women enlisted in the British military during this period. Others joined the merchant navy, and some travelled to the UK to work in munition factories.[2]

As well as being aware of developments at home, Manny had access to the British perspective on the war through the correspondence his older sister, Nellie dos Santos, kept with her British pen pal, Nellie Ramsbottom from Radcliffe, Manchester. Although, to my knowledge, none of these letters has survived, it is likely that they gave an account of the everyday challenges faced by the British people at the time, the daily rationing, the regular air-raids overhead and the nightly task of blacking out their homes. These letters may have informed Manny's decision to join the British war effort. We know from the home video that he was aware of the Ramsbottoms' situation and would visit them shortly after his arrival in the UK, although again we cannot be sure.

On 21 November 1944 Manny boarded a merchant ship in Georgetown and set sail for Trinidad. After three days at sea, on 24 November he arrived in its capital, Port of Spain, where he was issued with his military uniform. Manny proudly remembered that it bore the British Guiana badge on its shoulder pad. The Royal Navy record marks this day as the official date of his enlistment. From Port of Spain his journey continued northward onboard the *Benbow*, a troopship bound for New York City. This journey was broken up by a short stay in Guantanamo Bay, Cuba. By the time he disembarked the troopship at Pier

90 in New York, it was early December 1944. During his stay in New York, Manny later recollected to my father, he and his fellow new recruits followed closely the most recent reports from the western front, where the Battle of the Bulge was being fought. The outcome of this battle, an Allied victory, would prove decisive in shaping their own fate in the coming months.

The Royal Navy used a US Navy receiving station on Pier 92 in New York as a transit hub and it was from here that Manny continued his journey across the Atlantic. Manny recalled boarding the ocean liner, RMS *Queen Mary*, along with fifteen thousand other troops in early January 1945 bound for Gourock, Scotland. From Gourock he continued his journey by train to Glasgow then onto London and finally to Devonport, Plymouth, where he was allocated his port division for the duration of his service in the Royal Navy. Much to his dismay and in what can only be described as an anticlimax, Manny was ordered to take thirty days of family reunion and relief when he reached his destination. His own family being 4,500 miles away in Georgetown, he decided to visit the home of his sister Nellie's pen pal, the Ramsbottoms, in Manchester. He was issued with coupons to pay for his journey and arrived on their doorstep at 2 am one morning. There, he learned of the German bomb attack on the greater Manchester area a few weeks earlier, on Christmas Eve 1944. The V1 bombs had killed 42 people and injured 109 others. Manny remembered how the Ramsbottoms told him that one of these bombs, probably destined for a nearby chloride factory, had landed and exploded in a field just behind their home. Eyewitnesses estimated that it had left a crater between 80 foot and 100 foot across and 30 foot deep.[3]

Upon his return to Devonport, Manny was sent to Skegness in Lincolnshire to begin his military training. In Skegness he witnessed the incredible site of many Lancaster bombers setting out on their bombing campaign over Germany. By his own account, he was in awe of the sustained waves of these heavy bombers – each capable of carrying over ten tons of explosives, flying day and night over the Lincolnshire coastline towards the continent. At this stage of the war, the Royal Air Force (RAF) and the United States Army Air Forces (USAAF) had over 3,500 bombers to fly missions over Germany and on 13 February, during Manny's time in Lincolnshire, they launched one of the most devastating attacks of the war on Dresden.[4] A week later he arrived at HMS *Glendower*, a Royal Navy training camp, in Pwllheli, North Wales, to begin his basic seamanship training.[5] He claims that a lot of the recruits he met at HMS *Glendower* were army personnel absent without official leave, an indication, as Manny saw it, of how desperate the navy was for recruits. His time at HMS *Glendower* coincided with the surrender of Nazi Germany in May 1945. A month later, on 16 June, he began his training as a radar technician in Douglas, on the Isle of Man and on board three different training ships, including HMS *Valkyrie*, HMS *Renown* and HMS *Drake*. He remembered that King George VI and the Queen Mother came to inspect a military parade in which he participated. Sometime after this inspection his unit was sent to Torpoint, Cornwall, for radar gunnery skills training. Manny described the use of computer technology to track ballistic fire which allowed them to adjust the trajectory for accuracy. Gunnery training would have also typically included familiarization with various light arms and live firing targets. He also noted that, while he was in Cornwall, Japan announced its unconditional surrender on 15 August 1945.

Manny's post-war Mediterranean mission

After twelve months of military training, Manny returned to Gourock on 23 February 1946 to begin his tour of duty on board HMS *Chieftain*, a C-class destroyer. He and his comrades set sail for the Mediterranean on a particularly challenging mission – to restrict the flow of Jews into Palestine, then a British-mandated territory. In 1920 the League of Nations had limited the number of Jewish immigrants permitted to enter Palestine to 1,500 per month, but Nazi persecution of the Jews had led to many multiples of this number seeking refuge there. Anxious to expand the Jewish presence in Palestine and mindful of the suffering of Jews in German-occupied Europe, Zionists had established an organization, the Mossad l'Aliyah Bet, in 1938 to help organize the illegal transportation of Jews from Europe. Faced with a swell in demand at the end of the war, the Aliyah Bet set up mass camps in southern France, most notably in Marseilles, and trained prospective immigrants in methods of passive and active resistance.[6]

The crew of HMS *Chieftain* steamed from Scotland towards the Mediterranean in early spring 1946 with a view to halting the plans of these determined Jews. After short stops in Algiers, Malta and Benghazi, the ship continued to Tripoli, Libya. Manny recalled that the harbour entrance was blocked by twenty-three ships that had, he suspected, been deliberately sunk by the retreating German and Italian forces following the disastrous end to their military campaign in North Africa in 1943. The action hindered Allied access to the important North African port during the war. Manny identified the sunken ships as 'ammo ships' and described them as being completely shredded. This was testament to the violence witnessed in this area only a few years earlier when on 23 January 1943 the city and the surrounding province were captured by the British 8th Army after many hard-fought battles extending across the deserts of North Africa from Egypt to Morocco.[7] The crew, Manny recounted, was told that half a million men had drowned in the harbour and as a result they were warned not to go swimming.

Manny's Royal Navy record shows that he spent nineteen months as an acting able seaman on board two vessels involved in the British Mediterranean patrol – firstly HMS *Chieftain*, and then from August 1946, on HMS *Stevenstone*, a hunt class escort destroyer. While he mentioned that these ships were employed in patrolling the Mediterranean to stop illegal immigration to Palestine and escorting so-called Liberty ships to refugee camps in Limassol and Larnaca in Cyprus, he provided little commentary in his interview on the precise challenges this involved.

This is surprising, given that these ships were involved in two particularly difficult encounters with the immigrants. The first came unexpectedly in December 1946, when Manny was on board HMS *Stevenstone*. The Mediterranean fleet and patrols had been scaled back for the winter months, as it was anticipated that poor weather conditions would result in a significant fall in the number of illegal crossings being attempted. However, on 7 December a major rescue operation had to be launched to aid the shipwrecked passengers of the *Athina*, a Greek ship which left Bakar, Yugoslavia, on 26 November carrying 784 Jewish refugees. Adverse weather conditions in the Aegean Sea forced the *Athina* to seek shelter in the lee of Sirina, a small island off the coast of Crete. The ship struck rocks close to shore and sank shortly afterwards. Frightened passengers immediately scrambled overboard to flee the stricken vessel. Eight people, including three children, tragically lost their lives. The survivors managed to rescue a radio from the ship and alerted the Jewish authorities in Palestine and Athens to their dire predicament.[8]

The request for assistance was passed on to the British authorities who called on the RAF to parachute medical supplies onto the island and launched a flotilla of navy vessels including HMS *Stevenstone* to help in the rescue operation. Adverse weather conditions made it a very difficult and dangerous one. Survivors had to be secured with safety lines and hauled on board the rescue ships. Once rescued, the immigrants were transferred onto a Landing Ship Tank (LST) and escorted by HMS *Stevenstone* to an internment camp in Cyprus. Upon arrival in Famagusta, Cyprus, a small cohort of passengers refused to disembark and blocked the exit of the rest. Tear gas was employed to restore order and disembarkation then began under the supervision of the HMS *Stevenstone* crew. However, during this process a group of men attacked two sailors, and a shot was fired to disperse the men, causing injury to one person. After a spell in internment camps, the women and children from the *Athina* were eventually permitted to settle in Palestine in May 1947.[9]

The second incident was the famous capture of the *Exodus 1947*, a passenger ship which attempted to illegally land 4,554 immigrants in Palestine in July 1947.[10] This was the largest number of immigrants encountered by the Royal Navy during this period. The operation proved to be difficult and dangerous, not just because of the sea conditions, but also because of the stiff resistance mounted by the passengers. They used a rifle, axes, coshes, oars, crowbars, 12-foot scaffolding bars and an array of missiles to evade arrest. The Royal Navy responded with tear gas and gun fire, including a volley of machine-gun fire. News footage from the time shows a dangerously overcrowded and badly damaged ship subsequently docking at the port of Haifa. Three immigrants were killed, amongst them a 15-year-old boy, and three British sailors suffered serious injuries in the operation. The passengers were transferred to three other ships, which the HMS *Stevenstone* then escorted to refugee camps in Cyprus, before eventually being returned under protest to Germany.[11] Manny recalled one of these three ships, the *Ocean Vigour*, during his interview, only to note that it was a Henry J. Kaiser construction and that it was covered in barbed wire.

Towards the end of 1947 HMS *Stevenstone* began its journey home to England via Gibraltar and Tangiers. After serving almost two years on the Royal Navy Mediterranean patrol, Manny was discharged on 7 June 1948. He returned to British Guiana and secured employment with the central housing planning authority before emigrating to the United States on the advice of his sister, Nellie, who lived in California at the time. He worked with an advertising agency before enrolling on a radio and television course in San Francisco's City College with the support of his brother, Gregory. However, when Gregory was drafted into the Korean War, Manny needed to find the means to support himself. Even though he was not yet a US citizen, he enlisted in the USAAF, where he was assigned to a radar technology unit based on his limited coursework in radar technology. It was during his time stationed on a radar base on Martha's Vineyard, Massachusetts, that he met my father's aunt, Mary. Manny and Mary were married in 1957 and moved to California, where they raised their family. They were regular visitors to Ireland and, on their retirement, built their own house close to my family in An Cheathrú Rua, Co. Galway, and would spend up to six months of the year here in their later years. Manny sadly died in 2010 at the age of 85. *Ar dheis Dé go raibh a anam.*[12]

My memory of Manny is that of a kind, obliging and playful man who always seemed to have time for us. I am deeply grateful that my father decided to ask him about his early life in British Guiana and that Manny revealed so much more. When I undertook this project I felt a great sense of pride upon receiving his Royal Navy record, which confirmed and shed more light on details recounted in this chance interview. It is puzzling to know why Manny did not talk more about the challenges of preventing Jewish settlement in Palestine and especially the experiences with the *Athina* and the *Exodus 1947*, which were significant enough to inform subsequent naval policy and procedure. The omission is particularly striking, as Manny was known within the family for his attention to detail – given after fifty-three years he could recollect the pier numbers in New York City, the number of troops on board the RMS *Queen Mary* and how long it took to prepare two meals during his transatlantic voyage. It is possible that the experience was too traumatic to retell, yet my sense of him is that, if pressed, Manny would have been happy to expand on his experiences. The benefit of hindsight prompts a host of further questions that one might now wish to ask.

Notes

1   Interview by Seán Ó Loideáin of Manny dos Santos (September 1998), private archive.

2   Clair Wills, *Lovers and Strangers: An Immigrant History of Post-War Britain* (London: Penguin, 2017), 10.

3   See P. J. C. Smith, *Flying Bombs over the Pennines: The Story of the V-1 Attack Aimed at Manchester December 24th 1944* (Manchester: Neil Richardson, 1988); cited in 'Photos and Histories of Air Crashes, Air Raids and Other Wartime Stories'. Available at: http://aircrashsites.co.uk/air-raids-bomb-sites/v1-site-at-radcliffe-near-bury/ (accessed 24 August 2020).

4   R. A. C. Parker, *Struggle for Survival: The History of the Second World War* (Oxford: Oxford University Press, 1989), 162.

5   Manoel dos Santos, Royal Navy Service Record, JX645813.

6   Ninian Stewart, *The Royal Navy and the Palestine Patrol* (London: Frank Cass, 2002); United States Holocaust Memorial Museum (USHMM), 'Aliyah Bet', Holocaust Encyclopedia. Available at: https://encyclopedia.ushmm.org/content/en/article/aliyah-bet (accessed 24 August 2020).

7   Parker, *Struggle for Survival*, 177–82.

8   Parker, *Struggle for Survival*, 85.

9   Parker, *Struggle for Survival*, 86–8.

10 USHMM, 'Aliyah Bet'.

11 Stewart, *The Royal Navy and the Palestine Patrol*, 121–5.

12 'May he rest in peace.' Translated from Irish.

PART TWO

Lives under siege: Coping with occupation

9

A Spanish communist in the French Resistance: Uncle Luís and a German map

Sara Farrona

Allow me to take you back in time to a scene from my childhood. My World War II family story is the story of a German map dating from 1941, and how this map travelled 2000 kilometres from the place it was found to a small town in western Spain where I first saw it, and was captivated by, several decades after the World War. I can still picture myself looking at the map and feeling an electric current of curiosity and anticipation at discovering hidden secrets. The map was slightly cracked in some places and its borders had yellowed but apart from that it was perfectly preserved. I must have been about 8 or 9 years old when I first studied it because I could read perfectly well all the place names in Spanish and German, written with very fine and precise calligraphy. Some of those places were familiar, such as Mérida, the small city where I was born and which is today the capital of western Spain's Extremadura region, and the small town of Valverde de Mérida, about a twenty-minute drive away, which was where my grandparents and my grand-uncle Luís were from. However, many other places, although I have been there, I never thought as having had a real name because for me they were just pieces of land in the countryside. The level of detail of this map is in fact stunning. I can see myself moving my hand delicately to touch all the tiny fine lines and names depicted with beautiful coloured ink – brown, blue, yellow and red. The map had been in my family for more than forty years and, therefore, I must have heard about its existence before, but touching it as I described above is my first memory of actually seeing it. My story is a mixture of facts, imaginings and undisclosed secrets, but the map illustrates the absolute uniqueness of my tale. This is a story about a German map and my grand-uncle Luís, a Spanish communist who fought against Franco and helped the French in their resistance against Hitler.

An early morning in Bordeaux, 1980: End and beginning

It was still dark, although some light could be seen coming from the horizon one pleasant summer's morning in Bordeaux in 1980. In my mind's eye, I see my grand-uncle Luís standing close to the small Renault 5 belonging to his niece, Dori (who is my mother's sister), observing how Dori keeps anxiously reorganizing his belongings. There are not many objects but they still fill the small boot and back seat of the little car that had brought them to France almost two weeks before. It was still strange to think that only twelve days ago, when he arrived in mid-western Spain from France where he had spent half of his life, they had finally met for the first time. After the tiring car trip that brought them to southern France and the days they had spent together there, he was still astonished at how much she reminded him of his brother, who had always been stressed by the prospect of travelling. 'Uncle Luís, are you sure that everything is here?' she asked in Spanish, for the hundredth time. 'Oui, oui', he responds. All farewells had been said the night before to the few neighbours who had looked after him during the last couple of years since he had become a widower. Now, after forty years, he was more than ready to return to Spain. 'Then, come on, let's go. We still have a very long trip,' she replies while getting into the car, energetically closing the door. Without looking back, he also got in. Saying 'allez, allez' he encourages his niece to start the car, and they were off. Inside one of the suitcases in the boot, squashed among Luís's few clothes, is an old German map that is also travelling down to Spain with them.

Luís's early years (1915–31)

In 1915 Spain was still ruled by a monarchy; Alfonso XIII was king. Though Spain stayed neutral in World War I, it was impacted economically and socially by it. On 10 November 1915, my grand-uncle Luís was born in the small town of Valverde de Mérida in Extremadura. Extremadura is at that time – and probably still is – one of the poorest and most underdeveloped Spanish regions, but Valverde de Mérida is very close to the Guadiana river, which makes Valverde's lands part of a fertile valley; this allowed locals to cultivate crops, such as cotton, and to breed all sorts of animals. Luís had a brother, Manuel, who was two years his senior, although everyone called him by the typically Spanish nickname 'Manolo'. Their parents were Eusebia Farrona Farrona and Primitivo Cortés Ramírez and, therefore, in the Spanish way of preserving both father's and mother's surnames, their children became Cortés Farrona, two last names that have been weaved together repeatedly in our family tree. Primitivo was a peasant and a respected member of Valverde's community, as evidenced by his position as a justice of the peace. As the town was too small to have its own judicial officer, he mediated in minor neighbourhood disputes.

Luís was only three years old when he endured one of the most consequential events of his life – the death of his mother due to the Spanish Flu pandemic of 1918–19. Luís (see Figure 9.1 for his photograph as an adult) was too young to realize how this terrible event would shape his early life. After his mother passed away, he and his brother were cared for by Balbina, his mother's sister-in-law. Balbina was a strong-minded and resolute woman who, along with her husband Ángel, owned a bakery and food shop in the middle of town. They had a son, Teodoro, and two daughters. Whilst Balbina was not an affectionate foster mother to Luís and Manolo, she always treated them fairly. I myself

FIGURE 9.1 *Luís Cortés Farrona, in France, 1940*

can recall her in her last days as a stooped, ancient woman whom we used to call 'Bisa', the shorter version of great-grandmother ('bisabuela' in Spanish). Importantly, the new situation meant that the two brothers become even closer to their cousin Teodoro who was only half a year older than Manolo. Teodoro's serene and reflective personality meant that he came to fill the role of an older brother for the two boys. The three became very good friends and their life paths developed along similar lines, intersecting many times in the years ahead. The apex of these connections came years later when Teodoro's youngest son and Manolo's second daughter would marry. This couple were (and are) none other than my own parents.

Living through the Second Republic (1931–6)

In 1931, when Luís was 15, Alfonso XIII was effectively deposed ushering in a new regime known as the Spanish Second Republic. Many things have been written about Spain in the 1930s. Bear in mind, however, that I myself was born just after democracy was re-established in Spain in the 1970s. In consequence, as there remained deep (and still recent) divisions amongst Spaniards, the history that I and my generation learnt in school avoided the period of the republic which had ended in one of the darkest times of Spanish history, the Civil War (1936–9). In my family, we rarely discussed this time with our grandparents without a certain amount of unconscious self-censorship. In spite of this, I have still been able to get a few glimpses into the lives of Luís, his brother and their cousin in those times. For a family living in an underdeveloped, impoverished, rural area, education was highly important. It is striking that, at a time when most men barely knew how to write their name, even the women of my family, such as Balbina, were literate. That young Luís would embrace the new republic that, amongst many other reforms, proclaimed a new open education system and promised fairer land distribution may well have been inevitable. I imagine him at this time developing the ideas that would make of him the communist he became in adult life. In the course of this time, the three young cousins probably enjoyed a stimulating time studying and helping out with the local family business. During town festivals they were the ones setting tables and chairs on the street terrace in anticipation of the community celebration. A few years ago, my mother chanced upon a Valverde local journal. She was mesmerized to see a photograph of Valverde de Mérida's musical band from 1931 included in a 'Memories of the past' feature. In the picture, 18-year-old Manolo and his cousin Teodoro can be seen wearing spotless band uniforms and holding shiny musical instruments. It is a pity that we cannot be certain whether Luís is one of the figures in the image, although he also played in the band. The music gave the boys the opportunity to have fun taking part in festivals in Valverde and other villages close by.

Another important factor that may have also influenced their lives and decisions as young adults was that one of their uncles, José Ruíz Farrona, was a respected colonel in the Spanish Army. Indeed, Teodoro also enrolled in the army in an administrative position. Luís was probably influenced by his family's military history and by the politically charged atmosphere. In any case, as many others at that time, he could not stay removed from the circumstances in which he lived. Hence, when this period of democratic transformation riven with political and social conflict abruptly ended in civil war, he made what was for him the only logical choice – one which would define his future.

The Spanish Civil War and flight to France (1936–9)

If we, Spanish children of the 1970s, rarely heard about the time of the republic, then the period of the Spanish Civil War was even more taboo, a subject completely censored during my childhood. Talking about this time with my grandparents was avoided; it was obviously very painful for them to relive such dark memories. Teodoro, my closest grandparent, would almost never discuss those years. Manolo and Luís were more open to talking about the war; however the opportunity to hear from them about their experiences were scarcer as neither of them lived close by to the rest of the family. Therefore, from my point of view, this part of Luís's story is unfortunately full of gaps. I would give anything to have the opportunity to ask him about it again!

Luís was only 20 years old in the summer of 1936, when a section of the Spanish Army, led by General Francisco Franco, took up arms against its own democratic government, starting a terrible war. What made this war so bloody was the fact that people fought against their own – neighbours against neighbours, brothers against brothers; it opened a divide that is still prevalent in Spanish society today. Retrospectively, we could consider my family lucky, as most had decided to support the republican government thereby avoiding a family split. The family was not lucky in the short term however. Franco's nationalists defeated republican forces by March 1939, putting my family in a very challenging situation in which Luís had to take a desperate decision and in which others, such as Teodoro and Manolo, needed to revise their future plans. During this terrible war, Teodoro was an army sergeant and, being a socialist, stayed loyal to the government as part of the republican forces. Manolo and Luís also enrolled in the army to support the constitutional government. From this point on, the story becomes hazy. When the war had broken out in the summer of 1936, their uncle José Ruíz Farrona was stationed in Badajoz, the largest city of Extremadura, where he commanded the Castilla 16th Regiment. Teodoro was also working for the army in the same city, which was also where he met and fell in love with my grandmother who was working as a maid locally.

A few months later Teodoro was promoted first to sergeant and later to lieutenant rank, both indications of merit, before being transferred to the 199th Mixed Brigade, with which he took part in combat on the Brunete front (close to Madrid) where one of the war's most important battles occurred. In the summer of 1937, he joined the 63rd Mixed Brigade, which played a very important role in defending Extremadura, under the command of his uncle Colonel José Ruíz Farrona. By war's end, Teodoro had been promoted to captain. Manolo, meanwhile, belonged to the Unified Socialist Youth (JSU) (Juventudes Socialistas Unificadas), a political organization founded in 1936 as an amalgamation of the Socialist Worker's Party and the youth groups of the Communist Party. He was also recruited to the 'carabineros', an army corps famously loyal to the republic.

Where was Luís during the war? Of the three young cousins, Luís may well have been the most radical, with deeply held communist beliefs. He may have joined the JSU, with Manolo. His communist ideals did not dim over the years and, indeed, his experiences of war seem to have reinforced them. It is not difficult to understand his decision to join the republican forces. He took part in the Battle of the Ebro, a four-month-long struggle fought out between republican and nationalist forces from July to November 1938, in which, according to historian Antony Beevor, about thirty thousand soldiers loyal to the republic perished – Franco's victory there helping to seal the fate of the republic.[1] Amongst the wounded, Luís thereafter carried a long deep scar on his leg – which was a reminder of the Ebro.

By the end of the Civil War Luís's brother and cousin were captured as prisoners of war. Both cousins would be moved between different military prisons, Teodoro ending up in Mérida's and Manolo in Valencia's prison on completely opposite sides of the country. It is said in my family that they were incarcerated, not only because they were republicans but also because they were the relatives of José – holder of a prestigious place in the military high command. Indeed, while in Valencia at any rate, Manolo was held in the same prison as José. As fate would have it, though, being related to José may have also saved them from execution, as José's death sentence was eventually reduced to thirty years of imprisonment, which was still part of a wider pattern of very harsh treatment of the defeated side by the victorious nationalists. We believe that the commutation of the death sentence may have been due to General Franco's direct mediation, as he may have been an old acquaintance of José's; they had both held positions of high command in the army before the war and may well have been acquainted with one another in Spanish Morocco in earlier decades. Ultimately, after several months anticipating the worst, watching as many of their fellow inmates were removed, never to come back to the prison, both Teodoro and Manolo were released. They were free to follow their lives as best as they could, in a world that had completely changed around them.

Did Luís hear about the situation with his brother and cousin? Did he know that they had been made prisoners? I do not have an answer to these questions, but news across the country travelled slowly during those chaotic days. However, it is highly likely that Luís was aware of the terrible end met by many leftist comrades, as he decided to flee the country by the end of the war. As a wounded soldier, his flight through a crumbling republican zone must have been an odyssey. At some point, he managed to reach the north of Spain and crossed the French border – probably with the help of the Spanish Maquis, *guerrilleros*, who were able to hide out and seek shelter in the dangerous northern terrain, fighting against Franco's regime for many years to come. He was but one of many fleeing as part of *La Retirada* (retreat) of 1938–9, an exodus in which hundreds of thousands of Spaniards, civilians and combatants, fled, most of them on foot and with very few possessions. He and his compatriots had been of the belief that, once in France, they would be sheltered by France as it was a democratic sister-republic and neighbour; however, they were shocked and dismayed to be detained in one of a string of 'concentration camps' that the French government had established, often hemming them in on beaches behind barbed wire, where exiles lived in deplorable conditions, exposed to the elements. France's socialist-led Popular Front government of 1936–7 had been sympathetic to the Spanish republic but found it politically impossible to give it much more than rhetorical (and some covert military) aid. By 1939, French public opinion had become more suspicious of Spanish republican fighters. The French Republic's new government under Édouard Daladier considered them as a potential communist fifth column. Nowadays when I see photographs of the refugee camp in Lesvos, showing people escaping the misery of the war in Syria, I can only think that European history is just a repetitive succession of events from which we rarely learn.

Spanish maquisards, German maps and Vichy France

For pragmatic rather than humane reasons, by mid-1939, the French government offered these Spanish veterans a choice between joining the

French Foreign Legion or joining new 'foreign labour companies', with more compulsion applied from September 1939. At the time of the surprise defeat of France by Nazi Germany in June 1940, there were an estimated 120,000 to 150,000 Spanish republican refugees in the south-west of France. They were, as Julian Jackson puts it, 'among the earliest victims of the Vichy regime [the authoritarian and collaborationist French state established in July 1940], liable to be put into immigrant labour camps or sent to work in Germany: For many Spaniards resistance was a necessity as much as a choice'.[2] Cooperating over time with French Communists and other anti-German networks, these Spanish fighters played a unique role in the French Resistance being nothing less than, in Robert Gildea's words, 'the original *maquisards* [the term used to describe armed resisters who hid in hilly scrubland or *maquis*], a step ahead of the French by their experience of battle and hardship'.[3] Vichy propaganda in turn denounced the resistance for its recruitment of foreigners – ranging from Spanish republicans to Polish Jewish immigrants – whom they depicted as alien bandits.

This brings me back to Luís, who was amongst those Spanish who fought in the French Resistance. Added to his sense of justice was a survival instinct to escape the misery and horrendous conditions of the concentration camps where many detainees had died of diseases and starvation or had been deported to Nazi death camps. In my aunt Doris's house, there is a small blue notebook dated from 1944 to 1945 with annotations in Luís's meticulous calligraphy. It is likely that he wrote entries in the notebook during the last months of World War II, probably the most dangerous time to be a resistance fighter owing to the volatility of the retreating German forces. The notes written by Luís are essential to getting a sense of his movements during this period. They detail in writing how to build explosive devices, and there are drawings illustrating projectile trajectories. Indeed, many of the Spanish republican soldiers, who joined the resistance, contributed to the sabotage and blowing up of bridges, trains, roads and high-voltage power lines. The goal was to hamper the movements of the Wehrmacht. Our family is fortunate to have a rare photo, taken in France, of Luís and a group of Spanish republican guerrilleros – one of whom is proudly displaying a copy of a banned Spanish trade union newspaper for the camera (see Figure 9.2). In addition to the sabotage attacks noted above, as an experienced guerrillero, Luís may have also engaged in hand-to-hand combat when he participated in an incursion into local German headquarters. It was during one of these dangerous raids that he found something completely unexpected.

During World War II, Luís stayed in the south of France. His *carte d'identité* from 1945, which is still in my family, indicates that he was positioned in the 17th Military Region, an area corresponding to the Toulouse region, specifically in the Tarbes subdivision, a small city close to the Pyrenees. Toulouse was

FIGURE 9.2 *Luís (first from left) and a group of Spanish republican members of the French Resistance, 1944 or 1945*

(and remained after 1945) a major centre for the Spanish republican diaspora. Luís was a private in the 6th Security Battalion, a unit mainly active along the French border with Spain. Spanish guerrilleros were organized into a range of divisions that retained autonomy from the French Resistance though they shared the common goal of fighting Fascism. For them, liberating France was a necessary preliminary step for the liberation of Spain from Franco. Somewhere in the south of France, sometime after 1941, Luís and his comrades stormed a German headquarter killing the enemy in close combat. After the attack they would have had time to explore the building, searching for information that would help them in the struggle. I imagine the scene: Luís and his comrades frantically looking around, rifle still in his hand and adrenaline rushing through his body. There they find a series of German maps, and he freezes in front of one, almost in shock. He cannot believe that there, amidst the mayhem of this new, foreign world, he is encountering a fragment of his old life. He reads the names of the places that he so well knows, 'Mérida', 'Trujillanos', 'Don Álvaro', and for a brief moment time seems to stop – the distances between his old life and his new life disappearing.

Why would the Germans have had such a map? Until the very end of the war, the German military employed some fifteen thousand people, among them soldiers and cartographers, to produce more than 1.3 billion maps to assist German conquest and control of vast tracts of Europe. Amongst this mass production were some 1,500 making up the 'Deutsche Heereskarte von Spanien 1:50.000' ('German Army Map of Spain, scale 1:50,000'). In 1943, Franco's Spain remained neutral in the world war despite Hitler's request to join the German faction. The Spanish armed forces – Franco's – located on the French border overpowered a group of Spanish guerrilleros in the Pyrenees at this midpoint in the war and were surprised to find the guerrilleros in possession of German maps of Spain, of the type that had stopped Luís in his tracks. The Francoist secret service confirmed that the information on the maps had originated from Spanish sources and secretly printed in Germany.[4] The reasons behind such puzzling map discoveries, including Uncle Luís's, go back to the Civil War when Franco's nationalist rebels lacked good maps as the Spanish cartographic service remained in official republican hands thereby making good maps wartime treasures, maps at 1:50,000 scale being especially prized. In light of Nazi Germany's military aid to Franco, and the possibility of future conflict in Spain, the German secret service obtained access to information in Spain that allowed official German military map-makers to collate a 'Sonderausgabe' ('special edition') of detailed maps of Spain superior to those of their nationalist allies. These the Germans kept a secret from Franco's Spain. The maps contain a legend in German and Spanish. Copies of the 'Deutsche Heereskarte von Spanien 1:50.000' were stored in Berlin, Paris and also in southern France (the latter being a strategic location on the Spanish border), helping to explain Luís's chance discovery. The beautiful maps are still referred to by Spain's official ordinance survey.[5]

A Spanish exile in post-war France

Having been prominent in the liberation of several French regions in 1944, including Paris, some 150,000 Spaniards stayed in France after the war having been recognized by the Provisional Government of the French Republic in March 1945 as Nansen refugees, a special category protecting stateless persons.[6] One of these was Luís who eventually settled in Agen, not far from Bordeaux, where he was officially registered with the Office Français de Protection des Réfugiés et Apatrides. As for other Spanish republican exiles, a return to Spain promised only Franco's government's reprisals. Luís remained a communist, a heartfelt republican and a freedom-loving soul, exactly what the Spanish government was trying to banish. Unable to travel to Spain he got news of Manolo, Teodoro and other family members through the exchange of letters and photographs. It was in Agen that he got to know Marie Bru, known in my family as Aunt Pierrette. In 1951, she would travel to Valencia to visit

Luís's brother, and then, together with Manolo, visited Mérida to meet the rest of the family. This difficult solo journey likely had as its main objective the obtaining of a copy of Luís's birth certificate, as less than a year later they were married. For the rest of their years together, the couple enjoyed a relatively calm life. They had no children. Luís found employment as an industrial worker. He fraternized with other Spanish Communists as evidenced by his 1976 membership card of the 'Amicale des Anciens Guerrilleros Espagnoles en France' veterans' body. Such bodies had been officially closed down by the French government from 1950, which was anxious to conciliate Franco whose regime was by then incorporated into the same western camp as France in the Cold War. The dictator's death in 1975 opened new possibilities. In 1978 Aunt Pierrette died and Teodoro visited Luís not long after, insisting Luís to return with him to Spain to live with his family, who were willing to take him in. Another two years passed before Luís accepted Teodoro's persistent offer, finally deciding to return to his homeland in 1980.

Juana – and a rekindled romance

How must it have been to be back in Spain after forty years? Luís had left a country fractured and torn apart by war; he returned to a very different Spain. A left-wing party was in power and most people were proud of their young democracy. Much of the old country remained, yet so many things were new to him. He was 65 years old when he returned, yet despite only just having reunited with his family after so long, and having lived a life full of adventure, he did not hesitate to embark on a new escapade. I was just 4 years old when Uncle Luís arrived in Mérida in 1980 and, although we had thought that he was coming to stay for good, he only spent three years with us. I remember him clearly during this time. There was something strange about his manner; he had a tendency to retreat into a world of his own. Because of the years spent in France, he spoke a funny mixture of Spanish and French – a combination that resembled neither language! He was generally placid but very obstinate when he disagreed with something. As a child I was grateful that he treated me so patiently, and not in the condescending way that many adults have with children. He was very generous, happy to contribute to his long-lost family, but at the same time he was very independent, probably as a result of all the years living alone. My sister and I were happy in his company, as a treasured family photo shows (see Figure 9.3). He also seemed to crave love, and this, together with rediscovered memories from his youth, prompted him to look for old friends and, specifically, to search for Juana.

FIGURE 9.3 *Juana (author's aunt), Sara Farrona, her sister Ruth and Uncle Luís at Montserrat mountains near Barcelona, 1985*

Juana was four years younger than Luís. When the Civil War started, she was only 17 years old. Thinking about the woman who I met many years later, I am sure that even at that early age Juana was determined, a freethinker and maverick – perhaps those characteristics were the ones that attracted Luís. What I know for certain is that the war interrupted their romance. Though a staunch republican, Juana's gender meant she was not able to follow her political ideals like her male peers and join the armed forces to fight for her beliefs. Instead, she had to stay in Valverde. The republicans were defeated; she endured derision and humiliation from her own neighbours. They shaved her head, marking her out as a member of the losing side and undermining her integrity. Years later, she escaped the town that treated her so cruelly, running away from local subjugation and post-war poverty. She moved to Barcelona, a city that she would grow to love and know like the back of her hand. It is in Barcelona that Juana built a new life; she got married, had a daughter and worked as caretaker of a building on the vibrant central Paseo de Gracia Avenue.

Since the Civil War had separated them, Luís and Juana had completely lost contact. Once back in Mérida, Luís contacted a mutual friend in Valverde, who told him that Juana was now a widow, living in Barcelona. There might have been a new courtship, perhaps they reunited when Juana visited her relatives in Valverde or Luís visited her in Barcelona; the details are lacking. My family did not hear about Juana until Uncle Luís informed us that he was moving to Barcelona to be with her. He left everything behind, including the German map, which he gave to my parents, who had been very close to him – leaving his family in complete awe. In 1983 Luís and Juana were married in a small wedding ceremony; his brother Manolo was best man. Separation from his family was easier this time; the distance was shorter and news and visits were exchanged frequently during this period of his life. Our initial scepticism about the whirlwind romance was misplaced as Luís and Juana were a perfect match. This was most probably one of the happiest periods of Luís's life, until Juana's death after seventeen years of marriage. Luís's nieces, my mother and my aunt, supported him through this difficult time and, after many years, he finally returned to Mérida; his life's circle was complete. It was here, surrounded and cared for by family, that he would gradually forget all his memories.

Luís died in December 2005. He was 90 years old. The old German map still hangs in my mother's house, a reminder of his astonishing, awe-inspiring life.

Notes

I would like to thank Fernando Barrero Barzac for his interest in my story and for sharing his knowledge about the dark days of the Spanish Civil War helping me to fill in gaps in my knowledge. Diego Casillas Torres took the photographs of Uncle Luís's map and provided important clues about the map. Prof. Luís Urteaga contributed essential information to help me understand the origins of the map. Amelia Walker had the patience to read the text, correcting my mistakes and transforming it into a finer piece of writing. Francis García Ballesteros kindly helped to get high-quality scans of family photographs to illustrate my memories. My warmest thanks to my mother, my aunt Doris and my sister for sharing their memories in long mobile phone conversations in which they answered my countless questions, as I thank them also for the papers, letters and photos that they sent me, which inspired my telling of this story.

1   Antony Beevor, *The Battle for Spain: The Spanish Civil War, 1936–1939* (London: Penguin, 2006), 358.

2   Julian Jackson, *France: The Dark Years* (Oxford: Oxford University Press, 2004), 495; see also Evelyn Mesquida, *Y ahora volved a vuestras casas. Republicanos españoles en la Resistencia Francesca* (And Now Return to Your Homes: Spanish Republicans in the French Resistance) (Barcelona: S. A. Ediciones B, 2020).

3 Robert Gildea, *Fighters in the Shadows: A New History of the French Resistance* (London: Faber & Faber, 2015), 206–7.

4 Wolfgang Scharfe, '"Deutsche Heereskarte von Spanien": El mapa d'Espanya a escala 1:50.000 de l'Estat Major de l'Exèrcit alemany (1940–1944)', *Treballs de la Societat Catalana de Geografia* 57 (2004): 111–38. See also, Wolfgang Scharfe, 'German Army Map of Spain 1:50 000: 1940–1944', *Proceedings of the 21st International Cartographic Conference (ICC): Durban, South Africa, 10–16 August 2003*. Available at: http://maps.mapywig.org/m/m_documents/EN/W.Scharfe_GERMAN_ARMY_MAP_OF_SPAIN_50K_1940-1944.pdf (accessed 1 May 2020).

5 *Mapas y Cartógrafos en la Guerra Civil Española (1936–1939)*, ed. Francesc Nadal y Luís Urteaga (Madrid: Instituto Geográfico Nacional, 2013).

6 'The Painful Past of Spanish Civil War Refugees in France, 80 Years On', Interview with historian Geneviève Dreyfus-Armand, France 24 television, 9 February 2019. Available at: https://www.france24.com/en/20190209-france-spanish-civil-war-republican-refugees-la-retirada-80th-anniversary (accessed 30 April 2020).

10

A boy in small-town Germany from home front to Allied occupation

Hermann Rasche

The events of the Nazi era cast a long shadow over German families. For mine, the greatest challenge was the loss of my father, Heinrich Rasche. Conscripted into the Wehrmacht, he died in a Russian prisoner of war (POW) camp in Romania in August 1945. I grew up fatherless and an only child. My mother, Elly (Elisabeth) Rasche, remained a widow until her death in 2013. In other respects, however, the Nazi legacy was less problematic for my family than for many others. Nobody had held any position in the Nazi Party, apart from my grandfather's appointment as secretary in a very minor Nazi organization in 1943. Indeed there were several examples of opposition to Nazism on the part of family members, and Germany's capitulation and the subsequent Allied occupation were welcomed as acts of liberation by all around me. The bookshelves in our house were full of critical studies of the Third Reich, published in the post-war years. They made me aware of and interested in this part of German history at a very early age. The war years and their aftermath were common topics for discussion within my extended family. There were no obvious wounds, no silences or taboos, no mutual accusations and recriminations.

Few Germans enjoy this luxury. Historical research conducted over the past few decades has revealed widespread complicity by ordinary Germans in Nazi crimes.[1] This knowledge is difficult to bear at a collective level, but even more so when it threatens to tar beloved relatives as Nazi criminals. Research into the intergenerational transmission of memory in Germany has shown how the desire to exempt their parents and grandparents from complicity in Nazi crimes drove some young Germans to rewrite their families' past, often quite unconsciously. Claims that 'Grandpa was no Nazi' were common among the subjects interviewed as part of a large study into memory in the 1990s.[2]

While innocence must be a relative concept in Nazi Germany, the opposition of my family to Nazism is made the more plausible by the local context in which they lived. Our small country town, Vechta, and the surrounding area, the historic Grand Duchy of Oldenburg, were traditionally conservative in outlook, and the inhabitants were very conscious of forming a Catholic enclave in the predominantly Protestant north of Germany. A Dominican monastery and boarding school stood just across the street from us. There were very close, friendly links between 'town and habit'. This commitment to Catholicism and the Catholic Centre Party seemed to have largely immunized the people in our area against Nazism. Just 8.7 per cent of Vechta's Catholics voted for the Nazis in July 1932.[3] Our government district or Regierungsbezirk, the District of Oldenburg, was the only one in the whole of the German Reich where Christian crosses in primary schools were not replaced by the official portrait of the Führer, Adolf Hitler, in 1936. The Nazis tried it once but were physically obstructed and did not dare to try it again. This courageous act of resistance is still celebrated every year as the victory of the Christian cross over the swastika.[4] When the Nazis imprisoned two Dominican monks in 1935 on a trumped-up charge of financial embezzlement, there was uproar among the local people, and the Nazis released them soon afterwards; one of them, Titus Horten, died in early 1936 as a result of his inhumane imprisonment.[5]

There were, of course, some Nazis in Vechta. Yet, while three local party members were implicated in the burning and looting of the town's small synagogue in Kristallnacht, on 9 November 1938, the real perpetrators, two dozen Brownshirt (SA) thugs, had to be transported in from the outside. My mother often mentioned that, on the morning of 10 November, she saw that SA men from outside Vechta had thrown bed linen, duvets and personal clothing on to the main street from the upstairs window of a building, which contained a haberdashery belonging to two unmarried Jews, the Bloch sisters. Both of them perished in a concentration camp in 1944, possibly near Minsk. My youngest uncle, who was then seven and a half years of age, later recalled witnessing the destruction of the synagogue on his way to school nearby. He remembered seeing some of the support beams still smouldering – the local fire services were forbidden to extinguish the fires! – and people standing around and just staring at it. There was, he said, not much talk in his school of what had just happened. Classes went on as 'normal'.[6]

My father's war

I was not born until four years later, in 1942, in the midst of World War II. I was just that little bit too young to have any immediate, abiding personal memories of even the very last months of World War II. While I was born in the nearby town of Osnabrück, my mother and I had moved to Vechta, her home place, in the last year of the war. My father, a secondary schoolteacher, had been called up to the German Army at a relatively late stage, in 1943, when I was about ten months old. The last photo we have of him before he was stationed in France and in Croatia shows him holding me in his arms; I was just beginning to crawl. That was also the last time my mother saw him. The last letter from the front she was to receive from him was stamped 22 October 1944. As far I know, he and his battalion or company were captured by American forces in eastern Austria and then handed over to the Soviets, in accordance with arrangements made at the Tehran Conference in 1943. They were then transported, probably by rail, to a Soviet POW camp in Romania, in the city of Focşani, located 160 kilometres north-northeast of Bucharest. One of the few survivors of that camp witnessed my father's death in August 1945 and informed the German Red Cross. My mother got official confirmation of his death only in 1949, however. Up until then, she believed that he might still be alive (see Figure 10.1).

My father's premature death meant that I was robbed of the opportunity to ask him about his political sympathies and war experiences. Yet my mother made clear that he shared her family's hostility to the regime. She never depicted his death as anything other than an enormous, terrible and absolutely needless loss. She made sure I knew that he objected to the war. Very often, but especially on my father's birthday, 22 June, she almost ritualistically recounted that, when the German Army invaded Russia on that date in 1941, he was unable to get out of bed. She had to inform the local school and pretend that he was down with severe flu and too ill to teach his classes. According to her, he said something along the lines of: 'That'll end disastrously, it will be horrific, Hitler, this dirty pig!' ('Das wird schlimm enden, es wird fürchertlich werden, Hitler dieses Schwein!').

Sometime in the 1960s, I remember a former colleague of my father's providing evidence that it was not simply the invasion of the Soviet Union, a highly risky military campaign, that angered my father. This man told me that my father had made an anti-Nazi remark in a public place just after the German invasion of Poland in September 1939 and that he was very lucky not to have been interrogated by the dreaded and ruthless Gestapo as a result.

Indeed on the bookshelves of our home I found copies of books that had been banned and burned by the Nazis in 1933. Among them were works by

FIGURE 10.1 *Elly Menke and Heinrich Rasche on their engagement, 1939*

Erich M. Remarque (*All Quiet on the Western Front*, an international bestseller), Sigmund Freud, Thomas Mann, Karl Marx, Karl Kautsky, Kurt Tucholsky, Maxim Gorki, Romain Rolland and others. My father must have acquired them before 1933 when it was still possible to do so, and he kept them hidden. If he had been found out, it would most likely have cost him at least his teaching job.

Family memories of the war

My knowledge of these years was passed down to me primarily by my mother and her family. My maternal grandfather and the only adult male in our home during the war, August Menke, acted as a kind of substitute father to me. A financial controller with the Revenue Commission, he was a great source of information, being a voracious reader of books and magazines, especially those dealing with twentieth-century German history. Occasionally Grandfather mentioned that very early one morning, in the city of Oldenburg, he saw a goods train on a siding near the central station and people's faces staring out between the iron bars of the wagons. This train was most likely on its way from the concentration camp near the Dutch village of Westerbork to Bergen-Belsen. This image haunted him for the rest of his life.

His three sons, my uncles, contributed even more to the knowledge I acquired over the years. All were shaped by the war. Two had to serve in the army. They had almost diametrically opposed experiences. The younger of the two, Karl-Arnold, served on the Russian front line and had been involved in fierce fighting near Stalingrad. He survived and is alive to this day. He came back from Russian captivity only in 1949, totally emaciated. His parents hardly recognized their own son. When I saw him for the first time, he seemed to me like a frightening, walking skeleton. It took him several months to recuperate. He became a successful and highly respected lawyer. Only after his retirement and after his wife's death from cancer was he able and emotionally sufficiently 'unblocked' to relate his harrowing experiences. He ascribed his survival to a young Russian female doctor who took pity on him and cared for him.

By contrast, the elder brother, Nikolaus, known as Niko, served as a member of the marines near Narvik in Norway and had luckily not been engaged in any major armed conflict. He came through the war totally unscathed. After surrendering, he and his platoon came into British captivity. He was back in civilian life half a year later. Though by no means a Nazi ideologist, he nevertheless referred on certain occasions to the 'great times he had enjoyed in Norway'. That, of course, did not go down well with his brother who had seen the reality of a brutal war in Russia. There always remained a degree of friction and a latent animosity between these two brothers.

The youngest brother, Heinz-August, barely 15 years old in the dying days of the Third Reich, only just managed to avoid joining the so-called Volkssturm. This was a territorial army formed in the last months of World War II, consisting of old men and youngsters who were unfit for regular military service and totally unequipped – a bizarre attempt to hold the march of the advancing Allied troops. The local Gauleiter had issued an order that his age group join up. Discipline remained harsh even as Germany's defeat loomed. The situation was highly dangerous. Deserters were rounded up and severely punished, if not shot on sight. My uncle had to go into hiding in the woods during the day, sneaking back home at night to get some provisions before disappearing again. Two of his classmates were not so lucky and were rounded up by diehards, although luckily they survived the final months of the war. Of all the brothers, Heinz-August told me the most about the war. He probably had positive experiences with the British occupation army in the summer of 1945 and later studied History and English.

One of my maternal aunts, Adelheid, a district children's nurse, also contributed to my understanding of the family as anti-Nazi. She related an incident that happened one day when she called at a farm house unusually late in the evening to check on a potential case of measles. She entered the house unannounced through the open back door and heard the *bum-bum-bum* radio signal tone of the BBC foreign services. The father of the house instantly turned pale when he saw her entering, fearing that she could, and very possibly would, now report him to the Gestapo for listening to an 'enemy station', a crime which could easily have meant the death penalty. As quick as lightning he reacted, shouting at his innocent young son and giving him a smack behind his ears: 'You have been fiddling again with the radio stations. Don't do that ever, ever again.' But my aunt calmed him down when she assured him: 'We, too, listen to the BBC.'

The war was also remembered for the challenges it posed to everyday life and the successes in overcoming them. We always had plenty to eat. My mother took care of a big garden, she kept hens and goats, we had our own potatoes, apple, pear and plum trees; my favourite fruit as a young child were gooseberries, of which there were always plenty! We also had our own plot of turf. Tea and coffee became more and more of a rarity. My mother, as she was always proud to tell, ingeniously concocted a coffee-like *ersatz* brew from acorns. Jam made from turnips became a staple foodstuff in many households; so too were semolina dumplings. The longer the war went on, the more difficult it was to buy new clothes. But that was a very minor problem; women were always busy mending, repairing, knitting for families and friends.

Our town was in the flight paths of the Lancaster bomber groups on their way towards their intended targets, the industrial centres of Bremen, Hamburg and the shipyards further north. There was a small military airfield in our vicinity, which was attacked by Allied bombers. A few bombs went astray. One exploded close to our house, luckily causing only minor damage, breaking the stained-glass windows in the hallway. Sirens on roofs went off quite regularly to warn people about those fighter planes. My mother, my grandparents and one or two of our neighbours then hurried down into the basement, which had been converted into a makeshift air-raid shelter, using steel girders and concrete. I was, as I was later told, brought into this makeshift shelter on several occasions, peacefully asleep and blissfully unaware of things going on above us.

Memories of the aftermath

My very first conscious stepping out into the world around me – shortly after the surrender in May 1945 – remains very vividly with me till this day: Vechta, located in a primarily rural part of north-west Germany, was now in the British-occupied zone. The fairly spacious and comfortable house of my maternal grandparents – into which my mother and I had moved in the final year of the war to get away from the more vulnerable industrial centre of Osnabrück, which was also a strategic railway crossing point – had been taken over by British military personnel. Their task was to keep order, try and re-establish democratic administrative structures and, wherever possible, round up former high-ranking Nazis.

My grandparents, my young mother and I, her only child, were allowed to remain in an annexe to the house. The overwhelming majority of the inhabitants of our town had welcomed the 'Tommies', by which name the British were rather endearingly called. These soldiers apparently behaved impeccably, and they had plenty of time on their hands. Early memories tend to be vague and blurred, but my own very first memory goes back to that time in the spring of 1945 when two young British soldiers, who were quartered with us, were holding my hands. One of them gave me a red Cadbury sweet, the other one a green sweet, and they played football with me. I can still recollect the pungent smell of their khaki uniforms in my nostrils to this day. My later decision to study English language, literature and culture must have been, I am convinced, subconsciously motivated by these very positive memories. In fact, I undertook my first trip abroad not into neighbouring Denmark, Belgium or another geographically closer country but to Winchester in England.

Family lore also has it that British Field Marshal Bernard 'Monty' Montgomery, who had a base nearby, stopped his motorcade one sunny afternoon when my mother happened to be cycling by. I was sitting behind her on the child bike seat. Whether my mother assumed this was going to be a routine check or was somewhat alarmed, I do not know, but it turned out to be a friendly encounter. Monty's men apparently wanted to take snapshots for a photoessay that was to be published in some of those German newspapers which had been granted a licence to reappear after the war. A young local mother, her healthy child, a sunny day in late spring in a post-Nazi war-free countryside: This must have been in their eyes a very suitable image for the newly emerging democratic Germany. While I have never seen a copy of the photograph, I am relatively certain the encounter did happen. My mother made no great bones about it, but did mention it from time to time. I do remember – much later on when she was an older woman – us driving around between the city of Osnabrück and the hills of the Teutoburg Forest, when we were passing by an old, extensive manor house, called 'Gut Ostenwalde', Mother said: 'That's where your (!) Monty had his headquarters.' I checked the history of Ostenwalde, and it was in fact one of Montgomery's temporary headquarters.

My home town had come through the war years fairly unharmed. The inhabitants did not have to face any major physical catastrophes. Overall, they had experienced minimal physical damage or destruction, apart from several raids on a nearby military airfield. Friesoythe, a town not too far away, had been razed to the ground. Some fanatical SS officers had tried to defend Vechta in the last fortnight of the war, but they were shot dead by British snipers before they could inflict any further damage. Our local mayor, Georg Gerhardi, hoisted a white linen sheet on a pole to signal total surrender. Because he spoke good English, he was employed as a kind of go-between and interpreter. Those Nazis officials who had been more prominent in the local branch of the party tried to get rid of incriminating evidence, such as their uniforms, medals and party documentation, but they were found out. One of those functionaries was made to clean our public toilets with a tooth-brush! – to howls of laughter from passers-by. One well-known woman, however, a widow and a convinced supporter of the Nazi movement through all her professional life, killed herself by taking poison after she had been informed that her only son had 'honourably sacrificed his life in action defending his fatherland' in early March 1945 on the outskirts of Berlin.

I also remember from around this time sitting on my little stool beside one of our next-door neighbours who was crying bitterly. I did not know why, but my mother told me then that he had just received confirmation of his only son having been killed in the last weeks of the war. The high number of casualties of war in and around town was very noticeable. The Dominican monastery had by 1943 been turned into a central military hospital for severely wounded soldiers. It was kept on as a rehabilitation centre for three years after the war. Cripples in town were quite a familiar sight for us youngsters. Many had lost their legs, their arms; they were on crutches or in special wheelchairs. They were nursed back and reintegrated as far as possible into a society that had to redefine and rebuild itself. A number of them married local girls; some stayed on in town. Another aunt of mine, Elisabeth known as Lisbeth, married one of these convalescents from Thuringia. Her future husband, Hermann Goral, had been a decorated fighter pilot. He had been shot down in an aerial battle, but was able to save himself, although he had been badly wounded. He made a full recovery and became a professional (part-time) flight instructor in his civilian life.

In contrast to other parts of Germany which had been particularly badly hit, our mainly agricultural region had come through the last months of the war pretty well. I saw steam trains packed with people, some dressed in their former army coats, disembarking at the station. They were engaged in so-called 'hoarding trips'. In exchange for personal belongings such as jewellery, carpets, watches and cameras, they bargained for provisions like potatoes, bacon, meat and lard. American cigarettes were a popular substitute currency and served many as a means of bartering. There were a few unsavoury occurrences where some farmers took advantage of those needy people. On a lighter note I remember the legendary soccer team of Schalke 04 touring the provinces and also coming to our town. They played local teams in exchange for foodstuffs which they then distributed back home in the devastated Ruhr district. Schalke 04, seven-time German soccer champion before and even during the first two war years, defeated our amateur team 14:1 – the one conceded goal being celebrated for months to come.

I also remember a sizeable influx of refugees. Since there was no physical damage where we lived, with houses and the basic infrastructure mostly intact and the food situation relatively unproblematic, many refugees, mostly ethnic German expellees from Silesia, which was now Polish territory, were given temporary shelter. Local families had to take in certain contingents of homeless people. We had to accommodate two elderly women, unmarried sisters who received food and lodgings from us. Others, not quite so fortunate, found temporary emergency accommodation in overcrowded Nissen huts. I liked their strange-sounding accents and what I thought were very funny surnames. Among them was a relatively high percentage of Protestants. They did not attend 'my' church services, which I also found somewhat odd. The social divide along religious lines was still very strong and noticeable. And it was more than slightly frowned upon to go out with a Protestant girl. When a refugee died, they were not buried in the cemetery in the town reserved for Catholics but in another one located at the outskirts of town. This was known as the 'Russian cemetery' because it contained the graves of some civilian Russians, refugees from the 1917 Revolution, as well as a few soldiers from World War I. I also heard about a war cemetery some miles to the north. Only later in life did I visit this cemetery and came across the marked grave of the very first Allied Forces victim, a pilot with the RAF from Mallow, Co. Cork. He had been shot down over the North Sea (as it says on the granite gravestone) on 4 September 1939.

Some incidents were referred to in public only in hushed tones, such as the terror of a few marauding hordes of forced labourers, mostly from the eastern parts of Poland and the Soviet Union. They were now liberated and free to take the law into their own hands, taking revenge on whoever they regarded as their enemies and oppressors. Plunderings, lootings, even shootings of innocent people were a daily routine for a short while. But there were also cases of former forced labourers who had been treated well and with dignity. A few of them even decided to remain in Germany after their liberation. One of them, a young Pole from Białystok, Kowalski, seems to have paid regular visits to the local farm where he was a forced labourer. He became the coach of our junior soccer team. We addressed him affectionately as 'Kowi'.

The abundance of war matériel lying around in the local forests meant that we children could do much more than play football. My friends and myself played 'Cowboys and Indians' with steel helmets and rusty old revolvers. We found part of the wreckage of a fighter plane high up in the branches of an oak tree, under which we liked to light a fire; nearby there was a burnt-out tank, half immersed in marshy ground – for us children the perfect adventure playground! We used to swim in craters left by bombs near the abandoned airfield. Accidents caused by ammunition happened from time to time. Two brothers in our neighbourhood, whom I knew, were killed when they handled live ammunition that had not been cleared. I joined the junior Christian boy scouts. We were not supposed to wear any type of uniform; those days were definitely gone – at least for the time being. We were allowed to wear a necktie, however. But I kept my belt with the knuckles still bearing the swastika emblem – a new leather belt was difficult to come by (see Figure 10.2).

I entered primary school in 1948. About half my classmates had a similar background to mine: one-parent families, the fathers either killed in action or missing. Some had survived the war and returned from captivity in various places. The last two men were only released from captivity in 1953 and settled again in our town. I was, officially, one of 2.5 million half-orphans. I did not know what a father's role involved and therefore did not develop any feeling of loss or missing out. Living in a 'fatherless society' in Germany

FIGURE 10.2 *Elly and Hermann Rasche, c.1948*

around that time was nothing exceptional; I did not in any way feel 'different' or even stigmatized.[7] In fact, I considered and experienced my status as quite the norm. Once my father's death had been officially documented in 1949 my mother got a war widow's pension, which allowed her a decent, simple standard of living. Her situation was representative of that of so many other young widows: a high proportion of them did not remarry. Marriageable men had become scarce since millions had not come back from the war. My mother decided to look after her ageing parents.

Our school buildings had not been damaged in any way. Although we young pupils had felt no particular hardships and had not seen any severe rationing, CARE parcels with special 'goodies' were distributed in the schoolyard. A half-litre bottle of chocolate milk per day was given to each pupil, free of charge. We were also vaccinated against possible diseases. Our school had arranged a four-week holiday camp on an island off the coast of northern Germany in order to 'strengthen our lungs', as I remember one of our older teachers remarking. Among our teachers were a few war victims; some had lost limbs, some their eyes. Our mathematics teacher had had both his legs amputated above the knees and was walking on artificial prostheses, but he was still a keen and competent swimmer. Most of our teachers were women. Some 'Nazi teachers' made a career in the new Germany but, as far as I was concerned, denazification seems to have succeeded in our school system.

I remember Martin Bormann, eldest son of the infamous Martin Bormann senior (Hitler's private secretary), calling at our house a few times in the early 1950s. Martin junior had converted to Catholicism and later worked as a missionary priest in Africa. He was visiting one of our neighbours who had been a governess to the children in the Bormann household on the Obersalzberg, Hitler's mountain retreat. There she met her future husband who served as a member of Hitler's personal body guard team. 'Uncle Kurt', as I used to call him, was by now running a fairly lucrative family business. Once a highly decorated member of an elite Nazi corps, he had turned into a successful second-hand car dealer in a small and fairly insignificant town – a remarkable turnaround not untypical of the time.

The legacy of Nazism was thus all around us. Unlike other families, however, which failed to address Nazi crimes in the decades after the war, our family was spared the dramatic moment of confrontation brought on for some other families by the 1968 student revolt in Germany. Our process of coming to terms with Nazism was a continuous one, marked by very personal milestones. In 1979 my mother and her eldest brother Niko went to Focşani. It was very difficult in those Ceaucescu days to move around Romania but they managed to find a sympathetic taxi driver with some knowledge of German, who was able to point out the spot where those who had died in the camp were likely to have been buried. At that stage it was just an indistinct mound, close to the city dump. After the demise of the Ceaucescu regime and thanks to the initiative of some locals and the International Red Cross, the plot was converted into a dignified 'German Soldiers' Cemetery', to use the official designation. It contains the graves of 2,997 German soldiers, of whom 1,726 are known by name. My father's name does not appear on the register, but his death had been verified by an eyewitness. It was a fitting place to mourn his loss thirty-four years after the event.

Notes

1 Ian Kershaw, *Hitler, the Germans and the Final Solution* (New Haven, CT: Yale University Press, 2008); Till Bastian, *Furchtbare Soldaten: deutsche Kriegsverbrechen im Zweiten Weltkrieg* (Munich: C. H. Beck, 1997); Wendy Lower, *Hitler's Furies: German Women in the Nazi Killing Fields* (London: Vintage, 2014).

2 Harald Welzer, Sabine Moller and Karoline Tschuggnall, *'Opa war kein Nazi': Nationalsozialismus und Holocaust im Familiengedächtnis* (Frankfurt am Main: Fischer Taschenbuch, 2002).

3 Jeremy Noakes, 'The Oldenburg Crucifix Struggle of November 1936: A Case Study of Opposition in the Third Reich', in *The Shaping of the Nazi State*, ed. Peter Stachura (London: Croom Helm, 1978), 213.

4 Noakes, 'The Oldenburg Crucifix Struggle', 210–33.

5 'Titus Maria Horten', *Gedenkbuch für die NS-Opfer aus Wuppertal*. Available at: https://www.gedenkbuch-wuppertal.de/de/person/horten (accessed 30 July 2020).

6 On attitudes towards Jewish victims of Kristallnacht in Vechta, see Maria Anna Zumholz, 'Der Kreuzkampf – Katholisches Milieu und Widerstand: der Kreuzkampf im Oldenburger Land', in *Katholisches Milieu und Widerstand: Der Kreuzkampf im Oldenburger Land im Kontext des nationalsozialistischen Herrschaftsgefüges*, ed. Maria Anna Zumholz (Berlin: LIT, 2012), 68–70.

7 Hermann Schulz, Hartmut Radebold and Jürgen Reulecke, *Söhne ohne Väter: Erfahrungen der Kriegsgeneration*, 3rd edn (Berlin: Ch. Links, 2009).

11

A child's view of war: Nazi occupation, Resistance and civil war in north-eastern Italy, 1943–5

Enrico Dal Lago

On a July morning [in 1944] … among the women of the Lago area … [a rumour spread that] the Germans and the Fascists had arrested and taken away all the men they could find. Mom immediately called il Nane *and told him to 'run now to papa … and tell him to hide because this time the Germans will take away every man they find'.* Il Nane *ran to the path … and, as soon as he did this, he heard bullets whistle just past him. Realising he was the target [of a German machine gun] … he threw himself on the ground and, slithering on the grass, … he entered the woods. He could, therefore, reach papa, who was working in the field, and tell him what Mom had said to him.*[1]

The excerpt above is from my father's memoir of his childhood in north-eastern Italy during World War II. At the time of these events, my father, Olinto Dal Lago (Figure 11.1), lived with his family near Vicenza, in the Veneto, and was only 11 years old. He was nicknamed 'il Nane' ('the Dwarf'), because

FIGURE 11.1 *Olinto Dal Lago, 'Il Nane', pictured in 2010s*

he was short for his age. He was the youngest of four brothers and the only one who had not gone to the mountains to fight with the Resistance but had stayed behind with his family.[2] His parents were peasants; his father worked in the fields while his mother worked at home in the Lago area of a little village called Nogarole Vicentino. The excerpt describes a common occurrence in northern Italy in the summer of 1944: Nazi and Fascist soldiers' searching for partisans amongst the local population, followed by the arrest and deportation of the men and by the execution of civilians as an exemplary punishment for the community's lack of cooperation with the occupier and for its support of the Resistance. Fortunately, in this case, my father was able to warn my grandfather and tell him just in time to hide, thanks to no small courage on his part since he had to avoid German bullets directed at him. The brutality of the war, shown in this excerpt, the daily experience of the Nazi occupation, the deportations and the massacres, and the constant fear for his life and for the lives of the members of his family, left my father with traumatic and unforgettable memories of the period 1943–5, which he passed on to me and to my brother when we were children and which, a few years ago, he decided to put in writing in a little book, from which the above excerpt is taken. Published in Italian, naturally, the book's title may be rendered into English as 'Resistance Told to the Children, 1943–45: The memories of *il Nane*,

Caterina Dal Lago

La Resistenza
raccontata ai ragazzi

1943-45
I ricordi del Nane,
bambino di 10 anni

FIGURE 11.2 *Illustrated cover of Olinto Dal Lago's memoir of his wartime childhood*

a Ten-Year-Old boy'.[3] (See Figure 11.2.) This book was edited and published by his sister Caterina and he wrote it primarily for the benefit of his granddaughter and other children of her age, of which more later. This essay is based mostly on my father's memories of his World War II experiences and, to a lesser degree, on the impact they had on me, when I first heard them from him at the age of 10 or 11, about the same age my father had been in 1943–4.

A descent into civil war

In the autumn of 1943, the Italian government switched sides in the middle of World War II, shortly after having overthrown the Fascist dictatorship and imprisoned Benito Mussolini. After an initial period of confusion, following the 8 September armistice between Italy and the Allied Forces – during which the Italian soldiers were overwhelmed by their former German allies, now-turned enemies, while the Nazi troops occupied the entirety of northern and central Italy as far south as Rome – the Fascist government was restored, following Mussolini's liberation by the Germans, under the name of 'Italian Social Republic' (*Repubblica Sociale Italiana* or *R.S.I.*) sometimes called the 'Republic of Salò', from the name of the Lake Garda town where it had its headquarters. The restored Fascist government acted as the legitimate authority in northern and central Italy and considered as deserters all those who did not follow its call to arms. These deserters were, effectively, the individuals and groups who became partisans and organized the Resistance against the Nazis' occupation and their Fascist collaborators. Though it was little more than a puppet regime, the Fascist Republic of Salò was, nevertheless, a government made by Italians and with Italian soldiers and therefore the period 1943–5 in northern Italy witnessed not alone a war waged by Italians against the German Army and the Nazi occupation but also a true and simultaneous civil war between Italian Fascists and Italian partisans, as the history-writing of this period has acknowledged since the 1980s.[4]

The 1943–5 civil war literally divided families, communities, towns and villages, and its impact was very strong in my father's little village in the Veneto, where the majority sided with the Resistance but a few – known by everybody to be Fascists – acted as ruthless collaborators with the Nazi authorities, despite their own ties with the local community. While the Allies advanced slowly and with much difficulty up the Italian peninsula after their landings in the very south of Italy in September 1943 opposition to the Nazis and Fascists in the occupied areas, in the period between the autumn of 1943 and their final liberation at the end of April 1945, was mainly provided by irregular guerrilla groups of partisans who, especially in the mountainous regions, engaged in a prolonged conflict with the German Army and the Fascist soldiers. While they were not formally part of any army, most of the partisans had military experience and they tried to create a semblance of military structure in their formations – with different levels of hierarchy and with commandants in charge of rank-and-file combatants, all with specific battle names. Thus, the eldest of my father's brothers, Pietro Dal Lago (nicknamed 'Pierin' (Little Peter))[5] was a partisan commandant in the Resistance in charge of a group of young volunteers, under the nom de guerre 'Pacifico' (meaning 'peaceful'), while my father's third eldest brother Egisto was nicknamed 'Tranquillo' ('calm').[6] The occupied region of the Veneto, and specifically the area where my father's family lived, was where the Wehrmacht had its headquarters in northern Italy, at Recoaro, under the command of General Albert Kesselring. The Veneto was also where the Fascist Republic of Salò's navy had its main operational centre. In this region, partisans such as my two eldest uncles fought the Nazis and Fascists in a particularly brutal guerrilla campaign-cum-civil war which resulted in many victims amongst the civilian population.

Italy's troubled 1970s and the moral meaning of Resistance memories

It was in the mid-1970s, which was a very particular time in Italy, when, as children, my brother and I first heard my father's stories about his childhood and about his brothers' participation in the Resistance and the effective civil war of 1943–5. Considering only thirty years had elapsed since World War II, memories of the occupation were still fresh in the minds of many people. Those of us in the younger generations were very much influenced by how much time and effort the politicians – the most senior of whom had been partisans – and civil society invested in remembrance of that tragic era, especially with regard to the Resistance struggle against Nazis and Fascists. In Italy, this remembrance had particular features because the post-war Italian Republic had been founded as a result of the collapse and then defeat of the Fascist regime and its Nazi allies in World War II. Therefore, remembering World War II meant at once not only celebrating the costly struggle that had led to the victory of democracy over dictatorship, in which the Resistance had made a substantial contribution, but also reasserting the importance of the democratic values on which the Italian Republic was founded.[7]

This was particularly important in the mid-1970s, since Italy was then trapped in a seemingly never-ending spiral of violence, often on a mass scale, equally fuelled by groups at the extreme right and at the extreme left. This violence kept the entire country in a continuous state of apprehension as every day the papers and the TV brought news of terrorist attacks against particular individuals or of a massacre caused by the explosion of a bomb in a crowd. Hundreds of people lost their lives in Italy in those years, the so-called *Anni di piombo* ('years of lead'), and the terrorist attacks and massacres of this period – collectively called *Strategia della tensione* ('strategy of tension') – have been now found, after many years and inquiries, to be part of major plans to destabilize the relatively recent democratic institutions of the Italian Republic with the ultimate goal of preventing the Italian Communist Party, the largest in western Europe, from becoming part of the government and perhaps even of establishing another extreme right-wing dictatorship.[8] And since Neo-Fascist groups were at the heart of these plans, as were also extreme left terrorists such as the infamous Red Brigades, this reassertion of the validity and stability of democratic principles through the continuous remembrance of the Resistance's victory over Nazis and Fascists, at the cost of several thousands dead, assumed a particularly important contemporary meaning.[9]

Even if I was only 10 or 11 years old in 1976–7 (my brother being three years older than I), the connections and the parallels, emphasized by both media and politicians, between the partisans' struggle against the Fascists in 1943–5 and the struggle against the 1970s terrorists, seen as the 'enemies of the Republic' – as in the title of an important recent book[10] – did not escape me. There is no doubt, therefore, that my brother and I listened to my father's stories on the Resistance and World War II interpreting them in the different, but equally difficult and tragic, context of the mid-1970s in which we lived. In Piedmont, the region in which I was born and raised, the terrorists were particularly active in the 1970s. At the same time, the brutal 1943–5 civil war between Fascists and partisans which my father had witnessed in the Veneto had had its wartime counterpart in the Piedmont region where he now lived with us, his family. The Nazi occupation had left indelible traces on the local population in both regions.[11] Though my father's stories related to the Veneto, the entire environment around me had already prepared me to understand them, since they were similar to many other stories still told by many eyewitnesses of the events of World War II in Piedmont. More widely still, such common experiences informed the literary output of great authors, such as Italo Calvino, Beppe Fenoglio and others, whose works we read at school.[12] The context of the mid-1970s, in which I lived therefore, was as crucial as the context of the war years for my understanding of my father's memories when I heard them for the first time.

Childhood in a time of terror

The first vivid impression I have of my father's memories relates to his recollections of the tragic events following the 8 September 1943 armistice between Italy and the Allied Forces, with the Nazi invasion of northern Italy:

In the days around 8 September 1943, *Il Nane* listened to the adults [who were] having heated arguments over what was happening in Italy. They talked about the king [Victor Emmanuel III], who had arrested Mussolini. ... The men especially expressed their fears [saying]: 'What will the Germans do now?' The next day, it became known that, from the Brennero [an Alpine pass], columns of German soldiers had reached our northern cities, and especially the barracks where our soldiers were stationed.[13]

One of those soldiers in the barracks in Piedmont was my father's second eldest brother, Danilo,[14] about whom the family did not know whether he was alive or dead, until 'one day ... suddenly Danilo appeared across the fields ... all dishevelled, covered in mud, and in a state of shock'.[15] He told the family that he had been arrested by the Germans and put with others on a cattle wagon but had miraculously escaped, dodging bullets. Wandering for days and nights, he had finally managed to board unseen a train bound for the Veneto. My uncle Danilo's tale is similar to that of many Italian soldiers who, left with no instructions from their government or their superiors, were caught unaware by the German Army at the time of the armistice. On the other hand, Danilo was one of the minority of these men who managed to avoid being sent to concentration camps on one of those infamous cattle wagons, a possibility which terrified me when I heard this tale first since I had learned about the concentration camps in school – where we read the books written by camp survivor Primo Levi.[16]

My father's memories then jump to the spring of 1944, describing through the eyes of a child, the beginnings of the Resistance movement in the area around Vicenza, which originated as a movement of opposition to the Fascist Republic of Salò's call to arms:[17]

> In the spring of 1944, in Nogarole and in the nearby villages, there were meetings among the young who were of military service age to discuss what to do ... [then] it became known that ... the first groups of partisans were taking shape. ... [Subsequently] at the beginning of June, in the area between Tezze, Arzignano, Chiampo and Nogarole [all villages close to each other], the first 'round-up' by Germans and Fascists looking for *rebels* [deserters] took place. In the following days ... many of the young left their home, among them also Pierin, *il Nane*'s eldest brother.[18]

The Nazi and Fascist retaliation against the communities and families who helped their sons and daughters turn partisans, and with them the Resistance, then started and intensified before reaching its peak in the summer of 1944, the period which my father's memory quoted at the start of this essay refers to. For the entire period between July and September, the Germans implemented a policy of carpet round-ups, combing systematically, with a large number of soldiers, every inch of the territory between the Wehrmacht headquarters and Nogarole:

> The soldiers proceeded combing everything, as if they formed an immense human *rake*,[19] which searched lawns, fields, woods, houses, leaving no stone unturned … with their weapons ready, they entered in one house after the other … in the barns, they pierced the hay with their bayonets, in the basement they often broke bottles … if they found evidence that *rebels* had been hosted, they burned down the house. … One of the scariest *round-ups* was the one that, on 9th September [1944], hundreds and hundreds of Germans and Fascists conducted all over the Lessini mountains … in order to defeat once and for all the *rebels* in the region. … For the entire day the air was filled with cannonballs, mortar shots, gunshots and hand grenades … when, as the night descended, the Germans left … they said that dozens of partisans had died.[20]

My grandmother Ilena feared that Egisto and Pierin, her two sons in the Resistance, had been killed by the Germans but then, the following night, Egisto came back and told the family that, luckily, Pierin had been sent on a mission with his patrol before the Germans struck and that he had managed to save himself by hiding under a bridge until the next day. 'After the round-ups of that tragic summer', writes my father, '*il Nane* heard that the Germans and the Fascists had managed to instil terror everywhere among the people'.[21] This period between the summer and the autumn of 1944, significantly, marked the peak of the Nazi terror tactics and of their massacres against civilians in the occupied areas all over northern and central Italy. The worst massacres occurred at Sant'Anna di Stazzema in Tuscany (12 August 1944), with over 560 people killed, and at Marzabotto in Emilia (29 September–5 October 1944), with over 770 dead.[22]

As these war atrocities were routinely commemorated in the media in the 1970s and we also learned about them at school, my brother and I could see that my father's memories were entirely consistent with the view of this period then prevalent in Italy – a view that glorified the Resistance as a great popular movement led by partisan heroes against the brutal occupation of the Nazis and the criminal collaboration of the Fascists. This was, essentially, the foundational myth of the post-war Italian Republic which, back then, very few questioned. The truth, however, was much more complex, and at least some of it was not known by many: that is the reason why there is nothing in my father's memories about wrongs and even crimes committed by the partisans. Only in relatively recent times, as a result of the longer temporal distance from World War II, has Italian public opinion begun to nuance this view, prompted to do so by several Italian scholars who have begun investigating and telling a more objective history of the events in Italy in 1943–5 – squarely recognizing that those events were part of a true civil war between Italians, not just part of a war of liberation conducted against Nazis and Fascists. Like all civil wars, therefore, this one also saw atrocities and war crimes on both sides – meaning that not all partisans were upstanding moral heroes and not all Fascists were simply criminals – and often personal vengeance was more important than any ideological motivation as a reason for the occurrence of atrocities and crimes.[23]

But back then, in the 1970s, neither myself nor my brother – and equally not my father, who was just a boy in the 1940s – knew anything about this, and the story, simple but effective, of the great popular revolt of the Resistance led by larger-than-life partisan figures against the barbaric German invaders and the brutal Fascists fed our children's fantasies in ways not dissimilar from a fairy tale with a clear contrast between all the good characters, at the centre of whom was my father's family on one side and all the bad characters on the other side. Also important is the fact that this view, which fitted perfectly a child's sensibility in portraying in relatively simple and straightforward terms a very complex series of events, because it was told by my father as a child's memory to us children, could only portray the Resistance as one single monolithic movement of heroic partisans fighting against the oppressor. But even in this case, as my brother and I discovered later, the reality was far more complex, and the ideological divisions among the partisans not only were very deep, but they also represented the early iterations of the political and party conflicts that characterized Italy in the 1970s.[24] These, then, were even replicated in microcosm in my father's family, in which, as in the country at large, there were both Christian Democrats and Communists – that is, the two most important majority party and opposition party in Italy throughout the period between the late 1940s and the early 1990s – among those who fought against Nazis and Fascists. When my brother and I initially heard, as children, my father's childhood memories, we certainly had little knowledge of these internal divisions among the partisans, but we also found it comfortable to imagine the partisans all united in the one overarching objective of liberating the country from brutal occupation and dictatorship.

Boy helper of the Resistance and a narrow escape

In my father's memories, one of the episodes related to the Resistance and to the partisans' fight against the occupation that stands out, and one which I also well remember him telling, is about when his eldest brother Pierin, the partisan commandant named *Pacifico*, gave him an important task, effectively involving him in the Resistance despite his young age. It happened during the winter of 1944–5, which was unusually harsh and cold and which had forced the partisans to come down from the mountains and hide their weapons until spring came, when better weather would allow them to continue the fight against Nazis and Fascists. On that occasion, Pierin took the weapons of his patrol and hid them in a hole in the ground behind the family home. He only told my father – that is, his little brother – about this, and charged him with the task of taking out the weapons from their hiding place in the sunny days and leaving them out for a while so that they would not rust. My father says that 'proud for the task he was assigned, *il Nane* never said a word to anybody', though his secret could have easily gotten him killed.[25] This might have been the case particularly on a day in February when, as he was putting back the weapons in their hiding place, he saw soldiers coming towards their house:

> He hurried to put everything back in its place, making sure nobody saw him; then, running and breathless, he rushed to the house, shouting 'the Ger …', but the word died in his throat; sitting in the kitchen, four soldiers were eating bread and salami, served with awe by his mother Ilena. … 'Thank God,' *il Nane* thought, 'they didn't go to the back of the house, otherwise they would have discovered the weapons and the hiding place.'[26]

This occasion, in which my father narrowly escaped being discovered hiding Resistance weapons by the Nazis, and perhaps even being killed along with his family, was part of a sudden and unexpected round-up that occurred in the area around Nogarole, in February 1945, 'the first [round-up] of the new year'.[27] During that period, as the terribly cold winter finally gave way to the spring, and the Resistance was able to resume its guerrilla warfare, the civil war of Italians against Italians – that is, partisans versus Fascists – intensified, and there were often sudden appearances of Fascists' squads looking for partisans hiding in their families' houses. One of those squads caught by surprise an uncle of my father called Zio Santo, who was hiding two of his children, my father's cousins, together with other partisans in his barn. The Fascists discovered them and first shot one of his children and then killed the other one, after threatening my father's uncle, and killed the other partisans a little while later. This was not only a particularly traumatic event for my father and for his family and community but also one of a number of war crimes committed in that area by Fascist soldiers who, as in other similar circumstances, killed five partisan prisoners after they had surrendered.[28]

At the beginning of 1945, the number of partisans all over northern Italy was growing exponentially; they would reach more than 200,000 by April of that year.[29] At the same time, the actions of the Allied Forces against the

Nazi occupation of northern Italy intensified, and so did the carpet bombing of cities whose industrial production was essential to the Nazi war machine. One of those cities was Vicenza, and its bombing could be seen clearly from the countryside where my father's family lived:

> It usually happened at night and it was preceded by an incredibly long siren, which the entire region could hear in the silence of the night. After the siren stopped, a few minutes later, the dark sound of hundreds of bomber planes seemed to shake the sky, while the immense cloud formed by the machines, distinguishable in the dusk like small lights in the sky, slowly approached the city until they were above it and then they released hundreds of bombs. In falling, the bombs ignited [huge] flames which reddened the sky in a sinister, but also striking, way.[30]

The combined action of partisans, under the leadership of the *Comitato di Liberazione Nazionale*, or *CLN* (Committee for National Liberation), and of the Allies, culminated in the large-scale offensive of mid- to late April 1945, when the Nazis were expelled from northern Italy and the Fascist government was ended once and for all with the death of Mussolini. In the weeks preceding these events, 'the news spread among the people' – in my father's words – 'that the Allies, after freeing first Rome [on 4 June 1944] and then Florence [on 11 August 1944], were rapidly advancing towards northern Italy'. Foreseeing imminent defeat, in April, large numbers of German soldiers departed from the Veneto to try to reach the Brenner pass, which led to Germany. As they left, though, the Nazis did not give up without a fight: 'groups of partisans had tried to confront them and the outcome had been one of very harsh combat', as the German soldiers took hostages and continued to kill people in retaliation. Eventually, the day of the final liberation came on the last Sunday of April 1945:

> After the 11am mass, the church square in Nogarole filled with partisan patrols, still alert to the possibility of a last attack by the Fascist squads, and yet already celebrating the Liberation that had just happened. That morning, the bells of all the churches in every village tolled happily for a long time and, after so many years of living in fear, the people stayed in the square, enjoying the end of the war which they had awaited for so long.[31]

From 'il Nane' to the Italian children of today

More than sixty-five years after the end of the war, my father decided to put down on paper his memories for the benefit of his granddaughter Giulia, then a teenager. He wrote the stories about the events I have referred to in this essay as they came to him and as he remembered them, talking in third person about himself as *il Nane*. A few years later, when he thought he had completed his collection of memories, he showed it to his sister Caterina, a former schoolteacher in the region of Piedmont. Caterina decided that it was worth publishing a book out of them and bring it to the schools to teach the schoolchildren about the Resistance and the Italian civil war of 1943–5. She herself could have had little in terms of personal memories of the period, since she was only 4–6 years old at that time, but she grew up with the memories of her older siblings, whom she admired, and the cult of the Resistance and the partisans – which was so strong in the Veneto in the aftermath of World War II. As a mother and a teacher in Piedmont, she did her best to convey to her own children and to the schoolchildren the importance of remembering that tragic period as the foundational moment of Italian democracy. My father also made a similar contribution in this sense as a schoolteacher and, eventually, as principal of a junior high school in my home town.

Like my father I too have pursued a career in education, albeit in a different way, becoming a historian working at a university. I ask myself what impact my youthful listening to our father talking about those terrible years in northern Italy had on my own scholarly interests? Certainly, this experience gave to my brother and myself a strong sense of the importance of the past as a living memory conditioning the present. In my own case, it was certainly one of the main factors that inspired me to become a historian and, eventually, also to publish a book on another earlier, but much lesser known, civil war which occurred in southern Italy in the years 1861–5.[32]

As I stated at the outset, my father's act of writing down his World War II memories formed the basis of the book *La Resistenza raccontata ai ragazzi* (2017), which my aunt Caterina edited and to which she added documents and other snippets of family history and explanatory material on the Resistance – all of which added to the book's teaching value. Moreover, the book was illustrated with drawings done by children; in fact, three of Caterina's own grandchildren contributed artwork. The young illustrators succeeded in expressing in visual terms the essence of my father's memories with their direct and straightforward style, which really gives the impression of his wartime childhood experience (see Figure 11.2). For these reasons, the book has proven particularly appealing to children and it has had quite a lot of success as a teaching resource in the schools of my area. It certainly is a unique document in its own right, presenting the terrible events of 1943–5 in Italy – with their combination of brutal Nazi occupation and civil war between the Resistance and the Fascists – as seen through the eyes of a 10-year-old child who happened to be born and raised in one of the areas of northern Italy where World War II was at its most lethal and cruel, especially with regard to the many victims among the civilian population.

Notes

1   Olinto Dal Lago, 'Raffiche di mitragliatrice [Machine Gun Bursts]', in *La Resistenza raccontata ai ragazzi. 1943–45: I ricordi del Nane, bambino di 10 anni* [Resistance Told to the Children. 1943–45: The Memories of *il Nane*, a Ten-Year Old Boy], ed. Caterina Dal Lago (Ivrea: Bolognino, 2017), 24. All translations from the above book are my own.

2   Altogether, there were nine Dal Lago children, four boys (Pietro, aged 21 in 1944; Danilo, 20; Egisto, 17; Olinto, 11) and five girls (Rita, 15; Teresa, 14; Pierina, 10; Caterina, 5; Onelia, 4).

3   See full bibliographical details in note 1.

4   See especially Claudio Pavone, *A Civil War: A History of the Italian Resistance* (London: Verso, 2014), [originally published in Italian in 1991]; and Gianni Oliva, *I vinti e i liberati, 8 Settembre 1943-25 Aprile 1945: Storia di due anni* [The Vanquished and the Freed, 8 September 1943–25 April 1945: A History of Two Years] (Milan: Mondadsosi, 1994).

5   Pietro Dal Lago (1923–2014) was a partisan commandant in the legendary *Brigata Stella* (Star Brigade), and was in charge both of recruiting volunteers and also of leading them in a number of high-risk actions. He was awarded the rank of sub lieutenant in which he fought during the last months of the war (September 1944–April 1945); later, in 1966, he received from the Italian government the 'War Merit Cross' for his role in the Resistance. See his obituary published by ANPI Vicenza, regional branch of veterans' organization the National Association of Partisans of Italy. Available at: https://www.anpi-vicenza.it/pietro-dal-lago-pacifico-1923-2014/ (accessed 15 March 2020).

6   Egisto Dal Lago (1924–2013) was only 17 years old in 1944 when, in my father's recollection, he 'disappeared from home. … Later, the family came to know that he had left to join the partisans and that Pierin, not succeeding in convincing him to go back home, had enrolled him with the [battle-] name *Tranquillo*'; see Olinto Dal Lago, 'Egisto Dal Lago, "Tranquillo" ', in *La Resistenza raccontata ai ragazzi*, ed. Dal Lago, 54.

7   On these points, see especially Miguel Gotor, *L'Italia nel Novecento: Dalla sconfitta di Adua alla vittoria di Amazon* [Twentieth-Century Italy: From the Defeat at Adwa to the Victory of Amazon] (Turin: Passaggi Einaudi, 2019), 156–71. It is worth mentioning the importance of the international dimension of the post–World War II Italian Republic, which, after the defeat of Fascism, had become a founding member of a democratic European Community, together with post–Nazi West Germany, itself a federal republic. The two former dictatorships and enemy countries were now on the same side of the Iron Curtain, being also both crucial strategic members of NATO and thus heavily influenced by US foreign policy (the main reason why extremist left terrorism was particularly strong there – with the Red Brigades in Italy and

the Red Army Faction in West Germany). Yet, in the historical memory and in popular culture of 1970s Italy, the brutality of German occupation during World War II was very much alive and this was apparent from a number of historical studies, novels and movies – the latter ones influenced by the great 1940s and 1950s works of neorealism – which were still produced about the war in the 1960s and 1970s.

8 See Guido Crainz, *Il paese mancato: Dal miracolo economico agli anni ottanta* [A Missed Country: From the Economic Miracle to the Eighties] (Rome: Donzelli Virgolette, 2005), 363–411.

9 In the region of 29,000 people lost their lives in the Italian civil war of 1943–5; see Gotor, *L'Italia nel Novecento*, 137.

10 See Vladimiro Satta, *I nemici della repubblica: Storia degli anni di piombo* [The Enemies of the Republic: A History of the Years of Lead] (Milan: Rizzoli, 2016).

11 See *Dizionario della Resistenza* [Dictionary of the Resistance], *Vol. 1: Storia e Geografia della liberazione* [History and Geography of the Liberation], ed. Enzo Collotti, Renato Sandri and Frediano Sessi (Turin: Einaudi, 2000); and *Vol. 2: Luoghi, formazioni, protagonisti* [Places, Units, Protagonists] (Turin: Einaudi, 2001).

12 See Alberto Asor Rosa, 'La cultura', in *Storia d'Italia, Vol. 4: Dall'Unità a oggi*, Part 2, ed. Ruggero Romano and Corrado Vivanti (Turin: 1975). For examples of this literature, see especially Italo Calvino, *The Path to the Nest of Spiders* (London: Collins, 1957) [originally published in Italian in 1947]; Beppe Fenoglio, *The Twenty-Three Days of the City of Alba* (Hanover, NH: Steerforth, 2002) [original Italian edition 1952] and *Johnny the Partisan* (London: Quartet Books, 1995) [original in Italian in 1968].

13 Olinto Dal Lago, 'Quei giorni intorno all'8 Settembre 1943', in *La Resistenza raccontata ai ragazzi*, ed. Dal Lago, 15.

14 Danilo Dal Lago (1927–2015).

15 Dal Lago, 'Quei giorni intorno all'8 Settembre 1943', 16. On the significance of the 8 September 1943, see Elena Aga Rossi, *Una nazione allo sbando. L'armistizio italiano del Settembre 1943 e le sue conseguenze* [A Nation in Disarray: Italy's September 1943 Armistice and Its Consequences] (Bologna: Il Mulino, 2006); and Gotor, *L'Italia nel Novecento*, 122–8.

16 See especially Primo Levi, *If This Is a Man* (London: Orion Press, 1959), which was originally published in Italian in 1947.

17 On the different phases and features of the Resistance movement, see Santo Peli, *Storia della Resistenza in Italia* (Turin: Einaudi, 2006).

18 Olinto Dal Lago, 'La Repubblica di Salò', in *La Resistenza raccontata ai ragazzi*, ed. Dal Lago, 19–20.

19 The Italian term for round-up is *rastrellamento*, which comes from the word *rastrello*, meaning 'rake', as in a garden rake.

20 Olinto Dal Lago, 'I terribili *rastrellamenti* dell'estate 1944' and 'Lo spaventoso *rastrellamento* della Piana', in *La Resistenza raccontata ai ragazzi*, ed. Dal Lago, 23; 27–8.

21 Dal Lago, 'Lo spaventoso *rastrellamento* della Piana', 29.

22 See Carlo Gentile, *I crimini di guerra Tedeschi in Italia, 1943–1945* [The War Crimes Committed by Germans in Italy, 1943–1945] (Turin: Einaudi, 2015); and *Zone di Guerra, geografie di sangue: L'Atlante delle stragi naziste e fasciste in Italia (1943–1945)* [War Zones and Maps Made of Blood: Atlas of the Nazi and Fascist Massacres in Italy (1943–1945)], ed. Gianluca Fulvetto and Paolo Pezzino (Bologna: Il Mulino, 2017). Collectively, ten thousand people died as a result of Nazi massacres in Italy in 1943–5.

23 Fundamental in this respect remains Pavone, *A Civil War*; according to Pavone, three wars were fought in Italy in 1943–5: a 'patriotic war' of liberation from the Nazis; a 'civil war' between partisans and Fascists; and a 'class war' to remake Italy along the Soviet model. See also Mirco Dondi, 'Il conflitto interno al movimento di Resistenza' [The Inner Conflict in the Resistance Movement] in *La Resistenza italiana: Storia, memoria, storiografia* [The Italian Resistance: History, Memory, Historiography], ed. Mirco Carrattieri and Marcello Flores (Florence: Goware, 2018); Renzo De Felice, *Rosso e nero* [Red and Black] (Milan: Dalai Editore, 1995); and Renzo De Felice, *Mussolini, l'alleato, Vol. II: La Guerra civile (1943–45)* [Mussolini, the Ally, Vol. II: The Civil War (1943–45)] (Turin: Einaudi, 1997).

24 On the continuity between the ideological divisions among partisans and the post-war parties in Italy, see in particular Roberto Gualtieri, *L'Italia dal 1943 al 1992: DC e PCI nella storia della Repubblica* [Italy from 1943 to 1992: Christian Democrats and Communists in the History of the Republic] (Rome: Carocci, 2006); and Aurelio Lepre, *Storia della Prima Repubblica: L'Italia dal 1942 al 1992* [A History of the First Republic: Italy from 1942 to 1992] (Bologna: Il Mulino, 1993).

25 Olinto Dal Lago, 'Il rigido inverno 1944–45', in *La Resistenza raccontata ai ragazzi*, ed. Dal Lago, 31.

26 Olinto Dal Lago, 'Rastrellamento a sorpresa', in *La Resistenza raccontata ai ragazzi*, ed. Dal Lago, 34–5.

27 Dal Lago, 'Rastrellamento a sorpresa', 35.

28 Olinto Dal Lago, 'La strage dei Grilli' [The Massacre of the Grilli] in *La Resistenza raccontata ai ragazzi*, ed. Dal Lago, 36–8. Grilli was the name of the family that inhabited that particular area.

29 See Gotor, *L'Italia nel Novecento.*

30 Olinto Dal Lago, 'I bombardamenti su Vicenza e Verona … e nugoli di bombardieri verso il Brennero' [The Bombing of Vicenza and Verona … and Flocks of Planes towards the Brenner Pass] in *La Resistenza raccontata ai ragazzi*, ed. Dal Lago, 46.

31 Olinto Dal Lago, 'Le settimane della Liberazione' [The Weeks of the Liberation] in *La Resistenza raccontata ai ragazzi*, ed. Dal Lago, 50.

32 Enrico Dal Lago, *Civil War and Agrarian Unrest: The Confederate South and Southern Italy* (New York: Cambridge University Press, 2018).

12

A Greek tragedy: A small village at war

Constantinos G. Efthymiou

Like many others who grew up in Greece in the 1970s and 1980s, I was conscious from a young age of the terrible shadow that the World War II period cast over the community where I lived. Perhaps that is why I have long been drawn to the poetry of Odysseus Elytis (1911–1996), who became a Nobel Laureate for Literature in 1979. His haunting poems meditating upon the heroism and the suffering of Greek women and men during World War II resonate deeply with me, for reasons that shall become clear in the course of this chapter. Particularly powerful for me is his image of the defiant hand of a resister whose last act is to daub the slogan 'BREAD AND FREEDOM' on a village wall.[1] This story that I recount here of occupation and resistance in a village – my home village of Platystomo located in central Greece – during World War II is very largely based, therefore, on the narrative accounts of those times given by my late father Georgios who, as a youth, participated in the national resistance against the occupation of Greece by the Axis powers in the years 1941–4.[2] Over the years, the level of detail in the version of the story I tell here has been enriched by the tales I first heard as a child from my mother Eleni (Figure 12.1) and other older people from my village, stories which I have checked again in some cases in more recent times as I began to write this chapter. This variety of oral accounts helps to build a narrative framework which reflects all the darkness of those terrible years in Greece, marked by famine, executions and massacres, as well as the heroism, solidarity and compassion shown by people during the war period. My father was just 20 years old when

FIGURE 12.1 *The author Constantinos Efthymiou with his mother Eleni Lambadiari, c.1975*

he was recruited as a member of the left-wing United Panhellenic Organization of Youth (EPON), the youth branch of the National Liberation Front (EAM). Stressing patriotism, resistance and future social reform rather than Marxism to the rural population on which it depended for support, EAM and its military wing, the Greek People's Liberation Army (known as ELAS), sprang in part from the previously small Greek communist movement. Communists had been repressed by the right-wing Greek government of the 1930s. ELAS became the largest partisan group fighting the Nazis in occupied Greece but it was not the only armed resistance movement. On the national level, its main rival was EDES (the National Republican Greek League) which, like ELAS, wanted to liberate Greece but rejected communism. The potential for future conflict between the two factions was clear. My father's youthful involvement with EAM, the first movement above, is a key part of the story I tell here.

A village and a dynamited railway bridge in central Greece

Let me set the scene for my family and community's story; the setting is my village of Platystomo, located in a valley in the region of Fthiotida in the administrative region known still today as Central Greece. In the early 1940s, Platystomo had a resident population of about six hundred people. In this rural community, people's main activity was agriculture, as it remains to some extent to this day. Farmers grew wheat, tobacco plants and also produced vegetables, amongst other foodstuffs. The village had one primary school, while a secondary school was located a short distance away in the small town of Spercheiada. The wider region of central Greece (in which is found Platystomo) is one which witnessed a lot of military activity during World War II, especially as it was the main field of operations of EAM – the movement my father supported. To this day Greeks recall the blowing up of the Gorgopotamos railway bridge on 25 November 1942 – a site less than 50 kilometres away from the village – as one of the major acts of sabotage successfully carried out in Greece during the war. It is notable that this daring operation was conducted jointly by the partisan groups of communist-backed ELAS (the military section of EAM) and its sibling rival EDES, with the support of twelve British commandos from Churchill's Special Operations Executive (SOE). The partisan groups overpowered the Italians guarding the bridge, while the experienced British special forces rigged explosives onto the railway bridge before destroying it. This sabotage was not just a blind partisan action but obeyed a broader strategic logic by helping to cut off the main overland supply routes for German forces in Greece, the Mediterranean theatre and of course the North African theatre of the conflict. For a while, supplies across the Mediterranean via the great Greek port of Piraeus were interrupted.

The contrasting Italian and German occupations

The fact that this important railway viaduct was manned by armed Italian as well as German guards in 1942 reminds us that Greece experienced military aggression from both Fascist Italy and Nazi Germany during World War II. Having annexed Albania in 1939, Mussolini launched an ill thought-out invasion of Greece from there in October 1940, which the Greek Army successfully repelled – pushing the Italians back across Greece's north-western borders. Greece remained vulnerable to further attack though notwithstanding belated Allied help. Hitler ordered the Wehrmacht to attack Yugoslavia and Greece in April 1941. On 27 April the Germans occupied Athens and established a collaborationist government there, the previous government and Greek king having fled into exile. As the swastika flag was raised over the Acropolis, remnants of the Greek Army and of a British, Australian and New Zealander force numbering fifty thousand were evacuated by sea to the island of Crete, then under British occupation (though subsequently lost to the Germans in mid-1942). Defeated Greece was subjected from April 1941 to a tripartite occupation by Germans, Italians and the Bulgarians who had allowed the Wehrmacht to use their territory to launch Hitler's Balkan campaign.

From 1941 till the spring of 1942, my home region of central Greece belonged to the Italian-controlled zone before it passed under direct occupation by the Germans from 1942. (After Mussolini was deposed and the new Italian government quit the alliance with Hitler in September 1943, all Italian zones in Greece reverted to the Germans who now occupied the whole country.) At the local level, people remembered the two occupations differently. My father used to say that the Italian occupation was relatively mild; Italian soldiers carried mandolins and guitars instead of weapons and were polite and friendly with civilians, abstaining from acts of cruelty. Active in the left-wing EPON (the United Panhellenic Organization of Youth), my father used to carry concealed proclamation leaflets calling for the liberation of Greece from the Axis powers. Many times he crossed paths with Italian guards but was never subjected to any form of inspection by them. In contrast, the Wehrmacht inspired dread in the region's rural population; when they marched up village streets, the thunderous sound of the disciplined soldiers' heavy boots struck fear into those who heard them. The coming of the Nazis established a contemporary 'Greek tragedy' as it became linked with what was called a 'line of blood and murder'. German forces treated civilians as potential enemies and when attacked by partisan groups, they retaliated by exterminating various villages. The memory of the massacre of Distomo is still alive and intense. Distomo is a village in central Greece, a little more than 100 kilometres from my home village, where the SS troops executed 228 civilians on 10 June 1944.[3] More villages like Kalavrita and Ypati experienced the same fate. Against the rules of the war the victims were unarmed civilians and not soldiers. The mourning and the news of the massacres spread fast across the villages, establishing a reign of terror. This pattern was repeated across the country. According to the *Penguin History of the Second World War*, the total number of hostages executed in Greece numbers about 45,000 and the Germans, Italians and Bulgarians between them executed another 68,000 Greeks during the occupation period as a whole.[4]

Aris, man of war, and the growing sway of ELAS

A pivotal personality in the creation of ELAS, and its successful growth in the region of central Greece, was a larger-than-life figure known to Greeks as Aris. Originally from Lamia, capital of Central Greece, I can picture him moving across the region, on the run in 1942, establishing control of the territory. His real name was Thanasis Klaras but he adopted the nickname Aris to style himself after the Greek god of war. Aris's partisans' aim was the deliverance of Greece and the establishment of a democratic constitution. At this time, Aris visited our village regularly and sometimes used an old abandoned windmill outside the village as his lair. To the villagers Aris is a hero. People still talk about how, with his very long beard, he looked like an Orthodox bishop. The people revered him like one: my mother remembers how kids of her own age would line up to kiss his right hand in a formal expression of respect and gratitude normally reserved for clergymen. Aris was often accompanied by a real priest, Fr Germanos Dimakos. I met this priest years later, when I was a kid, when he was an abbot of a famous monastery of the region. In fact, many priests took an active role in the resistance just as, at the national level, Archbishop Damaskinos of Athens is credited with saving many Greek Jews from deportation by the Nazis.

With armed resistance taking root there, the mountainous areas of central Greece were unwelcoming places for German occupiers; so the ELAS carved out areas where armed Greek forces had a large degree of control even if the risk of German counter-insurgency attacks remained. Within a short time the EAM became a type of alternative government in parts of Greece, providing new institutions and democratic rule in its territory. They even held elections in which, for the first time in Greek history, women, including the women of Platystomo and other regions controlled by the resistance, had the right to vote, like the men, to elect representatives to a national assembly which would assemble on the summit of Timfristos, the nearest summit totally controlled by Greek People's Liberation Army. Platystomo itself was dubbed 'Little Moscow' in these years because of the village's support for communist-leaning ELAS. The relative security ELAS partisans felt in its vicinity can be glimpsed in a rare surviving contemporary photograph showing four local fighters at rest from their normally tough life (see Figure 12.2).

A cultural renaissance also occurred as part of this democratization and my father, being a member of the partisan youth, took part in amateur theatrical groups that gave performances in the village school and in neighbouring villages. A world of hope was rising up beside the terror of war.

Executions and reprisals in Platystomo – 1943 – and a return visitor

Our sun-scorched Greek landscape is also the ideal field for a Greek tragedy. The war's cycle of blood intruded on the village and its neighbourly farmers.

FIGURE 12.2 *ELAS partisans near Platystomo during resistance period (from left, men identified as Tsimpanoulis, N. Zazas, Th. Zazas and S. Efthymiou)*

Near our village was a spa facility with a luxury hotel that was used as a residence for the commanders of a German battalion which guarded a wood-cutting factory. When they were in charge, the German officers had interactions with the locals, purchasing milk and bread or using the villagers' cars or carts for their transportation needs. These Germans could be both cultured but also serve the brutality of Hitler and the cruelty of Nazism. Some of the officers were highly educated scientists or engineers; they listened to Beethoven, Mozart and Wagner, and some of them had a background in classical and ancient Greek studies, having read Homer and the ancient poets and their tragedies. Yet they might have also witnessed or even taken part in massacres. How can the human conscience become so blinded by ideology, I ask myself? One family memory relates to a German occupier who showed human emotion in an extreme situation. My mother remembers, as a girl of about 6 years old, seeing the tall officers with their impressive military uniforms. She is able to recall one of the enemy soldiers in particular in an incident that characterizes the psychosynthesis or the inner feelings of one of these men. This particular Wehrmacht officer stood in the village square and embraced her and other children while tears rolled down his cheeks. The tearful officer explained to the startled onlookers that his emotions were stirred by the thought of his own children back in Germany. The sight of a Greek child revived the memory of them. Human nature overcomes national boundaries and distances, for a while at least.

Sometime later, in April 1943, a partisan group carried out an impressive operation. Disguised as civilians they managed to capture eleven of the German officers and soldiers stationed in Platystomo. The hostages were transported to the nearest mountain of Iti and executed. The retaliation for the executions of the German officers was harsh. The Wehrmacht forces burned the village and the neighbouring small town of Makrakomi. The people of Platystomo, warned by the partisans, left the village and dispersed into the hills and the mountains. Four older people, who were infirm or had limited mobility, remained in the village where they were slaughtered by the troopers – amongst them an elderly priest, Fr Demetressas. A friend of my father's, Demos Matsoukas, who was only 6 years old at the time, was an eyewitness to these acts. While helping his father, a shepherd, who was minding sheep a few kilometres away, Demos saw the troops arriving and ran to the village to raise the alarm, though by the time he reached it, the villagers had already fled. Demos entered the old priest's house where Fr Demetressas was lying in bed. When the soldiers entered the room, the terrified boy Demos hugged the old man. The troopers asked for Demos to get out of the way but, rigid with fear, he clung to the priest and made no move to stand aside. Fr Demetressas, fearing for the safety of the child, got Demos to leave him alone with the intruders and gave him his blessing. It was the priest's last act; Demos tarried in the front yard of the house until after a while he heard the gunshot that killed the old man.

While these horrors were unfolding in Platystomo, my mother was hiding with family and neighbours in the nearby hills. In the panic, families had been separated and some of her own family were seeking sanctuary in a nearby village. She slept for several nights under the bushes trying to remain silent, as they tried to not reveal their hiding places to German troopers. She can still recall the terror and the pounding of her heart, that of a 6-year-old child, hidden within sight of events in the village. At night, the German troops put up flares to make visible lurking partisans or civilians. The rockets' terrible sounds and glow are etched in my mother's mind. The people of the village returned to their houses after several days when the troopers had been withdrawn. The destroyed houses were rebuilt with the help of a company of British special operatives who were assisting the partisans – who had their headquarters in the nearby mountain village of Asvestis.

Several decades later, Dr Hermann Frank Meyer, a descendant of one of the executed German officers, retraced the steps of his father who had been a primary teacher in Germany before serving as an officer in occupied Greece. Meyer, himself born in 1940 and thus hardly out of infancy when his father was shot, visited the village Platystomo, the last residence of his father whom he could only know through family memories. Peaceably enough, considering the difficult history, this son of the occupier met and talked with people who had met his father during his time in our village. He later wrote a book in German about this remarkable experience.[5]

Ariadni's martyrdom

Another character in the blood-drama was Ariadni, a woman whose name harked back to antiquity, which helped make the story of her life and death even more captivating for me when I was a kid. In our region Ariadni Dalari was – and is – a heroine and a martyr. Even before the war, this exceptional woman was the first female dentist in central Greece which was a conservative and patriarchal rural society. A native of our neighbouring town of Makrakomi, she treated the poor during the war – often not taking payment while at the same time secretly assisting the resistance. In 1944, at the age of 33, she was betrayed to the Gestapo, who interrogated, tortured and executed her. Ariadni's fate was like that of two Athenian girls executed the same year – Electra Apostolou and Iro Konstantopoulou. These two women got national recognition, which sadly eludes Ariadni who is best remembered in our region. All three names, Ariandni, Iro and Electra, are derived from ancient times and these brave women met their ends owing to the violence of the age. In an earlier age, Greeks might well have thought that Nemesis, the goddess of revenge, would be stirred to deal out retribution to the wrongdoers for the crime of the women's executions.

Purge on the left in a Greek village

The Italian anti-Fascist thinker and activist Antonio Gramsci had called this age of dictators the 'era of the monsters'. This small village of Platystomo looks like a theatre of that wider turmoil spanning the globe. Not only were the partisans and their allies, the British commandos, operating against the German troops, but violent struggles between different political fractions of the Greek Communist movement also made themselves felt in our small village. Although the EAM had a diversity of political hues within it, the major political force driving it was the Greek Communist Party (KKE). As elsewhere, a minority of Greek Communists were supporters of the political line taken by Leon Trotsky whom Stalin had had assassinated in Mexico in 1940. Greek Trotskyists were active supporters of the national resistance, including three men in our village who identified as Trotskyist Communists. Two of the men were the brothers Costas and Alekos Efthymiou (who were in fact cousins and friends of my father). Their comrade Nakos Panopoulos was the third. The trio formed our village's link with the partisan units of Aris, with whom they collaborated closely. When some British commandos were being landed on the hill of Lavanitsa, just 4 kilometres away, it was they who organized the rendezvous with the parachutists and transported them safely to Aris's headquarters in the mountains. As during the Spanish Civil War of the previous decade so also in Greece did Stalinists target and assassinate dissident communists. Nakos and Alekos were captured and executed by a militia group with this specific purpose. Today, a monument placed in the central square of the village bears their names alongside those of all local victims of the war. I try to imagine what it must have been like for these two men who fought the Nazis, as they awaited execution by their own comrades. These innocent victims thus added to the trail of blood and the Erinyes, the Greek goddesses who triggered pangs of conscience, must surely have been stirred by these happenings.

The joy of liberation, the shadow of civil war

The German troops finally left central Greece on 18 October 1944. People from the whole region gathered in Liberty Square in the city of Lamia, where Aris gave a major speech marking the liberation on 29 October. For this landmark event, my father walked with others 35 kilometres from Platystomo, staying overnight in the village of Lianokladi, close to Lamia. It was a great celebration and people opened their houses to host the travellers. Next day Liberty Square was packed for the first time in four years – fear gone, people were full of hope for the dawn of a new, peaceful and prosperous era. It was not to be – as, within months, violence broke out between communists and anti-communists. For the next five years Greece experienced recurrent political violence between right and left, beginning in Athens in December 1944, followed by the full-scale Greek Civil War, usually dated from 1946 to 1949, itself part of the emerging Cold War struggle between East and West. It left many scars on Greek life.

As a child, listening to all these narrative accounts of World War II was a fascinating process. This narrative framework, which has been transferred from the ancestors to the descendants, is part of a previous long cultural tradition which originated in the Homeric era and over the centuries created myths, legends, literature and history. Today, it is positive to note that, since 2017, a joint team of scholars at the University of Athens and the Freie Universität of Berlin have been compiling a wealth of oral history about occupied Greece, making their findings available on the internet in Greek, German and English.[6] Behind the stories I have shared here from my parents and the people of Platystomo lie not only fear and terror but also longings for peace. The World War II generation kept the memory alive so that, in time, the people of Europe decided to collaborate willingly in order to leave behind the divisive past and create a new united Europe – our common home. Villages like mine are part of the difficult history that made such a 'Europe' necessary and a living sign of hope.

Notes

This chapter is dedicated in loving memory of my father Georgios Efthymiou (1923–2019). In addition, I would like to record my special thanks to my mother Eleni Lambadiari for her narrative accounts of the war years. I would like to acknowledge the guidance of this volume's editors (and my colleagues) Dr Róisín Healy and Dr Gearóid Barry. Gearóid's help with the proofing was especially valuable. Elias Zazas kindly shared the photograph of the local partisans and Fotis Ntallis reproduced it for me in suitable quality. Finally, particular thanks go to Dr Constantina Papatriantafyllopoulou (School of Chemistry, NUI Galway) for her critical proofreading of this essay.

1   See Elytis's long poem 'The Axion Esti', in *The Collected Poems of Odysseus Elytis*, trans. Jeffrey Carson and Nikos Sarris (Baltimore, MD: The Johns Hopkins University Press, 1997), 119–90.

2   For a short and reliable overview in English of Greece's place in the course of World War II, see Peter Calvocoressi, Guy Wint and John Pritchard, *The Penguin History of the Second World War* (London: Penguin, 1999), 169–77; 307–10. See also the following national studies documenting the war years and their aftermath in Greece: Eleanor Hancock and Craig A. J. Stockings, *Swastika over the Acropolis: Re-Interpreting the Nazi Invasion of Greece in World War Two* (Leiden: Brill, 2013); Mark Mazower, *Inside Hitler's Greece: The Experience of Occupation, 1941–44* (New Haven, CT: Yale University Press, 1993); Mark Mazower, *After the War was Over: Reconstructing the Family, Nation and State in Greece, 1943–1960* (Princeton: Princeton University Press, 2000).

3   Subsequent to its liberation in autumn 1944, Distomo featured in a hard-hitting photoessay in a bestselling American magazine; 'What the Germans Did to Greece', *Life*, 27 November 1944, 21–7.

4   Calvocoressi, Wint and Pritchard, *Penguin History*, 307–8.

5   Hermann Frank Meyer, *Vermißt in Griechenland: Schicksale im griechischen Freiheitskampf 1941–1944* (Missing in Greece: Human Destinies during the Greek Liberation Struggle, 1941–1944) (Berlin: Verlag Frieling, 1992).

6   'Memories of the Occupation in Greece'. Available at: http://www.occupation-memories.org/en/index.html (accessed 31 March 2020).

13

A Russian Jewish family remembers the Siege of Leningrad

Irina Ruppo

'When they told us the war had started, we ran to the park. We were so young, 12, and 13, we were excited, we ran to find foreign spies.' Granny Lucia first told me that story sometime in the late 1980s on Soviet Victory Day, 9 May. At the time my family was living in Leningrad (before that and now again called St. Petersburg), a place of incredible beauty, which I also knew from school to be a 'hero-city that withstood the siege'. This is where my paternal grandmother Lucia and her sister, my maternal grandmother Raya,[1] grew up (see Figure 13.1). Their stories were part of the city's history, but they also stood apart from the official narrative.

When I first heard these stories I thought of them as part of family tradition. At once scary and comforting, they were reminders of earlier times when people were more stoical. I was around 8. I thought my grandparents and their guests were a bit funny: they fussed over tea sets as if they were priceless treasures and over freshly cooked potatoes with butter as if they were delicacies, but I was admonished for finding this amusing. Those people, I was told, had been through great hardships. Suffering and heroism were hidden behind their love for simple food, good appearances and of nice things like porcelain figurines on the bookshelves and china tea sets. Lucia's and Raya's stories of the famine, the bombings, of Raya's near-death experience during the evacuation were some of mine and my mother's earliest memories.

FIGURE 13.1 *Sisters Lucia and Raya Greenberg, Leningrad, c.1940*

They were also the most stable part of our identity, unthreatened by the Soviet state's subversion of individual freedoms. Patriotism was thwarted by the threat of being arrested for such innocuous acts as reading banned literature. Being Jewish meant different things for different generations: my grannies knew some Yiddish and remembered family members observing religious customs, whereas my parents experienced Jewishness not as a religion but as an ethnicity and a source of constant discrimination. Being often rewritten, official history provided no anchor for self-definition. Granny Raya's Siege of Leningrad stories alone provided a seemingly genuine link with history and served as place-based mythology.

However, family lore opened only a narrow view into our city's history. My grannies never mentioned the role of the government in the death by hunger of over one million people who found themselves trapped in Leningrad. Nor was the Holocaust ever mentioned, in spite of all of my family members being Jewish. I remember Granny Lucia mentioning seeing anti-Semitic flyers dropped from German planes, but that story was told without any reference to the mass killings of the Jews in the occupied parts of the Soviet Union. Raya seems to have started telling her stories earlier. My mother (Raya's daughter) remembers hearing about the siege as a child but my uncle, Lucia's son, remembers that Lucia refused to talk about the war. Their mother, Sofia, mentioned the war only in occasional snippets rather than stories.

In the late 2010s, shortly after the death of her husband, my Granny Raya, Raisa Kazachkova (née Greenberg), decided to type up her memoirs on a PC and print them out as a book for her family. Her experiences of the Siege of

Leningrad occupy a large part of the book. As I read it, I noticed that the familiar stories felt different. More questions emerged relating to the meanings of these memories for a family whose members live in several distant countries across the globe. In retelling part of Raya's story here, I would like to uncover some of these meanings.

Adventures, bonfires and air raids: How the war became real

Raya and Lucia Greenberg lived in a communal flat in Zoologicheskiy Pereulok on the Petrograd side of the river Neva in central Leningrad, with their mother Sofia Greenberg and grandmother Elizaveta Abarbanel, who were both widows. With only a year between them, the sisters were opposites of each other. The dark-haired and dark-eyed Raya loved rough-and-tumble with the boys, reading books and telling stories to young children. Lucia had auburn hair and blue eyes. She loved maths and excelled at school. She was quieter, more patient and more reserved than Raya. Both retained memories of a happier and prosperous childhood, of private German lessons and stays in the dacha in the summer, all of which came to an abrupt end when their father died when they were only around the ages of 6 and 7. At the start of the German-Soviet War in June 1941, Lucia was 13, Raya was 12, their mother was 36 and their grandmother was only 53 years old. For the sisters, the war was exciting, as was their short-term evacuation. 'Before September', she writes,

> war was just stuff in the newspapers and on the radio. Big-bellied barrage balloons hung above the city. That was fun. The children were taken out to the country because of the danger. But what danger? Wasn't war going to be over soon, once we have bashed the Germans? The kids talked about the best capital punishment for Hitler. It was like being in a Pioneers' camp [communist scout group]. We had fun. There was great food. We picked wild raspberries (there were thickets of them) and had them with cream for supper. We got up to all sorts of mischief. In the evening we wrapped ourselves in bedsheets, became ghosts and scared the passers-by.[2]

The Leningrad authorities' decision on mandatory evacuation of children was a disastrous move. Several groups of children were transferred not to safety but into the path of the German troops, and many families were separated and parents prevented from retrieving their children.[3] Luckily, for Raya and Lucia, the evacuation was only a pleasant adventure.

They came back, started school on 1 September, and a week later, on 8 September 1941, the first air-raids started:

This was the first time that we heard the horrible whistle of the falling bombs. We all ran outside. There was a huge bonfire … The rollercoasters were burning in the park. They burned well because they were made out of wood. It was unbelievably beautiful. Sparks flew all the way up to the sky. We didn't think it was scary. The grown-ups were panicking, but we marvelled at how strange and beautiful it was. And from another part of the city came black clouds of smoke. That was the food warehouses burning. Can you believe that? All the food for all the people in the city was stored in one place. Everything was burnt to a crisp in one day. They were saying that for days afterwards people who lived nearby picked up sweet earth and ate it.

For Raya, as for most Leningraders at the time, the burning of the Badayev warehouses symbolized the start of the war and provided an explanation for the famine that followed. Even though the widely-held belief that these storage units held all the city supplies is not factually correct, it is an indication of the city administration's failure to protect food supplies from air raids.[4]

The air raids made the war real. Raya recalls coming out of the bomb shelter into a different world:

There wasn't a single house left untouched. One of the walls of the house across from us was sliced clean off. What was once inside, was outside. A big clock with a heavy pendulum hung outside. Another house now had a couch hanging outside. We stopped going to the shelter after that. What was the point? Whatever will be will be. Some people were buried in the shelters. Nobody went looking for them. There wasn't anyone to look for them.

The war changed the family dynamics. The frequent visits to see their aunts and cousins stopped immediately, and with them the occasional encounters with Jewish tradition. The sisters were brought up as atheists, as were most children in the Soviet Union, but Raya recalls making the traditional *matzot* for Passover during one of those visits and hearing her paternal grandmother recite prayers in a 'strange language', which was probably Hebrew. Before the war, the sisters spent most of their time with their grandmother, Elizaveta. Their mother Sofia was away in the evenings. Sofia had always loved fashionable clothes (to the degree it was possible to be fashionable in the times of radical austerity), good company and beautiful things. Raya recalls how she and Lucia used to 'play at being Mom'. They stood in front of the huge mirror in the hall, put on imaginary lipstick, 'powdered' their faces and then pretended to leave the house with a pretty purse clutched in one hand. Once the war started, they would see their mother even less. She got a job at a hospital, had to volunteer to help build city fortifications, and spent a great deal of energy trying to get things for the family on the black market. Sofia was the daughter of a successful jeweller; her late husband managed a sweet factory. As an old woman she often spoke with nostalgia of the short time of the New Economic Policy (1922–8) and of the beautiful things she had once possessed. After 1928, trade, entrepreneurship and keeping valuables became illegal. However, the family might have secretly kept a few objects, which helped them to survive. Raya told me about her mother's partially successful attempts at finding food and necessary commodities for her family: 'one day she came back with an iron stove', another time, she brought in sunflower-seed peels ('fit for a feast'), and once she brought something that 'looked like cheese' but turned out to be soap.

'Dying in different ways', September 1941–March 1942

As the bombings continued Raya and Lucia went to school, but things soon changed:

> There were fewer and fewer kids in the class. Inkpots froze over. Winter came soon. There was no electricity or running water. Soon temperatures dropped to an unheard of -30C, and everything stopped. Snow wasn't white. It was yellow because the plumbing was broken. Tramcars were left in the middle of the roads and looked like they had never been used. There was no more food. At all. … At the start of winter, the standard bread ration was 125 grams per person. The bread was heavy and sticky.

The most important thing, for Raya, were the 'add-ons', the little slices of bread added to the main slice to make up the exact measure of 125 grams. Those little slices could be eaten on the way back. At home, she watched Lucia and her grandmother eat their bread slowly, savouring each crumb. She wanted to be like them, but ended up swallowing her pieces too fast. Lucia had been a fussy eater. She was patient too and saved a few breadcrumbs using a small mirror. Raya had always had a great appetite, and now she was losing her strength fast. For a while, her memoir focuses on the outside. She writes about queuing to fetch water from a hole in the ice on the frozen Neva. People came with 'kettles and small milk pails (we did not have buckets in the city)'. People began to die in the streets. One time a corpse blocked the entrance to their house. Another time, she saw a person fall down dead as she stood in the bread queue. As Raya was the first to lose the use of her legs from hunger, her narrative soon moves inside into the communal flat.

> In the room beside us, a little girl cried all the time. She stood under a portrait of an old man and twisted her finger beside her nose, probably in imitation of an old woman praying. 'Dear god, dear god, give us a bit of bread.' She and her whole family died. Other neighbours had a big red cat that everyone loved. Then she disappeared. Her owners ate her.

As the temperatures continued to drop, all the windows were shattered and the stove had to be used for boiling water. The sisters survived by 'lying under a heap of coats, clothes, and blankets. All [their] conversations were about food'. It felt strange that there was so much 'different food' before the war. It seemed unnecessary. The sisters daydreamed about bread; how good it would be to have bread once victory was achieved, 'maybe just a few different things, but mostly bread'.

Taking clothes off was unthinkable. Their mother shaved off the sisters' hair, but lice still appeared. 'We itched so much that we bled,' Raya writes, 'Still, that's when I read *Anna Karenina* for the first time, and I thought I understood everything.' Raya grew up to become a teacher of Russian literature and language; the comment about Tolstoy's novel is not only about the survival of culture in a place where children got 'used to death' and where 'nobody had any strength or empathy' and 'nobody cried – there were no tears'. The point here is also about her identity being formed by and in spite of the war.

Reading the memoir made me realize that the war stories my family grew up with were in fact more about identity and growing up than about what they might have been perceived to be – namely stoicism, or heroism or suffering. The sisters were teenagers at the start of the war; by its end, they felt that they had had a lifetime of experiences in the four years from 1941 to 1945. Unlike their mother, they were protected from political realities and did not participate in her constant search for means to survive; their attention turned within, to growing up and to dying. 'All of us,' writes Raya, 'were dying in different ways.' Grandmother Elizaveta lay down and did not get up anymore, Lucia was able to walk but was covered in sores, and Raya was barely able to move; both 'turned into skeletons'.

Shortly before their grandmother died, the family got a visit from her niece, Frida. The visit was unusual. Other survivors' testimonies suggest that people had no energy for visits and that, moreover, 'people were afraid to invite others to their places … and many wouldn't open the door'.[5] Frida, however, came in:

She was all swollen [from the hunger]. I don't know how she made it to the fifth floor. She told us that her parents and sisters had died and that her brothers were at the front. … Later, we found out that Frida didn't make it home.

It is not clear from Raya's narrative why Frida came for a visit. Was she saying goodbye or hoping to find shelter? The story of grandmother Elizaveta's death is similarly stark:

Granny died first. She shouted for three days. She was asking for something sweet. Mom swapped our china tea set for a bottle of sweet medicine. Sometimes, granny cried … saying she did not want to die before she got a letter from her son Borya. He was at the front. He died. The telegram arrived the day after granny died. Mama carried granny's body down the stairs. She held her by her head, and her legs thumped on the ice-covered stairs. She left her in the street. You couldn't bury your dead unless you could pay in bread. A truck picked her up along with the other corpses.

This happened in 1942. I remember my great-grandmother, Sofia, who was in her eighties when I was a child, talking about using a sled to bring her mother's body to the cemetery. It is hard to know which version is the right one. Raya writes that the sound of her grandmother's feet hitting the stairs stayed with her forever, but she admits that she does not know how she remembers it. She was bed-bound in their room when it happened.

'There are more good people than bad': The family's evacuation

Some details in Raya's story of the family's evacuation from Leningrad also do not match Sofia's version. Evacuation was arranged for the staff of the hospital where Sofia worked. Raya explains that they had to leave in a hurry and had no time to sign a form confirming their residency at the communal flat. The story my mother heard from Sofia is different: apparently when she visited the residency administration the woman on duty took one look at her and said: 'We want no more Jews here.' Sofia turned and left. Her intention was to call in again the next day, when a different person would be in charge. Begging was not her nature. However, evacuation happened the following day.

Sofia pulled Raya on a sled. Lucia walked beside them. They were picked up by big trucks and driven across the frozen lake Ladoga:

This was at the end of March 1942. The ice on the Ladoga lake started to melt. The truck that was driving behind us sunk into the lake. I saw it. When we were brought out to the mainland, we were fed. Chocolate, sugar, porridge. This caused many to die. I remember how they offered me a massive lump of sugar. I felt queasy. My stomach didn't accept food. They put us into narrow wagons. … We lay next to each other – young and old together. We only moaned a bit, nobody cried, not even children, and the air smelled of chlorine.

Raya recalls the journey, the stations along the way where boiling water was available and where people were asked to strip so their clothes could be disinfected, and how good it felt when somebody shouted: 'look, a dog', because 'dog' and cat' were old, forgotten words. Where her story differs from her mother's is the point at which they were asked to leave. In Raya's version that happened during the journey:

When people died they threw them off the train. A doctor told Mom she should get off to bury me (I heard him say that and I did not care at all). As always there were all kinds of people. One woman said to Mom: 'Get off, your daughter will soon die, and you won't throw her off, and I don't want to be stuck next to a corpse.' Another woman gave us a sled (we left ours behind) so that when she got off Mom could pull me to a house.

However, my mother's memories of Sofia's account suggest that this journey never happened because Sofia was not allowed to board the train with Raya. She was given a choice, leave with one daughter or stay behind with both. This version tallies with other reports of people being forbidden from taking dying family members on the trains.[6]

What is true is that Sofia and her daughters were left in the countryside. They wandered in the snow until they found a small house. Raya explains how they survived:

There are more good people than bad. I know this. Mom came out and got to a village. A woman took us in. She let me drink water in which potatoes had been boiled. Then gradually, she let me have baked milk [a Russian recipe]. I survived. I was saved by Lucia, Mom, and that woman, and then later, on another train, I learned how to walk.

I do not think they were ever able to track down the woman who helped them. Once Raya recovered, Sofia managed to get them onto another train; they travelled to Stalinsk, in Siberia, where their cousins lived. Sima was one of Raya's father's sisters.

Auntie Sima's husband, Mikhail Goryanov, was at the front. She had two kids, the lovely four-year-old Stalinka and little Gerochka, and they had a two-room apartment, and her mother also lived with them. And then we came. …

When we came in, we looked like skeletons (even though we'd been eating for a month) she [Auntie Sima] fell on her knees and said: 'I am not kneeling before you but before the whole of Leningrad.' She helped us to wash ourselves, gave us something to eat. She made us beds on the floor because there was nowhere else. She sat across from us. She saw how, when I fell asleep, my neck bent like that of a goose, and she burst into tears. How did she manage? Her kids looked well; she must have had food for them. But there was hunger in Siberia too.

In Stalinsk, the sisters attended school. Sofia got a job in a canteen. Every day, she smuggled out millet porridge in a little oilcloth bag hidden under her clothes. Raya notes that she did not realize that 'the best porridge in the world' could have cost their mother a prison sentence or a death penalty: 'We never gave a thought to Mom's worries, and she didn't say much. We just ate. We only understood the risks she took afterwards. I've been trying to make this porridge here, but it's not working out. That porridge smelt of Mom's oilcloth.'

Raya's account of the time after the siege is very sparse. Her memoir soon moves to the great joy of Victory Day (9 May 1945) and the journey back to Leningrad, where, upon arrival, the family had to split up: Sofia found a place, sharing a bug-infested room with a mentally ill elderly lady, and Raya and Lucia found sleeping arrangements at their workplaces, which in Raya's case was on a large shelf in a factory that produced galoshes. They also got help from their paternal aunts who had also survived and lived in Leningrad.

Telling stories and writing books: How written memoirs impact family memories

Until I saw Raya's text, I did not realize that my grannies' experience of the siege was limited to a few months (September 1941–March 1942) and that the family spent most of the war years in Siberia. Such was the immediacy of these stories, that they seemed to encompass the totality of Raya's and Lucia's experiences and our family's past. But there is a great deal of those years that remains hidden from view. The narrative closely mirrors the stories Raya had told her children and grandchildren. When I talked to my uncle about Lucia's memories, we realized that the few stories she had told him also found their way into Raya's memoir. At some point, the sisters began to share

FIGURE 13.2 *Author's grandmother and memoirist Raya (Raisa Kazachkova) in later life*

stories, the individuality of their experiences becoming blurred by the act of reminiscing. Moreover, in writing her memoir Raya did not resist the effects of this blurring; her work is less a reconstruction of forgotten details than an exercise in preserving existing narratives (see Figure 13.2).

Yet seeing these familiar narratives in print was, for me, an unusual experience. As text, Raya's stories accentuate precisely what was obfuscated through the oral retellings. The gaps and inconsistencies in the narrative become more obvious, the individuality of the experience, the fact that it is Raya's story more than Lucia's or Sofia's story, or part of collective family memory, becomes more apparent. As text, the memoir also draws the reader's attention to the meanings and motivations of the writer, and the context of the writing. I wanted to understand the meanings behind Raya's text in order to re-evaluate the role of her memories in our family. The 'meaning of family stories', writes R. Š. Slabáková, 'can perhaps be found not so much in the details of their content but in the message which is transmitted through them.'[7] If these stories had been part of our identity before they were written down, what role do they have as text?

When thinking about Raya's motivations for writing, I am reminded of Piankevich's point that studying the family in 'siege conditions' means looking at the period when 'the experiences of multiple years could occur in a single day'.[8] That notion of compressed time is also found in Raya's memoir. She notes that she and Lucia 'had experienced in those four years enough for a whole decade'. I suspect that having lived through contracted time, Raya was able to use her memories of the war to understand not only the early trauma but also the more recent pain sustained over a longer period.

The years before Raya began to write were difficult not only for Raya and our family but also, it appears, for a great deal of the Russian population. In an article tellingly entitled 'The Dying Russians', Masha Gessen explains that in 'the seventeen years between 1992 and 2009, the Russian population declined by almost seven million people, or nearly 5 percent – a rate of loss unheard of in Europe since World War II'. Gessen notes that during these years the mortality rose, so that 'the average St Petersburg man lived for seven fewer years than he did at the Communist period'.[9] People died of unrelated causes: heart attacks, cancer and strange accidents that were so frequent that people became accustomed to death. While studies of the period have been carried out, their explanations for this sudden rise in mortality are not conclusive, suggesting an array of unfortunate coincidences and psychological factors.

Even though most of us emigrated to Israel, our family was not exempt from these upsetting trends. Lucia's husband Aleksander Ruppo (my grandfather) died in 1991 of a heart attack. My great-grandmother Sofia Greenberg died in 1992 in a tragic accident. In 1993 my father Yuri Ruppo (Lucia's eldest son and Raya's nephew) died of cancer at the age of 39. In 2005, Raya's son (Mikhail Kazachkov) died by suicide. My grandmother Lucia, who had been in deep depression since 1993, died in 2008 of complications brought on by chronic under-eating. David Kazachkov who was Raya's husband died of cancer in 2010. Looking at the list of names reminds me of a conversation that Gessen had with another American reporter.

> I cried on a friend's shoulder. I was finding all this death not simply painful but impossible to process. 'It's not like there is a war on,' I said.
>
> 'But there is,' said my friend, a somewhat older and much wiser reporter than I. 'This is what civil war actually looks like. It's not when everybody starts running around with guns. It's when everybody starts dying.'[10]

The similarities between Gessen's observations of Russia and what happened in my family makes me think that Raya wanted to use her memories of World War II to understand that other hidden war that took so many of her loved ones.

Writing in Israel, after the dissolution of the Soviet Union, Raya reviews her life: 'I described how badly we lived in the Soviet Union,' she writes, 'but did we ever notice that we lived "badly"? Did we reflect on what this "badness" might mean apart from the memories of the War when we all suffered?' In another passage, she refers to Stalinist repressions and describes herself and other survivors of the regime as 'zombies'. 'Some people were killed', she writes, 'and some were zombified', so that people were not able to notice injustice, or miss freedom, and were satisfied with petty rewards and promotions. Raya adds, 'We once thought that Victory Day will usher in a triumphant future, but it remained as a tearful memory'. Raya's attitude is that of guilt. She was not able to understand how 'zombified' she was; nor was she able to prevent any of the deaths that happened to her family members. Raya writes about the great lie that the Soviet Union sold its citizens, but her method of examining that lie is not through discarding possible untruths but rather through the recitation of her repertoire of stories.

As oral stories, Raya's and Lucia's experiences of the siege fit the pattern of family stories observed by Slabáková, whereby ancestors are 'presented as people who managed to overcome danger and were able to transform their suffering into something positive'.[11] What I had known were oral stories of courage and survival as staid and familiar as my grannies' china sets and bronzes. As text, the stories are both more troubling and more meaningful. They are self-reflective; they engage with the subjects of identity, death and loss, subjects that were of primary importance to their author. Moreover, the connections between their content and the circumstances of their composition hint at the incompletely understood long-term effects of the war on Leningraders and their children. The devastation of the war, the text seems to suggest, was not completely over in 1945. It reveals that Raya's memories are also casualties of the siege and its aftermath. Her stories bear the marks of chronic obfuscation, whereby idealized narratives were repeated and more troubling aspects of her experience were forgotten. The stories' very incompleteness, therefore, serves as an indictment against a Soviet regime which not only failed to safeguard its citizens against one of the worst disasters in the twentieth century, but which prevented them, through the culture of fear and silence, from fully voicing and understanding their own experiences.

It is impossible to predict how and whether the Leningrad story of the two Greenberg sisters will continue to circulate in our family, which is not overly large and whose members are scattered across several countries – Russia, Israel and Ireland. At the moment, Raya's text serves to underscore the cross-national connections between our individual lives and historical traumas and injustices.[12]

Notes

1   The sisters' full names were Lucia Immanuilovna Ruppo (née Greenberg) and Raisa Immanuilovna Kazachkova (née Greenberg). For personal reasons, I did not use the standard transliteration system for their names, preferring Greenberg with its Russian-sounding long 'e' to 'Grinberg' and Lucia, cognate with the English Lucy, to the awkward-looking Liusia.

2 All quotations from Raya's text are from her unpublished Russian-language memoirs, *Bez Prodolzheniya* (2010) and *Prodolzhenie bez Prodolzhenya* (2012), which were printed in several copies and distributed to several family members. All translations are mine.

3 Anna Reid, *Leningrad: Tragedy of a City under Siege, 1941–44* (London: A & C Black, 2012), 96–101.

4 Reid, *Leningrad*, 162.

5 Vladimir L. Piankevich, 'The Family under Siege: Leningrad, 1941–44', *The Russian Review* 75, no. 1 (2016): 116.

6 Piankevich, 'The Family under Siege', 107–37.

7 Radmila Švaříčková Slabáková, 'Moral Heroes or Suffering Persons? Ancestors in Family Intergenerational Stories and the Intersection of Family and National Memories', *Journal of Family History* 44, no. 4 (2019): 439.

8 Piankevich, 'The Family under Siege', 108.

9 Masha Gessen, 'The Dying Russians', *The New York Review of Books*, 2 September 2014. Available at: https://www.nybooks.com/daily/2014/09/02/dying-russians/ (accessed 28 January 2020).

10 Gessen, 'The Dying Russians'.

11 Slabáková, 'Moral Heroes', 438.

12 Raya passed away on 9 February 2020. I was fortunate in having been able to see her and talk to her (and to discuss her memoir and this piece) shortly before her death. This essay is dedicated to her memory.

14

Slave labour and its legacies: My maternal grandparents' journey from Ukraine to Germany to Belgium

Sylvie Mossay

Slave labour was an essential part of German military planning in World War II. The regime had to bring foreign labourers into Germany to work in agriculture and industry, taking the places of the German workers it had sent to the front. While it initially solicited volunteers in occupied countries, from spring 1940 onwards it resorted to force. By 1944 one-third of the workforce consisted of foreign forced labourers. In total, they numbered twelve million. Two of these were my maternal grandparents. This chapter retraces their lives from pre-war Eastern Galicia (now part of Ukraine) to their forced deployment in the Third Reich, before finally being resettled in Belgium in 1947, along with my reflections on their experiences.[1]

Their memories of the war and its aftermath were passed on to me by my grandmother, my mother and my Ukrainian relatives. Weekends at my grandparents', occasional anecdotes, a trip to my family in Lviv in 1986, conversations with my mother and emails to my Ukrainian cousins all helped greatly. These subjective sources were in part corroborated both by papers in my family's possession and by the many documents which I received from the Arolsen Archives, International Center on Nazi Persecution, in Germany. These official records include Assembly Centre and Displaced Persons registration cards, United Nations Relief and Rehabilitation Administration nominal rolls of authorized movement of displaced persons, identity cards and various other correspondence. All of these assisted me in locating my grandparents in time and place both during and immediately after the war. Despite the wealth of information they contain, some questions remain unanswered.

My grandparents' pre-war life

My grandmother, Aleksandra Olena Doronko (Олена Доронько), was born on 20 May 1912 in Lyskiv, a small village in the Lviv region. Lviv is located in the historic province of Eastern Galicia, now western Ukraine, and has a history marked by the successive conquests of the region by foreign imperial powers. At the time of my grandmother's birth and up until 1918, it was part of the Austro-Hungarian Empire and known as Lemberg. After a short-lived western Ukrainian National Republic, it became part of the Second Polish Republic in 1919, when its official title was Lwów. It remained under Poland until the beginning of World War II when a Soviet (1939) and subsequent German (1941) invasion changed its status once again.

My grandmother lived with her parents, Kyryl and Pelagna Doronko (Кирил і Пелагна Доронько), and her older brother, Dmytro (Дмитро), in a rural village. Very early on, her life was marked by the devastation of war when her father was killed during World War I. This was to be the first of a tragic series of losses. After her husband's death, my great-grandmother eventually remarried and had two children, Ivan (Іван) and Tekla (Текля). My grandmother, Aleksandra, shared in the daily chores at home and helped her mother look after her younger stepsiblings. Although she was not unhappy, she remembered getting little attention from her stepfather.

At the age of 18, she married a local farmer, Pylyp Chorniy (Пилип Чорній), and her first daughter Anastasia (Анастасія) was born the following year in 1931. They lived in a little cottage with a garden, a couple of hens, some geese and a cow. They both worked hard and were content with their lot. In August 1936 they welcomed their second daughter, Maria (Марія), into the world. Their life as a family of four was to be short-lived. Pylyp succumbed to pneumonia a few months after Maria's birth. Tragedy struck again within a few months when 5-year-old Anastasia contracted gangrene. Having no means of transportation, my grandmother had to carry her to the nearest doctor located a couple of hours walk from their village. She died in her arms on the way. My grandmother was devastated, but had to stay strong for her remaining child. Further separation ensued in 1939 when, fearing the war, her brother, Dmytro, emigrated to Canada.

My grandfather, Wasyl Marczuk (Василь Марчук), was born on 1 November 1919. From correspondence files obtained from the Arolsen Archives, I can ascertain that he was born in Svarychiv, in Stanislavshchyna, a region which had just then been incorporated into the new state of Poland. Nowadays however this is a region in western Ukraine called Ivano-Frankivsk Oblast and it was also part of Eastern Galicia between the wars. His parents were Michel Marczuk and Maria Sahajdak. His last permanent place of residence was Kalush, 25 kilometres from his place of birth. His profession was recorded on separate documents as a farmer and as a 'tiller'. Before being deported, he was married with two very young sons. My grandfather spoke little and my mother never had any direct contact with his family back home, hence the lack of information.

My grandparents' deportation and life in wartime Germany

Despite the Nazis' anti-communist and anti-Slavic convictions, Hitler signed a pact of non-aggression with Stalin on 23 August 1939. Poland was invaded by Germany from the west on 1 September and by the Soviet Union from the east on 17 September. The following month, Poland was defeated and divided between the two invading powers. Eastern Galicia fell into the hands of the Soviet Union. In June 1941, however, Hitler broke his agreement with Stalin and attacked the Soviet Union in order to both expand further eastwards and crush communism. The Soviet Union was defeated and Eastern Galicia was annexed to the Nazi General Government of the Occupied Polish Territories in 1942. However, by this time, it had become apparent to the German leaders that the war would drag on. As most German male citizens had already been drafted by early 1942, more manpower would be needed to ensure the survival of the German war economy. The only way this could happen was through the mass exploitation of foreign labour. Fritz Sauckel was appointed plenipotentiary general for labour allocation in March 1942. It was under his ruthless recruitment and deployment programme that my grandparents were sent to Germany.

By August 1941, when the volunteer recruitment scheme had practically dried up in the newly occupied eastern territories, together with 'more severe measures such as arrests, beatings … raids and manhunts', each village and district were ordered by the German authorities to provide workers according to quotas to be filled by specific dates.[2] My grandmother never spoke about the living conditions under Soviet or German rule in Eastern Galicia during the war. All we know is that she did not volunteer to work in Germany, but rather was forced to report for labour in the Reich to the local authority, possibly in the county of Stryj near Lviv. She was given two days to go home to pack a bag and then return to be transferred to Germany. My grandmother pleaded with the local authorities to be allowed to bring her 6-year-old daughter, Maria, with her. She had already lost her eldest child and husband and could not conceive of leaving Maria behind. Much to her dismay, her request was dismissed out of hand. Heartbroken, but left with no other choice, she put Maria into the care of her own mother. Little did she know that she would only ever see her once more – thirty years later. She never got over their separation.

According to the work card and certificates that my grandmother submitted to the Displaced Persons (DP) Camp in Erlangen, Germany, in 1945, she was registered with the Regional Employment Office for Nuremberg, Bavaria (Landesarbeitsamt Bayern-Nürnberg) on 10 August 1942. She was subsequently registered with the Ukrainian Central Committee, an organization that mediated between the Ukrainian population and the German authorities, in Cracow in May 1944 and redeployed to Bavaria to work for the Bayreuth Division of the Reich Food Estate (Reichnährstand/Landesbauernschaft Bayreuth). No family member could shed light on her presence in Cracow in May 1944. Similarly, on her DP registration record, there is also a mention of a certificate from Lachowycsy, now Belarus. Although it was not uncommon for forced labourers to be moved around where they were needed in both the industrial and the agricultural sectors, it seems unlikely that she would have been sent to Belarus. Lachowicze (in Polish), also spelt Lyakhavichy (in Belarusian), could actually be Lyakhivtsi, a region in western Ukraine, where my grandmother could have worked before being sent to Germany.

As for my grandfather, he was taken in a round-up while walking in the streets near his home. Together with other villagers, he was forced into the back of a truck and deported to Germany. It was a common practice. A report written in autumn 1942 showed that, to reach the quotas, 'men and women, including teenagers … are reportedly picked up on the street, at markets and during village celebrations, and then speeded away'.[3] He said that he was scared and deeply saddened by the fact that he was not given the opportunity to say goodbye to his family. Based on the archive documents, he arrived in Prahadic, Sudetenland in April 1942. This region, which had a predominantly German population, had been annexed by Germany from Czechoslovakia in October 1938. My grandfather received a work card from the Volary Suboffice of the local Employment Agency (Arbeitsamt Prachatitz Nebenstelle Wallern) on 9 March 1943 and a Certificate from the Ukrainian Auxiliary Committee in Dolina, Poland, on 9 July 1943, which mentioned his place of residence at the time as Wallern in the Bohemian Forest – where he stayed until he was sent to Bavaria (see Figure 14.1). It is unclear why he had to register with the Ukrainian Committee in Dolina.

To my family's knowledge, both my grandmother and grandfather worked only as agricultural labourers after their deployment to Germany. Historians

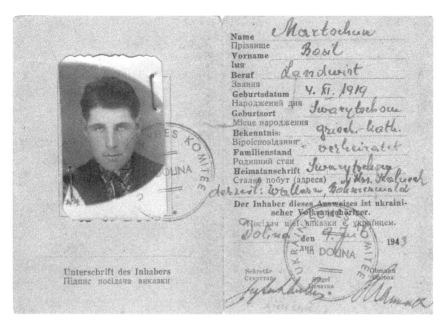

FIGURE 14.1 *Work card of Basil (Wasyl) Marczuk, 1943*

such as Edward Homze and Ulrich Herbert have described at length the horrific and cruel conditions to which labourers from the East, at the bottom of the Nazi racial scale, were subjected. They were seen as *Untermenschen* or subhumans, born to serve the German master race.[4] Conversations with my grandmother about her time in the Reich confirm this. She described long days working on the farm, exhaustion, mistreatment, harsh living conditions and hunger. She was deprived of everything and of every right, but it was the hunger that she remembered most. She was extremely badly treated by one farmer in particular. From her stories, we know that she worked in the fields during the day where she met other Eastern labourers. Depending on the season, she had to clear the land, plant or harvest crops and look after the cows. At times, she also had to carry out some household chores in the farmhouse. At night she used to sleep in an austere, cold outbuilding on the farm. She was prohibited from leaving the farm except to go to work in the fields. Semi-starved, she looked for ways to access food which the farmer was purposely locking away. Unsuccessful, she resorted to stealing the scraps given to the dogs in order to survive. This experience had a profound effect on her and is well known to her seven grandchildren in Belgium and Ukraine. My grandparents lived on neighbouring farms and met while working in the fields some time after May 1944. It would appear that my grandfather was slightly better treated and smuggled a part of his meagre ration, mainly bread, to give to my starving grandmother. It showed great selflessness at a time when everyone was lacking food. In spite of his generosity, my grandmother knew that if she stayed on this farm she would probably die. Escaping was not an option since, had she been caught, she would have been sent to a labour education camp or worse. As a last resort, one day she intentionally mishandled a cow in the hope that she would get injured. Her prayers were answered when the cow kicked back, hit her in the face and she was sent for treatment. She was then able to report the beatings and abuses, to which she had been subjected, to a German supervisor and was transferred to another farm in the area where she remained until the end of the war.

Life after liberation

When Germany surrendered in spring 1945, it was divided into four zones administered by the Allies – the United States, Great Britain, the Soviet Union and France. At the end of the war, the Allied Supreme Command (SHAEF) estimated that displaced persons, a category that included former inmates of concentration camps and prisoner of war (POW) camps as well as forced labourers, numbered 11,332,700.[5] The Allies organized assembly centres to try to bring together all the DPs. These facilities were placed initially under the authority of the military commands, before later being transferred to the United Nations Relief and Rehabilitation Administration (UNRRA). They provided basic food, housing and medical care and helped organize repatriation, where possible.

My grandparents reported to the Forchheim Assembly Centre in Bavaria, administered by the United States, in August 1945. By this time the Soviet Union, based on the Yalta agreement, had launched a campaign of total repatriation for DPs who had at some point been Soviet citizens. Their records reveal that, although Ukrainian and coming from Eastern Galicia, both my grandparents were registered initially as stateless, then Polish and later as Polish-Ukrainian by the authorities.[6] They more than likely claimed statelessness in order to avoid repatriation. Despite having left family behind, like many other Easterners, they feared being treated as collaborators, persecuted, sent to prison, exiled to Siberia or even executed by the Soviet government, if they returned home. Historian Miriam Rürup points out that this was not uncommon: 'The so-called Displaced Persons after the Second World War … preferred statelessness to forced repatriation to a country they feared or despised and so tried to rid themselves of any national classification.'[7]

My grandparents lived as a couple in the Forchheim Assembly Centre until September 1946 at which point they were moved to the Polish-Ukrainian DP camp in Erlangen, a former infantry barracks. The facilities were basic. The camps were cramped, but they had shelter and, more importantly, food. As shown on their DP records, they were also given some clothes. Furthermore, as many DPs were sick and the Allies wanted to avoid the spread of an epidemic, they also received a health check and were vaccinated. While in the Assembly Centre and in the DP camp my grandparents befriended many other Ukrainians, some of whom were also resettled to Belgium. My grandmother also realized at this time that she was pregnant and my mother, Anna Chorniy Marczuk, was born on 29 July 1946 at the hospital in Forchheim. Researchers at the Arolsen Archives were able to locate her birth certificate in December 2019. It was the first time that my mother had ever seen it. Her parents married formally some time before her first birthday.

At this stage, my grandparents were eager to leave the camp, but there was no work to be found. In agreement with the American and British authorities, Belgium was the first country to organize a large-scale recruitment programme among DPs to work in the mining industry – which faced a labour shortage. Although my grandparents had initially given Canada as their desired destination for resettlement, my grandfather enlisted in this programme and emigrated to Belgium in July 1947. My grandmother and my mother followed him three months later, once he had secured work and accommodation. Between 11 April and the end of July 1947, 14,000 DPs were given work in the mines.[8] The two largest groups were Poles and Ukrainians.

New beginnings in Belgium

My grandmother recalled that the journey by train to Belgium was very long and stressful. It took almost three days to become reunited with my grandfather. My mother, who was only fifteen months old at the time, was extremely sick with dysentery and dehydration. My grandmother feared that she was going to lose her. She said that if a doctor on board had not attended to her, my mother might not have survived. They disembarked at the then Liège-Palais train station, where a Ukrainian priest was on hand to help the new arrivals.

My grandfather was granted a house in the mining village of Retinne, in the Liège province, Eastern Wallonia. He was among the 'lucky' ones, as my mother remembers visiting Ukrainian friends who were living in the old military barracks left behind by the Germans. Belgium had been unable to fulfil its promise of providing proper accommodation to all the new recruits. Only a few weeks after my grandmother's arrival, my grandparents were asked to house a Ukrainian widow and her 8-month-old baby boy – Melania and Peter.

Melania's husband, who had been working in the mines with my grandfather, had been crushed by a coal cart shortly before they arrived. They stayed with my grandparents for three years and became family.

My grandparents' resettlement in Belgium was made easier through their membership of an existing Ukrainian organization, the Ukrainian Assistance Committee (Le Comité Ukrainien de Secours or UDK). Besides providing newcomers with material aid, legal assistance and helping with contacts back home, it organized cultural, economic and religious activities to promote unity in the Ukrainian community. My grandparents regularly attended local events and gatherings such as folk dances and concerts. As a child, my mother was herself part of a Ukrainian folk dance group. Religion was also very important. They went to a Greek Catholic service in Ukrainian every Sunday in Liège where they met their friends. I strongly believe that their faith helped them through the many hardships that they had to endure.

As anticipated, the work in the mines was extremely hard. Ukrainian miners reported in a survey at the end of 1948 that they found their working conditions unbearable. Indeed over half expressed a wish to leave Belgium.[9] In spite of this, my grandfather never complained. Growing up, my mother and her younger brother, born in 1949, saw little of him since he worked from 2 pm to 10 pm until he retired. In thirty-one years, he never took a single day off work. In his spare time, he was always outside looking after his vegetable plot and animals. To supplement his income, he mended the shoes of his colleagues. My grandmother also worked as a cleaner when my mother and uncle were at school. They proved to be extremely resourceful and hard-working people.

My mother always speaks about a simple but happy childhood. They were the only Ukrainian family on the street. Their neighbours were mainly Polish and Italian, all of whom had suffered the horrors of the war. My mother spoke Ukrainian at home. She also went to a Ukrainian school on Saturday organized by the Ukrainian Educational Society and learned to read and write in Ukrainian. It was important for my grandparents to pass on their heritage. She also picked up Polish playing with the other children and French at school. My grandparents also spoke Ukrainian, Polish and French. An unsuccessful immigration request to Canada dated 1954 shows, however, that my grandparents were still hoping for a better life than the one they had in Belgium. They had always hoped for a move to Canada, particularly since my grandmother's brother had settled successfully there.

At some point following the end of the war my grandmother first managed to make contact with Maria, although it is not clear how. Once this initial contact was established, however, they began exchanging regular letters. It is through this correspondence that my grandmother found out what had happened to the family members that she had been forced to leave behind. Her own mother died about two years after her deportation and Maria was placed in foster homes. Tekla, my grand-aunt, could not look after Maria because she had been sent to prison as she had fought for Ukrainian independence against the Soviet regime. When she was released, like other political prisoners, she was prohibited from returning to her local region. She was exiled east to Donbass, which was under Soviet control at the time and where her brother Ivan lived. Ivan had been conscripted into the Red Army during World War II and had been sent to Donbass to reconstruct the city as it had been destroyed during the war.

My grandmother also regularly sent parcels containing food and clothes back to Soviet Ukraine to both her own and my grandfather's family. She would often get upset reading Maria's letters. Her longing to see her daughter again prompted her to apply for a visa to go to Lviv to meet her. Despite approximately a dozen refusals by the Soviet authorities, she kept trying and eventually received her visa, in 1972, thirty years after her deportation. My mother recalls that my grandmother was both overwhelmed with joy and fear before her departure. She had left a child and was going to meet a grown-up woman who was herself married with three children. She spent three months in Lviv with Maria, her husband and her three Ukrainian grandchildren – Liubov, Oleksandra and Petro (see Figure 14.2). There were lots of tears – both of joy and of sadness. My aunt had been deeply affected by their separation and,

FIGURE 14.2 *Aleksandra Marczuk (centre), with Maria and her family, during her visit to Lviv, 1972*

although she understood the circumstances and had been well treated by her foster parents, she bore a grudge against my grandmother for leaving her behind. It was very hard for them both. My grandmother Aleksandra also got to meet her stepbrother and stepsister again. During her stay, my grandmother felt that she was being followed by the authorities. To her dismay, despite many further requests, she was never allowed back to the country.

As for my grandfather, he learned that his wife had died in an accident while working in a factory and that family members were looking after his sons. They remained in contact until his death but the letters were few and far between. These contacts were, however, very important to him. My mother only saw my grandfather cry twice – once when my grandmother passed away and once when she read him a letter from his sons a few years later.

My grandparents and I

From a very young age, I was drip-fed stories from my grandparents' past lives. Together with my sister I used to spend every Saturday at their house. It was decorated with many pictures of relatives in the Ukraine. My grandmother always shared their latest news with us. At the time, I did not fully understand the reality of their deportation, the separation from their home country and their loved ones and their effective political asylum in Belgium.

I have nothing but fond memories of the time that I spent at their place. Walks, playtime and food made up the weekends. My grandmother was a great cook and a great host. She cooked lovely traditional Ukrainian dishes such as *pirohi* (cheese-filled dumplings), *holubtsi* (cabbage leaves filled with boiled rice and meat) and my favourite meal, *placki* (potato cakes with a cottage cheese dip that I helped prepare). Most of the Ukrainian words that I can still recall are food-related. I remember my grandmother as being calm, but sociable, very kind and loving. As a child, I was bubbly, adventurous and full of mischief. While my father had little patience with me, my grandmother found my personality endearing. She was very fond of me and I loved her dearly. My favourite part of the day was the evening when she sat down next to me on the big green sofa. My sister sat in one corner, while I snuggled up to her to watch television in the other corner. My grandfather sat in his armchair. I remember him as a nature lover and a taciturn man. Since he only spoke very occasionally to me, I was a little scared of him – although I can honestly say that he never gave me any reason to be, and there is nothing that he would not have done to please me. As a grown-up, I often wondered if he had always been like that or if life had broken his spirit.

When my grandmother's health started to deteriorate around 1984, I was extremely upset. In 1986 while my grandmother was still alive, my mother decided to go to the Ukrainian Soviet Socialist Republic – Soviet Ukraine. I was 11 and decided to go with her for two reasons. Firstly, I wanted to make my grandmother happy by visiting her country and meeting our relatives. Secondly, I was very close to my mum. I feared that my grandmother's story could repeat itself and that she might never come back if she went without me. My paternal grand-uncle, Belgian-born and bred, who was retired and loved travelling, offered to accompany us. In the summer of 1986, after a long administrative process to obtain visas, we set off in a car overloaded with goods. We drove through Germany and Poland. At the Ukrainian border we were met by soldiers. Customs officials took my mother for questioning. My grand-uncle was requested to unload the car, which was then thoroughly searched. We had brought a dozen music tapes for the journey which I was asked to play in part to an armed soldier sitting next to me in the car. I was later told that they were looking for Western propaganda. We were finally allowed to enter Soviet Ukraine but not before a few of the officials had helped themselves to some of the goods we had packed. My mother also gave them Deutschmarks. She had been told by friends that, in order to avoid problems and unnecessary delay, a bribe would be necessary. Nevertheless, we spent four long hours at the border. It was a very scary first impression of the country we were entering.

On the way to my aunt's place, we passed through many rural localities. The fields were empty as it was only a couple of months after the Chernobyl disaster. The atmosphere was a little eerie. Arriving in Lviv, a taxi driver showed us the way to my aunt's address. When he stopped in front of an uninviting grey communist apartment block, we all looked at each other in apprehension. However, our initial shock was to be short-lived. We were warmly welcomed by Maria, her husband, Yaroslav and my cousins Liubov, Oleksandra and Petro. There was no awkwardness. It was like visiting family we had always known. Their flat was charming and well decorated in an eastern European style, in sharp contrast to the cold grim building. My cousin, Oleksandra, who was 23 years old at the time, spoke a little French and looked after me very well during the week. During the day we visited tourist attractions. My favourite places were the Museum of Folk Architecture and Life and the Stryisky Park. We travelled around Lviv on the packed yellow trams. I did not like the city itself as it was extremely busy and not very clean. The goods displayed at the butchers' and bakers' were unappetizing, and the shops were largely bare as it was only on the black market where most things could be bought. Every evening a feast prepared by Liubov was waiting for us. It reminded me of family gatherings at my grandparents' home. Around the dinner table my mother translated the conversations for me and my grand-uncle. Everybody went above and beyond to make our stay unforgettable. At night we returned to the hotel. We were not allowed to sleep at my aunt's place, and they were not allowed in the hotel. When my grandmother passed away the following summer, I was deeply saddened by her death and still miss her immensely. To this day, I keep a picture of both of us on my bedside locker. When Ukraine gained independence, my parents returned five times. However since every inch of our car was needed for supplies, I never went back. Maria and Yaroslav paid us a visit in 1991. My aunt's only request was to visit her mother's grave.

As a child, I was always fascinated by both my grandparents' and my mum's ease in languages and even more so now that I am a modern foreign-language teacher. I believe that this, coupled with my love of literature, played an important part in my choice of studies. However, one of my greatest regrets is that my mum has never spoken Ukrainian to me. We have often discussed this. As a child of immigrants, although she never suffered any discrimination in Belgium, she just wanted to fit in. As a direct result of my own experience, I made the conscious decision to only speak to my children in French even though we live in a bilingual country, where both Irish and English are spoken.

At secondary school, and later at the University of Liège, I studied languages, including German, and spent a lot of time in Germany where I made many friends. I also spent an Erasmus year in Bavaria during 1995–6 where I studied at the University of Bamberg. A US Army military base was still present there at the time – a remnant of World War II. The American flag flew in the city until 2014. I really enjoyed my time in Bavaria, visiting many places in the region including Erlangen, completely unaware of its significance in my grandparents' lives. I must admit that it came as a shock to me when I realized during my research that of all the places this is the one where my grandmother is most likely to have suffered the most.

World War II was part of the curriculum both at secondary and third levels. This was a part of history that interested me since my grandparents' lives had been affected by it. The crimes against foreign workers were understandably overshadowed by the stories of mass murder in concentration camps. It was only much later that I realized the extent of the atrocities committed against Eastern Foreign workers which deeply upset me.

My grandparents are a true inspiration to me and this project has been an emotional journey. The more I researched their lives the more important it became to me to give them a voice. They showed extraordinary courage and resilience in the face of overwhelming challenges, from surviving forced deportation and labour to dealing with separation from family and resettlement in a foreign country while remaining true to their roots. I never once heard them complain. Moreover, they did not show or pass on any feeling of hatred or resentment towards the Nazis or German people in general. The memory I keep of them is of truly good and admirable people.

Notes

I would like to thank my mother Annie and my cousin Petro in Lviv for sharing all their family memories with me, as well as the Arolsen Archives, International Center on Nazi Persecution, which provided me with precious documents. Without their help, I would not have been able to retrace my grandparents' experience during World War II and its aftermath. I would also like to dearly thank my husband, Brian, and my children, Emma and Oisín, who have accompanied me every step of the way on this project. Finally, I am very grateful to my brother-in-law, Jonathan, who encouraged me to pursue this family research.

1 Ulrich Herbert, *Hitler's Foreign Workers: Enforced Foreign Labor in Germany under the Third Reich* (Cambridge: Cambridge University Press, 1997).

2 Ulrich Herbert, 'Forced Laborers in the Third Reich: An Overview', *International Labor and Working-Class History* 58 (2000): 192–218.

3 Herbert, *Hitler's Foreign Workers*, 169.

4 Edward L. Homze, *Foreign Labour in Nazi Germany* (Princeton: Princeton University Press, 1967); Herbert, *Hitler's Foreign Workers*.

5 Herbert, *Hitler's Foreign Workers*, 377.

6 DPs were classified according to their citizenship, not by their nationality. Wolfgang Jacobmeyer, *Vom Zwangsarbeiter zum Heimatlosen Ausländer, Die Displaced Persons in Westdeutschland 1945–1951* (Göttingen: Vandenhoeck and Ruprecht, 1985), 75.

7 Miriam Rürup, 'Lives in Limbo: Statelessness after Two World Wars', *Bulletin of the GHI Washington* 49 (Fall 2011): 121.

8 M. Venken and I. Goodeeris, 'The Nationalizations of Identities: Ukrainians in Belgium, 1920–1950', *Journal of Ukrainian Studies* 31, nos. 1–2 (Summer–Winter 2006): 99.

9 Venken and Goodeeris, 'The Nationalizations of Identities', 99.

Index